CRITICAL MODERNISM

BICENTENNIAL
BICENTENNIAL
1807
WILEY
2007
BICENTENNIAL
BICENTENNIAL

Published in Great Britain in 2007 by Wiley-Academy,
a division of John Wiley & Sons Ltd

Copyright © 2007 Charles Jencks

Email (for orders and customer service enquiries): cs-books@wiley.co.uk

Visit our Home Page on www.wiley.com

Anniversary Logo Design: Richard Pacifico

Other Wiley Editorial Offices

John Wiley & Sons Inc., 111 River Street, Hoboken, NJ 07030, USA

Jossey-Bass, 989 Market Street, San Francisco, CA 94103-1741, USA

Wiley-VCH Verlag GmbH, Boschstr. 12, D-69469 Weinheim, Germany

John Wiley & Sons Australia Ltd, 42 McDougall Street, Milton, Queensland
4064, Australia

John Wiley & Sons (Asia) Pte Ltd, 2 Clementi Loop #02-01, Jin Xing
Distripark, Singapore 129809

John Wiley & Sons Canada Ltd, 5353 Dundas Street West, Suite 400,
Etobicoke, Ontario M9B 6H8

Wiley also publishes its books in a variety of electronic formats. Some
content that appears in print may not be available in electronic books.

Executive Commissioning Editor: Helen Castle
Content Editor: Louise Porter
Publishing Assistant: Calver Lezama
ISBN (HB) 978 0 470 03010 3
ISBN (PB) 978 0 470 03011 0
Page design and layouts by Liz Sephton
Printed and bound by Grafos SA, Spain
Picture credits: p 1 Anselm Kiefer, Mohnund Gedächthis, 1989, in
Hamburger Bahnhof – Museum für Gegenwartf, Berlin (photo C Jencks); p
2-3 E=mc2 outside the Altes Museum, Berlin, in the summer of 2006
(photo C Jencks); and pp 4-5 Peter Eisenman, Memorial to the Murdered
Jews of Europe, Berlin, 1998-2005 (photo C Jencks).

CRITICAL MODERNISM

where is post-modernism going?

CHARLES JENCKS

CONTENTS

PREFACE:
A REFOLUTION
IN FIVE PARTS

OPPOSITE [1] **Evolution's taste for hybrids.** A hybrid butterfly species, *Heliconius heurippa*, was recreated in the laboratory. This confirmed the hunch that sometimes speciation can occur by the merging of two branches rather than in the normal way, by divergence from a source. Here two species, one with white and the other with red marked wings, interbred and produced the red-white hybrid. This mixed species preferred to breed with itself rather than its parents' offspring. Creation is hybridisation, and post-modernists show the same taste for hybrids that evolution reveals. (Juan Gillermo Moñtanès, Mauricio Linares)

This book examines the five basic shifts in global civilisation that are well under way, the mix of cultural forms that are turning into more interesting hybrids and making us pause for thought. The lisp-like spelling of revolution above, an invention of Timothy Garton Ash, is itself one of these very mixed states and will be clarified below, but first let me enumerate the fundamental transformations taking place and explain the contents of this book.

Fundamental to the change is the shift in the modern world-view and with it of modernism, an ideology of economic rationalism and constant high growth. Both may yet have a decade or two to run but, with global warming and a host of related crises in train, they do not enjoy the usual fifty-year guarantee. This shift is accompanied by the rise of various post-modernisms, the hybridisation of national cultures into ones that are thoroughly mixed and in constant intercommunication, a process that generates the pervasive style of Post-Modernism in the arts, its double coding and cosmopolitan outlook. The third shift runs parallel to this hybridisation and concerns society. Here it is the blurring of social classes with the rise of a vast, inchoate group into which most people in the West slot themselves, the middle class, or what might be more properly called the muddle class, without being altogether pejorative. In large measure it is a sought-after, classless situation and one partly caused by a much deeper merger also going on, the melding of socialism with capitalism, perhaps the most all-embracing reality of our time.

The fourth shift, also parallel to these global trends, is the rise to power of transnational institutions – not only the NGOs and military institutions we all know like NATO, but also the supraregional bodies such as the EU. These are beginning to wrest power from that previously dominant institution that ushered in the modern world, the nation-state, though like the other changes in process, this is one more under way than complete. And finally there is the most exciting intellectual shift of our time, the big wave advancing beneath the surface wars of fundamentalism, that slow but inexorable movement from a traditional religious world-view to something more universal, cosmic and, in a few cases even spiritual. It relates to Gaia, the notion of the earth as a dynamic body constantly undergoing feedback in order to regulate itself. Indeed, it relates to the new conception of all matter and life as self-organising.

Such are the movements under way towards a more hybrid, integrated world – a mongrelised globe from one point of view – a world in constant and instantaneous communication across its boundaries. At the same time, I will argue, there is also at work a hidden tradition of reflection and reaction to all this cross-border modernisation, the Critical Modernism of my title. Unlike many of the other trends and agendas discussed here, this is not yet a conscious movement but an underground or tacit process, the activity of modernism in its constantly reflexive stage, a stage that looks back critically in order to go forward. If it becomes a conscious tradition, for reasons I outline at the end of the book, it will deserve the upper case designation of my title. As so often in history the negatively critical can shed its righteous anger and suddenly flip into the positively Critical (capitalised like all proper movements). This quick change points to the second, customary sense of the term, its scientific meaning as in 'critical mass', or 'critical bifurcation point', or a 'critical tipping point'. A good way to remember this secondary sense is the method nineteenth-century architects used as an *aide-mémoire*: the 'critical angle' of a roof, they recited, 'is roughly 30 degrees, the angle at which the rain runs off but the tiles don't'. Critical Modernism, as a two-headed term, carries the overtone that the many modernisms that have followed each other in quick succession may now have reached a 'critical' mass and become a self-conscious tradition.

All the modernisms, since the Christians first used the term in the fifth century, have claimed to be agents of progress fighting to overcome their corrupt predecessors (as the capsule definitions in the diagram opposite suggest). According to their view, these 'moderns' were morally

Modernisms

the key polemics

I **3rd–5th century – _Modernus_** Early Christians proclaim their ethical progress over paganism.

II **1450–1600 – _Moderna_** Renaissance usage by Filarete and Vasari on the superiority of the classical rebirth, distinguishing the 'good' revival (_buona maniera moderna_) from the 'bad' contemporary Gothic.

III **1600–1850 – Battle of the Ancients and Moderns** Again 'modern' means improvement over the ancient, invention within the classical tradition. The famous 'Quarrel' within the French Academy starts in the 1690s and lasts 200 years, while the British contrast progressive classicism with Gothic.

IV **1755 – Modernism as fashionable rubbish** Samuel Johnson's _Dictionary_ defines '_Modernism_: Deviation from the ancient and classical manner .... _Modern_: in Shakespeare. Vulgar, mean, common. "We have our philosophical persons to make _modern_ and familiar things supernatural and causeless."'

V **1900 – Modernism** A Roman Catholic movement examining tradition that was officially condemned in 1907 by Pope Pius X for atheism and having an exaggerated love of what is modern.

VI **1914–30 – Modern Movement** In literature the free verse, stream of consciousness and experiments by Pound, Eliot, Joyce and Woolf; in design the technical and social progressivism of those practising the International Style; in the arts the isms stem from Baudelaire and include Dada and Surrealism.

VII **1930–50 – Reactionary Modernism** The movements led by Mussolini, Franco, Hitler and Stalin that accepted the modern notion of the zeitgeist and a progressive technology and mass production.

VIII **1960s – Late Modernism** Tied to Late Capitalism. The proliferation of formalist movements, such as Op and Conceptual Art, and the exaggeration of abstract experiments in a Minimalist direction eschewing content. John Cage in music, Norman Foster in architecture, Frank Stella in painting, Clement Greenberg in art theory, Samuel Beckett in literature, and the _Pax Americana_ in politics.

IX **1970s – Post-Modernism** Stemming from the counter culture, was the double-coding of modernism with other languages to communicate with a local or wide audience. In literature, John Barth and Umberto Eco, in urbanism and architecture, Jane Jacobs and James Stirling, in the arts, Pop Art, Land Art and the content-driven work of Ron Kitaj, Mark Tansey and Damien Hirst.

X **2000 – Critical Modernism** Refers both to the continuous dialectic between modernisms as they criticise each other and to the way the compression of many modernisms forces a self-conscious criticality, a Modernism-2. Sceptical of its own dark sides, yet celebrating creativity, it finds expression in cities such as Berlin that have come of age under opposite versions of modernity.

NB. _Prefix-Modernisms_, emerging in the last hundred years, contest a single, monolithic modernism.

superior and often technologically or even hygienically more advanced than those that went before. Yet this progressivist reflex, while pointing to a real creativity, has also on occasion brought untold suffering and unspeakable folly. The destruction of cities, the collectivisation of agriculture under Stalin, the modernity of the Holocaust – to name three crimes – are some of the results of the reflex. The art market, with its shock of the marginally new, has infantilised a generation. Modernism has been the dominant cultural paradigm in the West since the Second World War and because of that dominance it might have become confident, and mature. But in many ways the reverse has occurred, with a regression to permanent adolescence. No doubt, the progressive side of modernism will continue, and should do so, but it is also time that it came of age, grew up and accepted the negative by-products that also attend its growth. Like post-modernism, it should be sceptical of itself – in short, a critical modernism. One can find this form of temperament operating constantly in my own field of specialisation, architecture, a subject to which I will return throughout and particularly in the last chapter.

A selective, critical response is needed to globalisation and post-modernism, and beyond that a careful attention to the possibilities. Now that post-modernism is no longer either a runaway fashion or despised corrupter of the modern faith, it is easier to attend to its peculiar charm and quality. This is its taste for the hybrid moment, the instant of creation, when two different systems are suddenly conjoined so that one can appreciate both sides of the equation and their union. As the usual conjunction of post-modernism, I have called this creative binding 'double coding' and it is similar to what the writer Arthur Koestler termed in a book of this name, the act of creation. The basic act he termed 'bisociation', that is the bringing together of two previously independent matrices, organisms or systems so that their hidden commonalty is discovered. Many fields retain a memory of this bisociation in their names, such as bio-chemistry and astro-physics (and I keep the hyphen in post-modernism to signal the same creative hybridisation). Unusual names should mark changing situations.

This is particularly important with complex political change. At the turn of the 1990s, when the communist world was beginning to unravel in Eastern Europe, the Professor of European Studies at Oxford, Timothy Garton Ash, coined some very striking terms to explain what a strange slide was going on. He wrote that the transformations were neither a full reform of communism nor a revolution away from it, but rather an unlikely mixture. 'Revorm', he called it, or the equally strange and hybrid, 'refolution'. I think the subsequent years have confirmed these insights. Much of the communist old guard holds on to some power and yet has accepted a quasi-democracy, different versions of capitalism and a host of new laws and institutions that decentralise power. These former autocrats have become cryptic pluralists, in all but name. In East, now Central, Europe so many individuals and policies have caught the through-train to the present EU that, with minimum bloodshed, the post-modern hybrids have turned out to be rather successful. Of course, this begs the question of how much of the communist past remains in each country and how much has changed, but it does underline the point that one needs to develop an eye for shifting slides, routes of movement more than points. One might also develop a taste for emergent forms of hybridisation, for that is what each pm revorm and refolution demands.

To dramatise the mixed transformations, bubbling above and below the surface, I have coined a new set of hybrid terms, or neologisms. Samuel Johnson, writing in the more relaxed and integrated culture of the eighteenth century, allowed an author only one new-fangled construction per book (and see his negative definition of 'modernism', above). I break his rule several times, not only because traditions are moving faster, but rather more to highlight the hybrid creations, to underscore their component pasts, and nudge the reader into taking note. Of course, Dr Johnson is right and neologisms are annoying, especially when there is an old word that can do the job. At the same time, language is remorselessly conservative and hides new realities behind tired labels. The reader will find I have coined the hybrid 'Socitalism' for this reason, to show how hundred-year-old 'socialism' and 'capitalism' have masked emergent realities and their fundamental combination. The new economy is the effective hybrid of socialised capitalism (not the reverse), one that is managed, packaged and run by the 'cognitariat', the thinkers and leaders who inhabit the knowledge-based industries that make the world turn. So it goes in several chapters, culminating in 'cosmogenesis', the hybridisation of cosmic evolution with the Genesis myth. This is not a term of mine but one coined in the late nineteenth century when a premature, ultimately abortive, synthesis was attempted. But, however forced and bogus the idea was then, I cannot think of a better phrase, so have used this old neologism.

Just as important to my purpose are diagrams and maps. In a single image they can clarify the shifts and slides under way with a depth and succinctness that would require a considerable number of words to accomplish. A good diagram, like a mathematical equation, can make a pattern of nature more understandable, and beyond this it can dramatise the most important forces at work, visually, according to their relevance. Today the most creative architects think, see and talk diagrams; they use computers to comprehend multifarious data that are then mapped. As has been shown in several cases, relevant diagrams can save lives. For instance, they revealed the link between particular water pumps and cholera in nineteenth-century London and they led to the solution of what caused the *Challenger* space shuttle disaster in 1986. Richard Feynman, the physicist who supplied the world with the famous Feynman diagrams of atomic particles, used analytical sketches (and a cup of ice water to hand) to show how the rubber seals on the shuttle were eroded by hot gas. Explanations are wordy diagrams. True, a diagram or chart always simplifies – and that is the point: to be the shorthand that saves a thousand words. I have used over twenty here, drawing or redrawing them to bring out the salient features of complex hybrids.

A few ideas, and some of the examples in this book, are modifications of previous work taken from four editions of a small tract known as *What is Post-Modernism?* This polemic was first delivered as a talk in Germany then published in 1985, and updated continuously since then, selling over 38,000 copies. This figure includes editions that were legal, such as the German, but not those from China and Muslim countries, which were presented to me, very graciously, well after publication. I remember one adept translator, who spent the day communicating my thoughts in Chinese to a world conference on architecture in Shanghai, in 1989. Unlike the thousand dark-suited conference-goers, he was dressed in excellent-fitting brown tweeds and, except for his Chinese face, looked every inch the sophisticated English academic. Waiting until the end of the day, he gave me translations of two different books on post-modernism, both mine, both pirated by the most advanced electronic means of reproduction. I was delighted and flattered, of course, by this form of exact plagiarism, an example of the instant globalisation I had been talking about (see also below, Chapter 3). In any case, the computer has indeed helped the rewriting here and for the fifth time, continuing what I have called an 'evolvotome' (a neologism that apparently I alone like). Now, however, the book has been completely revised and is over five times its original length. In effect, it is an entirely new book with a new argument and new title to mark the transformation.

The notion of critical modernism (lower case) was first broached in the year 2000, at the RIBA Annual Discourse and in various articles. I argued for the existence of a hidden pattern of modernisms critical of each other bubbling away under the surface but did not broach the question of this book, of whether such a pattern constitutes a conscious movement (upper case). An early version of this talk was published as 'Jencks' theory of evolution – an overview of twentieth-century architecture' in *The Architectural Review* (July 2000, pp 76–9), and in a more developed form as 'Canons in Crossfire, On the Importance of Critical Modernism', in *Harvard Design Magazine* (Summer 2001, pp 42–8). Another talk, and publication, on which I have drawn was given at *The Boston, Melbourne, Oxford Conversazione on Culture and Society*, 20–21 November 1998. It was for a conference called 'Post-Modernisms: Origins, Consequences, Reconsiderations', later published by Boston University (2002). My paper developed the opposition of its title, 'Restructive Post-Modernism versus Deconstructive Post-Modernism'.

An alternative subtitle for this book might have been the overblown – 'a personal and illustrated view of many trends and theoretical points'. Abstract ideas and evolutionary tendencies, for the most part, are here tested against the evidence, and against particular objects or works of art. In keeping with this course of illustrated enquiry, I have taken most of the photographs. My former professor Reyner Banham used to insist that for a critic 'being there makes the difference' – observing, taking note, avoiding the clichéd view, understanding what an artist or architect might be up to by seeing for oneself the object of investigation in the round and in its context. For what it's worth, I have seen and recorded almost every work illustrated here and helped render most of the concepts into diagram form. My PA, Gillian Innes, has also reconceived many of these charts and photographs on Photoshop, to simplify them and make them more self-explanatory. I am grateful for her patience and skill at this laborious form of digital enhancement, which improves the work of one quick sketch in ten counterintuitive steps. She has also been quick to spot the infelicities of my prose, as has Louisa Lane Fox, and also my editors Helen Castle at John Wiley and copyeditor Lucy Isenberg. Helen suggested this rewrite without knowing that it would expand the length of the last one greatly: the Fourth Edition has increased fivefold. I am indebted to her for seeing it through the many stations of life and supporting its new name and concept. As before I have tried to integrate text, image and caption together. For this careful textual knitting I am much obliged to the layout skill and design of Liz Sephton, the picture research of Calver Lezama and content editor Louise Porter. To my close friend, the literary agent Ike Williams, I am grateful for supplying Dr Johnson's definitions of the 'modern'.

Charles Jencks
November 2006

1. THE ORIGINS OF POST-MODERNISM

PM is Critical Modernism

America is modern, Europe is post-modern; the Ford Motor Company was modern, Amazon is post-modern; Tony Blair is modern (or, so at least is his mantra), Gorbachev was post-modern after a fashion; 'capitalism' and 'socialism' were modern when they were first used in 1810 and now the hybrid 'socitalism' is pm; Camembert is modern, Cambozola is post-modern and the recent Camelbert (like Brie but from camel milk) is very pm; Auschwitz was modern, Shock and Awe featured on television was post-modern; Minimalism is modern, Picasso was both.

In all parlour games, and oppositions between this and that, one has to be prepared for third terms, surprises, things that do not fit. No classification of a period ever covers the multiplicity of currents that flow through it, and all classifications simplify the character of the streams. Yet the paradox in each category clarifies important themes and without these it is hard, if not impossible, to see what is going on. Any classification is better than none, for it makes one turn over the evidence in a new way, think again.

Post-Modernism is written several ways, there are many more meanings to the term than these different spellings and, to make matters worse, these meanings change over time. Like 'Modernism' the usage and concept are dynamic, somewhat unstable, but nevertheless here to stay. Hence it is helpful to remember that there are three connected pms – Post-Modernism, post-modernity, post-modernisation. They support each other like members of an arch, but are quite different.

Post-Modernism, with its capital letters, was a movement in the arts, particularly in my chosen field, architecture, but it is also in the developed world today related to a prevailing social condition – post-modernity. This is the omnipresent reality, particularly in the West, of networking, social levelling, moral relativism, multiculturalism, global migration and media hype. Some experience it more as an illness to be suffered than a state to be sought after. Whether involuntary, or positively embraced as the force of pluralism, it is now chronic and here to stay because it is based on the underlying facts of the third term in the equation, post-modernisation. This is computer production and googling consumption as omnipresent as the air we breathe and as invisible as the electronic exchange of billions of dollars that passes over our heads every minute. Indeed, so much part of the background has this sort of post-modernisation become that it seems old hat, like the modernism of the factory and the International Style.

Yet this ubiquity of our three pms is deceptive, and it hides a deeper reality, the continuing power of the modern world. The modernist condition of expanding industry, mechanised warfare and nationalism is still, barely, in the ascendant, and is the most powerful world-view, with the USA its principal arbiter. Its chronic malady – ecological stress caused by economic success – is now irreversible and, like all social addictions, will not be given up without a possibly lethal trauma. Even when oilaholics like Bush acknowledge their addiction to the nation, they do nothing about it because it is too painful. The modern world, compelled forward by the imperative of continuous growth, is a juggernaut with no reverse gear. Every pm obstacle or treaty put in its path, from the Club of Rome Report on the *Limits to Growth* (1972), to the *Bruntland Report* (1987), to the recommendations of the Rio Earth Summit (1992) and the Kyoto Protocol (1995), is rolled over as if it is a mere bump in the road. In spite of increasing warning sighs and warming signs – such as the big Greenland glaciers sliding into the sea – the juggernaut accelerates ahead, celebrating the opportunity afforded by the new, thawing lands of the Arctic Circle.[1] [3] Modernism has another life. Here is virgin territory, not entirely owned, full of minerals and waiting to be exploited. New gas and oilfields in the Barents Sea, new shipping lanes to make a fortune, new virgin fishing stock waiting for high-tech nets, even new tourist sites. Global warming? Why worry, Go North!

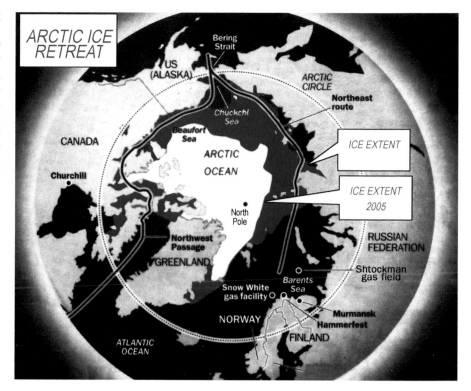

RIGHT [3] **Arctic melts, black gold rush starts.** The ice retreat, a visible sign of global warming for thirty years, brings with it not only a catastrophic rise in global sea levels but new wealth to the Norwegians and Russians. The latters Shtokman Field is the largest offshore gas reserve in the world. The rush for oil, new shipping passages and the scramble for unclaimed territory by eight nations, shows the modernist juggernaut ploughing ahead, come what may. (C Jencks after *The Times*, London)

Since the 1960s, when cultural post-modernism started, the global economy has doubled in size so often, made the rich so much richer and lifted so many out of poverty that it has become the only politically pragmatic paradigm of growth. In effect, for the modern world and its leaders, the model of Late Capitalism is accepted as an article of faith. Its tenets of controlled competition have been elevated to a religion; its oligopolies and multinationals accepted as the order of things; its World Bank and IMF operate as its missionary arms, and global modernisation is its First Commandment. In America it amounts to mortgaging the future in exchange for 3 per cent growth, a set of economic stimulus packages, living off credit, and a national debt running at 6 per cent; in China, Late Capitalism means an impressive 9 per cent growth, but at the cost of party control over investment and information. These two modern titans keep the juggernaut sliding ahead.

In this heady situation, post-modernism is, as it was in the 1960s, a loyal and cantankerous opposition, a modernism in its self-critical phase. More simply it can be Critical Modernism, a point that explains, at once, several paradoxes. It is why Post-Modernism will last for the foreseeable future, that is just as long as does Modernism, and it is why some of the most committed Post-Modernists are those who have left the High Church. They are apostates who understand from experience, and only too well, the inherent limitations of their former faith.

High Church? Religion? Apostasy? Are these adequate metaphors with which to think about something so secular as a cultural movement? Well, yes and no. No figures of speech are adequate to explain an epoch or movement – neither the 'Goths', those invading tribes who accidentally gave their name to a period, nor their successors engaged in a rebirth of ancient cultures, those supposedly of the Renaissance. The naming and classification of periods is a necessary fiction, one that brings out some major motivations, and one that simplifies the cross currents that are always flowing through history and channels them into a single stream. My own experience, as a student of architecture in the 1960s, typifies this channelling and, in turn, leads to a personal aside that illustrates the post-modern movement.

I was trained at Harvard under the tutelage of a group of Europeans, the second generation of Modernists led by the Dean of the architecture school, José Luis Sert, himself a disciple of Le Corbusier. Corb, as he was known, was also called the Pioneer of Modernism by a few historians, or the Hero of the Heroic Period – phrases that suggest his missionary role. As explained below (under *'Modernism as a Protestant Crusade'*), Le Corbusier was not just an architect, but like Mies van der Rohe or the other Pioneers, one with a calling, and therefore to learn architecture in a school such as Harvard was not simply to gain a skill but to adopt a way of life and thought, a hope and belief for a world transformed. His idealism, and that of the European Modernism of the early 1920s, was a moral force to be reckoned with, especially if one believed the intentions (social utopianism) and did not look closely at the results (disdain for local cultures). Around the world, Le Corbusier was the dominant force in most architectural schools at the time and I, like so many others, came under his commanding presence. Huge photographs of this Pope of Modernism were put up for his visitation to Harvard, iconic shots of the stern Calvinist with his owl-like glasses resting authoritatively on a furrowed brow. [4]

The many deaths of modernism

At about the same time, other currents were flowing through the school. Jane Jacobs had written her withering critique of Corbusian planning, *The Death and Life of Great American Cities* (1961), and another American, Rachel Carson, had fired one of the first shots of post-modern ecology, *Silent Spring* (1962). To my amazement, Sert and the Modernist apostles who dominated the other Ivy League schools had no convincing answer to either woman. In fact, like religions under attack, they simply ignored the criticism, and the way modern planning

ABOVE [4] **Le Corbusier and Walter Gropius, 1953.** Black-rimmed glasses and bow tie, two perfected object-types which Le Corbusier turned into icons for modern architects and their mission of abstraction, purity and mass-production. (© Dokumentation Le Corbusier, Stiftung Heidi Weber, Zurich)

and development were destroying cities functionally, economically and socially. This is why I felt it necessary to amplify the first very visual critique, the blowing up of Minoru Yamasaki's Pruitt-Igoe housing blocks, framing it as 'The Death of Modernism'. While others had noted the demise of the modern novel and other art forms, the photographs of these architectural explosions were indisputable and seen repeatedly on television. One could hardly deny such visible failures, especially when they were repeated in many other modern cities, and to this day. [5] The formulation was that 'Modern Architecture died in St Louis, Missouri on July 15, 1972, at 3:32 pm (or thereabouts) when the infamous Pruitt-Igoe scheme, or rather several of its slab blocks, were given the final *coup de grace* by dynamite … Boom, boom, boom.' This mythical moment and interpretation became a media event, after I announced it in 1977, in *The Language of Post-Modern Architecture*. It was repeated in countless languages, books and encyclopaedias, especially behind the Iron Curtain where modern housing was tied to the modern state and enforced as doctrine.

My factoid was believed because the world wished modern housing to die an ignominious death – I, of course, had no idea of the exact time in 1972. But the pseudo news bulletin, in our mediated society, had an electrifying effect. The architectural historian John Summerson wrote that this putative death was the most creative idea of Post-Modernism, because it liberated everyone from the false notion that the modern was the eternal present and therefore always with us, not the historical construct that it is.

ABOVE & RIGHT [5] **Pruitt-Igoe housing, the explosion seen round the world, 1972.** Such demolition soon became a recurrent ritual for modern blocks seen to have failed and one that continues today.

There were, inevitably, many other candidates for the original demise. Since modernism is the ideology of Henry Ford and bulk production, the most convincing argument was that the First World War was the true moment of death, since it produced killing at a rate never seen before. Russia suffered the most with 9 million casualties, followed by Britain with 7 million and France with 6 million. The overall count was 37 million. Although *the* modern institution par excellence – the nation-state – was the killing machine, and the idea of modernisation (progress at all costs) was a leading ideology, the diagnosis was not conceived that way. Rather, it was seen as ending the old order of Europe. Thus, when the War to End All Wars was over, it became an excuse for more modernism, not less. Indeed, post-1918 was the time when so many modern-'isms' sprouted that, as some wit claimed, their quick succession created so many 'wasms'.

Still, historians of the modern world had a good case: with its roots somewhere in the Renaissance, the nation-state was *the* engine of all modern life and, along with its factory methods of mass production, its destructiveness was unparalleled. The Second World War and what is called Total War (war against civilian populations) thus became further evidence for those trying to diagnose the contemporary pathology. The numbers game is horrific, but again it is how the media present the facts, as if bean counting (in the modern world) were the justification for belief. Thus, according to usual statistics, the Second World War killed 50 million people, Stalin in his project of enforced modernisation wiped out 35 million and Mao, pursuing similar goals, slaughtered 70 million. The death camps of the Nazis mass-produced 6 million dead. Each number becomes the foundation stone for the death of an ideology and the birth of a post-modernism; or perhaps, as with Israel, the emergence of a new nation-state.

Of course, post-modernism only grew in stature because it offered some positive, critical alternatives, and thus one could consider sociological and cultural explanations that placed its birth in the era of the 1960s. The pluralist counter-culture, feminism, the sudden dominance of the post-industrial workforce in America were all put forward as reasons. I found these arguments more persuasive and thus worked out a scenario of ten critical deaths, post 1960, that might become harbingers of a more positive paradigm. Some were very dramatic turning points, such as the nuclear meltdown at Chernobyl in April 1986, or the moment when Yeltsin turned his tanks on the remaining communist power structure and opened fire on 4 October 1993, at exactly 10:10 am. The clock on the top of the Supreme Soviet

OPPOSITE [6] **The White House turned red and blue.** Boris Yeltsin, the president, counter-attacked a hardline communist parliament resisting change, turning the tanks on the Supreme Soviet Building. The battle was between the neo-liberal oligarchs and the old Nomenklatura, two modernist leviathans, battling it out in a bloated modern box. As it happened, I arrived for an exhibition in Moscow on Post-Modernism just afterwards, and argued that they should refurbish the now blackened box in these tricolours to preserve a memory of the way events structure meaning: blue aluminium for the repaired part; red for the 187 killed inside; and white for the good intentions. But a year later the result was another whitewash. (Photomontage by Charles Jencks and Jason Rigby)

Building struck the time and, as I happened to arrive soon afterwards in Moscow for an exhibition at the Tretyakov Gallery, I got the precise moment right this time. [6] Most tipping points are not so clear-cut as this, and they are greatly amplified if the global media is in on the execution, as it was here.

To change a way of thinking takes a long time and a lot of blood. As physicists ruefully proclaim, because of the power of the old paradigm in science and the tenure system in the universities, 'physics proceeds death by death'. Or, as cardinals in the Vatican say, looking forward to a new Pope, 'where there's death there's hope'. Oscar Wilde wrote that 'experience is the name we give to our mistakes'. The list that follows is based mostly on ecological and economic mistakes and moments of political confrontation. Each is a moment of learning the hard way:

Ten Deaths of Modernism – Post-1960

1	**1968** May riots, French students attack Bigness
2	**1969** Civil Rights and Vietnam protests
3	**1971** Oil spill; **1986** Chernobyl; **1992** Exxon Valdez
4	**1972** Blowing up of Pruitt-Igoe and housing estates
5	**1973** Oil Crisis – nationalism and cartels of OPEC
6	**1978** Brazil, Mexico, Third World Debt
7	**1979** End of Keynesian economics, the Modern Settlement
8	**1980** Solidarity in Poland rises against Totalitarianism
9	**1989** Fall of Communism in Eastern Europe
10	**1993** 4 October Yeltsin storms Supreme Soviet

This eclectic list shows the chronic problems of the old paradigm, and reveals a pattern. However, it also suggests the ability of modernism to survive crises, an almost infinite capacity to absorb lethal blows. It was only in architecture, where mass-production values confronted differing ways of life, that the issues seemed clearer, and the death of modernism was accepted. Or, as the debate grew, so it seemed.

Two views of post-modernism

In 1979, the French philosopher Jean-François Lyotard published *La Condition postmoderne*, a book that had an extraordinary global reception and one that launched a different sort of post-modernism, as the reader will find. Later, in *The Postmodern Explained to Children*, he wrote that 'Auschwitz … is a crime opening up postmodernity' and claimed that it was the tragedy of the Holocaust that also sealed the fate of metanarratives.[2] The grand narratives that underlie social cohesion – socialism, progress, belief in religious doctrines, or, for intellectuals, belief in Enlightenment reason, even the credibility of science – were faiths to which it was no longer possible to adhere. Following Critical Theorists Lyotard wrote that grand narratives were used ideologically by powerful institutions to legitimise their authority; for instance, the march of socialism was employed by communist countries to quash dissent. He pointed out that in the post-modern period, the knowledge industries had taken over from the traditional productive industries, and their metanarratives dominated over local micro-narratives. By 1980, with the Venice Biennale on the subject and as the post-modern gathered strength and became a world movement, we found common ground between our views: the need to defend the small, the local and the plural against the large and the hegemonic; the importance of irony and language games in furthering difference. But he supported an artistic version of 'the sublime and the unutterable' as post-modern goals, while I found them evasive, pseudo-religious and really Late-Modern as ideals.

On such points Lyotard and I were critical of each other; ours were contrasting accounts of the fledgling movement perceived by him (more as a 'condition'). Where he defined post-modernism as a slackening of modernism into eclecticism, I found a positive hybridisation that I called 'double coding'. The divergences widened and so there were attempts to bring us together, in face-to-face debate. In spite of several close encounters of the conference kind, satirised in David Lodge's post-modern novel, *Small World*, Lyotard and I never met, in the physical sense, but we had one very convivial parody of an encounter, in the electronic sense, that clarifies the two major types of post-modernism. The pretext was a BBC radio programme of 1995, in which I interviewed several post-modern scientists, among them Ilya Prigogine and Stuart Kauffman.[3] However, the best Lyotard and I could manage was to sit together in different studios, he in Paris, I in London. After exchanging the customary pleasantries, and my being charmed by his French politesse, we attacked our main difference. The exchange went something like this:

CJ   Metanarratives have hardly ended. Rather people believe many more things today, beliefs have proliferated!

J-FL   After the Holocaust, one cannot believe in continuous progress, economic or social, nor the Kantian notion that democracies don't make war, nor so many other metanarratives of modernism …

This was the moment I had been waiting for, the argument I was proffering in the BBC programme, and so I countered with a ready-made answer: 'But today we have a new metanarrative, coming from the post-modern sciences of complexity and the new cosmology, the idea of cosmogenesis, the story of the developing universe, the notion that the evolving cosmos is a single, creative, unfolding event that includes life and us in its narrative, one that locates culture in space and time.' [7] I was fascinated to see how he would respond. Just as he started off, in a positive direction agreeing with much I said, the producer entered the studio and said the corporation had double-booked the room. This was double coding with a vengeance: we must leave, immediately.

In spite of attempts to find another place for recording, we never finished this promising beginning. The moment was lost just as it was reaching a climax, *cultus interruptus*. With Lyotard's death a few years later, I reflected ruefully that our non-meeting had been in some ways

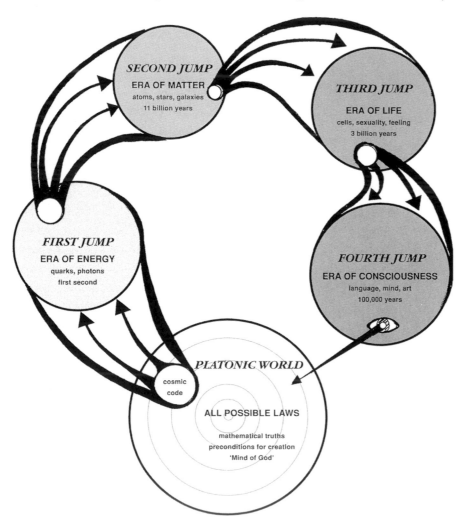

LEFT [7] **The Universe in Four Jumps: energy, matter, life, consciousness.** Each of the four worlds emerges unpredictably from a small part of its predecessor and our world is the first to look back and reflect on the underlying causes and laws. The post-modern sciences of complexity, as opposed to the modern reductive sciences, investigate these holistic laws of emergence. (C Jencks)

very post-modern. It was fragmentary, contested, mediated and then destroyed by the media, and thus I consoled myself with the thought that he would have derived some ironic pleasure from the interrupted consensus. For him, as for so many others, postmodernism (streamlined as a single word) was a condition more than a movement, it 'was a war on totality'. Dissensus, the struggle of micronarratives, or for me, pluralism, were at the heart of the various post-modernisms, and we shared the view that these minorities should oppose the modern juggernaut. This common agenda is worth emphasising. Critical pluralism always plays a role whenever the term is used. I keep the hyphen and avoid the streamline to underscore this plurality.

Post-modern speaks us

Which of us was closer to the truth, or the better diagnostician, was not the only issue at stake, because in the early 1980s the concept started to multiply like a linguistic virus and infect most people with a slightly different meaning, positive and negative. It was this differential usage that gave the phrase energy, and virulence. As so often with keywords, they were speaking through us. Language, as many have observed, is a social contract that no one writes, that no group or academy controls. Like the economy or fashion, words emerge and become socially accepted through reuse, and in this conventional sense we did not choose 'post-modern', it chose us.

Positive movement, negative condition and description of an epoch – these three formulations drove the concept in conferences, books, scholarly papers and lead articles. Today a list of pm book titles would fill a thousand pages; a full bibliography would become a small encyclopaedia. In spite of the dislike of the name it has become the label for seventeen anthologies I possess, and a search on the Internet would probably produce another fifty.[5] The term is now almost as ubiquitous and misunderstood as its parent, the modern. By 1992, the British newspaper *The Independent* recommended its use to mean anything you care to think about the present.

Like Modernism, it achieved a kind of linguistic lock-in on the future tense. The notion of lock-in is well developed in biology, product design and technology. For instance, the keyboard I am writing on – QWERTY (the first six letters of the 1890s' typewriter) – achieved lock-in more than a hundred years ago, in spite of being sub-optimal from several functional standpoints. Now computers, which have no movable gears (the prime reason for QWERTY) and other digital instruments, follow this convention. Many species, or industrial

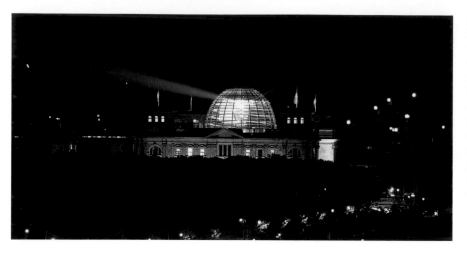

products, reveal this mixture of universal function and contingent compromise, and both get locked-in by evolutionary development. The five major religions, growing up in a period when magical thinking was possible, have had lock-in on collective worship ever since, and given their head start and monopoly all attempts to create competing religious have been marginalised.

'Post-modern', sub-optimal though it is in certain respects, achieved lock-in because of its semantic one-upmanship. Since modern comes from the Latin *modo* meaning 'just now', post-modern trumps it by meaning 'just after' just now. Or, it carries a spatial and temporal superiority of being 'beyond, contra, above, ultra, meta, outside-of' the present. The impossibility of this makes it maddening – and all the more desirable. Indeed, the paradox of being more modern than modern generates anger, as if it could overcome Oscar Wilde's jibe at the latest new thing: 'Nothing is so dangerous as being too modern, one is apt to grow old-fashioned quite suddenly.'

Put positively, the attack on the present tense is motivated by the idea of living across time, in a historical and cultural continuum that stretches into the future, living in a greater dimension than one period. It denies the flatness of 'presentism', and insists that memory and cultural DNA are built into the universe in a way that modernism underrates. In this case it is the 'post' of the term that relates to '*posterity*'; the desire and delights of living across cultural zones. [8] It is also a rebuttal of nostalgia because, while acknowledging the past, it does so in a way that is ironic and non-revivalist. The 'post' sees both traditional culture and modernism in its rear-view mirror.

PM also carries an overtone of spiritual and political transcendence, a desire to go beyond contemporary stalemates, the pettiness that freezes disputes at a low stage of resolution. Going

(I) PRE-HISTORY – 1870-1950 POST-MODERN AS MODERN PERIOD IN DECLINE (OR RARELY) ULTRA-MODERN

Post-Modern, 1870-1914. John Watkins Chapman, Rudolf Pannwitz
Post-Industrialism, 1914-22, Arthur J Penty
postmodernismo, 1934, Federico de Onis
post-Modernism, 1945, Bernard Smith
post-modern house, 1945, Joseph Hudnut
Post-Modern Age, 1939/1946, Arnold Toynbee
Postmodern poets, 1946, Randall Jarrell
Post-Historic Man, 1950, Roderick Seidenberg
post-Modern sciences, 1954, Arnold Toynbee
postmodernism, 1954, Charles Olson
Postmodern Fiction as Decline, 1959, Irving Howe, 1960 Harry Levin
post-capitalism, 1959, Ralf Dahrendorf

(II) 1950-80 PM DEFINED POSITIVELY AS COUNTER CULTURE, DOUBLE-CODING, 'POSTS', PLURALISM AND DECREATION

postbourgeois, 1963, George Lichtheim
postmodernist worldly writers, 1963, William van O'Connor
post-civilisation, 1964, Kenneth Boulding
post-scarcity economy, 1966
Post-Modern religion, 1968, John Cobb
Post-humanist anti-elitism, 1965 Leslie Fielder
post-modern period, 1968, Amitai Etzioni
Poststructuralism, 1969, Jacques Derrida
post-collectivist politics, 1969, Sam Beer
post-liberal era, 1969, Sir Geoffrey Vickers
Post-Christian, 1970, Lewis Feuer

post-traditional societies, 1970, SN Eisenstadt
post-economic man, 1970, Herman Kahn
post-tribal societies, 1971, Eric Hobsbawm
POSTmodernISM/mystical silence, 1971/1975, Ihab Hassan
Postmodern American poetry, 1971, David Antin
Postmodern literature, 1972, William Spanos
Post-Marxism, 1973, Daniel Bell
Postmodern American poetics, 1973, Charles Altieri
Post-Industrial Society, 1973, Daniel Bell
Post-Modern Architecture, 1975, Charles Jencks
post-modern dance, 1975, Michael Kirby
Post-Modern science, 1976, Frederick Ferre/Stephen Toulmin
postmodernismus, 1977, Michael Kohler/Jürgen Peper
post-materialism, 1977
Deconstructive postmodernism, 1979
La Condition Postmodern, 1979, Jean-François Lyotard
Postmodern fiction as replenishment, 1980, John Barth

(III) 1980+ PM CONDITION ATTACKED, PM CULTURE ANTHOLOGISED, PM GLOBAL MORALITY DEFINED

postminimalism, 1979
post-performance art, 1980s
Post-Modernity Destroys Meaning, 1981, Jean Baudrillard
postmodern sublime, 1982, Jean-François Lyotard
Post-National Economics, 1983

Postmodern Pluralism, 1983, Matei Calinescu
Postmodern irony & enjoyment, 1983, Umberto Eco
Postmodernism, The Cultural Logic of Late-Capitalism 1984, Frederic Jameson
Post-Fordism, 1984
Post-Feminism, 1984
Postmodern *weltanschauung*, 1984, Hans Bertens
Postmodern Culture, 1984, Hal Foster
Po-Mo, 1985, pejorative phrase in use
Post-Logical Positivism, 1985, Mary Hesse
Post-Modern Aura, 1985, Charles Newman
Constructive Postmodernism, 1986, David Ray Griffin
postmodern excremental culture, 1986, Kroker/Cook
postmodern politics, 1986, J Arac
Post-Darwinism, 1987
Postmodern society, 1987, Scott Lash, Anthony Giddens
postmodern poetics, 1988, Linda Hutcheon
Postmodern geography, 1988, Edward Soja
The Condition of Postmodernity, 1989, David Harvey
Post-Cold War, 1989
Post-history, 1990, Francis Fukuyama
Ecological postmodernism, 1989, Charles Birch/Charlene Spretnak
Postmodern global ethic, 1991, Hans Kung
Post-Modern agenda, 1992, Charles Jencks
Postmodern Ethics & Morality, 1992-3, Zygmunt Bauman

ABOVE [9] **Seventy Posts and their three phases.** The first use was unsystematic and often referred to a new period when the modern lost direction. The second defined the concept positively in terms of pluralism, decentring and counter-cultures, while the third phase analysed the negative post-modern condition and the various positive movements. (C Jencks)

beyond the modern means, in spatial terms, getting above the provincial landscape to achieve an overview, climbing a hill to see the bigger picture and then climbing out of that, in turn. In this sense, it is yet one more inheritor of Romanticism.

Such continual transcendence underlies the 'posties' that have been around since the 1880s, and one of the first, 'Post-Impressionism'. As the diagram of Seventy Posts suggests, [9] there is a type of futurism involved here, a continual revolution where each stage achieved entails both the past and the future stage. Thus post-industrial implies industry transcended but still present. Common to these seventy usages is the notion of *posteriority*, the transition from a known classifier to an unknown but suggestive future. Post-Christianity implies Christianity evolving on a global scale into a new hybrid, something that retains the valuable teachings of Christ, but cuts them away from the non-credible beliefs, and orients to a cosmic future.

Post-modern chose us in the 1980s because it was so precise and ambiguous at the same time; accurate about the port we left and richly suggestive about the destination to which we are headed. The direction comes from both the past cultural weighting and the pull of a future that will be different and critical of the present. Thus it has, as one of its core meanings, the motivation of double coding: the continuation of modernity *and* its transcendence. For literary critics, such as Linda Hutcheon, post-modern writers appropriate previous forms of literature in order to 'interrogate', 'subvert' and 'problematise' them. (She excuses such 'linguistic barbarisms' as having become 'an essential part of the discourse of postmodernism'.) Irony, parody and metafiction are the main ways this literature inscribes itself into the dominant while, at the same time, distancing itself from the mainstream. Again, these typical strategies of double coding make pm a *critical* modernism.

One should stress these subtle relationships because so often, especially in the style wars between modernists and traditionalists, pm finds itself caricatured on one extreme side or the other, when its intention is to be pluralist and cut across the antinomies. It does not, as the philosopher Jürgen Habermas contends, reject the Enlightenment project; that is, the social emancipation of humanity, increasing freedoms and universal rights. Rather, it rejects the totalising arguments with which universal rights are imposed by an elite on a subservient minority (along with so much else). Modern liberalism fought for the universal rights, which the developed world now partly enjoys. Post-modern liberalism argues that the agenda of multiculturalism, and the rights of minorities, should be asserted where they do not diminish the rights of other minorities.[6] In this sense it is the direct heir of its parent, modernism, and could not have occurred previously, nor existed without the prior assumptions of universalism. It is true that these two ideas of liberalism are sometimes in conflict, but that does not make either of them invalid. They are both necessary to the concept of a just society.

This double identity may result from the genetic connection between the two camps, especially on a cultural level. The initial Post-Modernists in literature, architecture and philosophy were first trained with the tenets and methods of Modernism, and then went beyond this training by going back to the past, or sideways to a local culture, or anywhere outside the present boundaries of space and time. They did this for philosophical reasons, and also for quite ordinary ones: because they had a different sensibility and a taste for heterogeneity. Post-Modernists simply enjoy variety and take pleasure in the mixture of cultures. They consume across the unities of time, place and background, high-life and low. Peter Blake perfectly captures the pleasure of opposites in his painting of three British artists meeting on the beach of Venice, California. There is a mock-heroic meeting with the grand Mr Hockney, based on a nineteenth-century allegory, but now placed amid the skaters, fast food and palm trees. [10] And Post-

OPPOSITE [10] **Peter Blake, *The Meeting or Have a Nice Day Mr Hockney***, oil on canvas, 39in x 49in, 1981–3. The taste for heterogeneity supports the pluralism. Depicted is an ironic meeting of 1960s' Pop painters in 1980s' Venice, that is, the one in California. This new version of Courbet's *The Meeting or Bonjour Monsieur Courbet* is both a contemporary comment on Classicism and a classical composition in itself. The meeting is between three representational artists – Howard Hodgkin, Peter Blake and David Hockney – the last with a brush rather than a staff in his hand. The squatting girl's pose is taken partly from a skating magazine and partly from classical sculpture. The meeting commemorates a historical act, if not a grand public one, as the nineteenth-century Classicist would have preferred. The artists, ethnic groups, skaters and palm trees are all set in serene contrast. (© Tate London 2007)

Modernists adopted this strategy of heterogeneity to build another tradition, something better, yet still, as the other side of the hyphen suggests, partly *modern*.

Perhaps this explains the schizophrenic streak within the emergent tradition; it certainly clarifies the latent energy, and paranoia, of the label. If modern means up-to-date and is used this way unselfconsciously, then it has a privileged grasp on progress. Modern computers are, by this definition, the most highly developed and immediately privileged over previous generations, that is, in so far as we assume a progressive view of technology (which is to say very far). Thus *post*-modern becomes even more up-to-date, modernism +1, supermodernism, and this evolutionary superiority is why Modernists continued to get upset by the term. It rendered them old-fashioned according to the same logic with which they had consigned the past to the scrap heap of history. While Modernists had rendered local cultures obsolete, their own logic was now suddenly thrown into question by the paradoxical nature of this new equation, which claimed to be both ahead *and* behind the times. The heat of their reaction, their anger, was the spark that ignited the debate in the late 1970s and kept it burning through the 1980s. This was another paradox of Post-Modernism, to thrive because of the paranoia directed against it, to be amplified by Modernist outrage (or, was it a secret love, that dare not speak its name?). Whatever the case – secret love, or love-hate – the virulent name provoked ever-greater response, until the whole world took note.

Screams in the cathedral

In October 1981 *Le Monde* announced to its morning readers, under the section of its newspaper ominously headed 'Decadence', that a spectre was haunting Europe: the spectre of Post-Modernism.[7] What Frenchmen made of this warning as they bit into their croissants is anybody's guess, especially as it came with the familiar Marxist image of a ghost looming over their civilisation (and their coffee) – but they soon forgot the phantom and looked forward to the next morning's 'Decadence' column, for in our culture one ghost grows boring and must be quickly replaced by another. [11]

      The problem, however, became that critics – especially hostile, Modernist critics – would not let this spectre dissolve. They keep attacking the phantom with ever-increasing hysteria, making it grow into quite a substantial force that upset not only *le petit déjeuner* but also international conferences and price quotations on the international art market. Clement Greenberg, long acknowledged as the theorist of American Modernism, defined Post-Modernism in 1979 as the antithesis of the Modernist canon: abstract formalism, the purist concentration of each art form on its own means of expression – the flat canvas, or the aesthetic of 'flatness' for painting, etc. By contrast the dreaded challenger lowered aesthetic standards, and this was caused by 'the democratization of culture under industrialism'.[8] Like the 'Decadence' columnist, Greenberg saw the danger as a lack of hierarchy in artistic judgement, although he did not go so far as the Frenchman in calling it, simply, 'nihilism'. Another art critic, Walter Darby Bannard, writing in the same prestigious *Arts Magazine* five years later, continued Greenberg's crusade against the heathens and restated the

ABOVE [11] *Strada Novissima, Venice Biennale, 1980.* This exhibit, which travelled to France and the USA, put Post-Modernism on the global map and gave the French reporter indigestion. It brought back the street, ornament and colour to architecture, emphasising difference within a shared urbanism. Leon Krier's facade is in the background. (C Jencks)

ABOVE [12] Philip Johnson and John Burgee, **The AT&T Building, New York, 1978–82**. The building first branded as a Chippendale-Highboy became a monumental focus for Post-Modern loathing. Today it seems a rather mellow New York skyscraper. (C Jencks)

same definition, but with more brutal elaboration. 'Postmodernism', he wrote, 'is aimless, anarchic, amorphous, self-indulgent, inclusive, horizontally structured, and aims for the popular'.[9]

Given the standardised nature of these attacks one wonders why he left out the epithets 'ruthless kitsch', or the customary comparison with Nazi populism, which the architectural critic Ken Frampton usually adds to the list of Post-Modernism's sins. Ever since Clement Greenberg asserted his famous opposition between 'Avant-Garde and Kitsch', certain intellectuals have been arguing that it has to be one thing or the other, and it is clear where they classify Post-Modernism, although of course if it is 'horizontally structured' and 'democratic' it cannot be, at the same time, Neo-Nazi and authoritarian. But consistency has never been a virtue of those out to malign a movement.

In the early 1980s the Royal Institute of British Architects (RIBA) hosted a series of revivalist meetings, which were noteworthy for their vicious attacks. In 1981 the Dutch architect Aldo van Eyck delivered the *Annual Discourse* entitled 'Rats, Posts and Other Pests', and one can guess from this appellation how hard he attempted to be fair-minded (the 'Rats' referred also to the Rationalist wing of the 'Posts'). He advised his cheering audience of Modernists in a capital lettered harangue, 'Ladies and Gentlemen, I beg you, HOUND THEM DOWN AND LET THE FOXES GO' – tactics not unlike the Nazi ones he was deploring, although the hounds and foxes gave this pogrom a Wildean twist.[10] If Van Eyck advised letting the dogs loose on Post-Modernists, the older Modern architect Berthold Lubetkin confined himself, on receiving his Gold Medal at the RIBA, to classifying them together with homosexuals, Hitler and Stalin. 'This is a transvestite architecture,' he said in a lightly veiled attack on Philip Johnson and John Burgee's AT&T Building, [12] 'Heppelwhite and Chippendale in drag'.[11] And he continued to compare Post-Modernism with Nazi kitsch in subsequent revivalist meetings in Paris and at the RIBA, equating Prince Charles with Stalin for his attack on Modernism.[12] One could quote similar abuse from old-hat Modernists in America, Germany, Italy, France and the rest of the world. For instance, the noted Italian critic Bruno Zevi saw Post-Modernism as a 'pastiche … trying to copy Classicism' and 'repressive' like fascism.[13] Harry Seidler, the Australian architect, used metaphors of sexual deviance, gender ambiguity and disease to damn the movement, themselves tactics of the 1930s, calling post-modernism 'architectural Aids'.

We can find in such howls of protest something like a negative definition emerging, a paranoid definition made by Modernists in retreat, trying to hold the High Church together, issuing daily edicts denouncing heresy, keeping the faith among a confused following. It was true that, through the 1980s and early 1990s, they kept control of most of the academies, sat on most of the aesthetic review boards, dominated the establishment and repressed as many Post-Modern artists and architects as they could. But many of the creative young were interested in neither suppression nor the previous orthodoxy, and the horizontally structured marketplace became the setting for an open-ended pluralism. In international competitions the entries were fairly split between modern, post-modern, traditional and other approaches, and that generality applies as much to sculpture, painting and new forms, such as Performance Art, as it does to architecture. The door was wide open, as it was in the 1920s, when Modernism had knocked down the previous academic barriers, and challenged the 'ruling taste'.

The irony, not lost on either side, was that the old-time Modernists were determined to be just as paranoid as their Beaux-Arts persecutors had been before them. Indeed, the slurs against Post-Modernists occasionally sounded like the reactionary vitriol poured on Le Corbusier and Walter Gropius in the 1920s, that is, the attacks of the Nazis. Did history repeat itself, but in a new key? Were these smears a kind of unintentional appropriation of fascist tactics? If so, irony upon irony, that would mean Modernists were becoming lazy Post-Modernists, unaware of their borrowings, and therefore worst of all – 'PoMo'. (That abusive phrase, with its sexual innuendo, came in use by 1985 to refer to unconscious parody, unknowing pastiche, kitsch borrowing.)

Whatever the case, the slurs did not do what they were supposed to do – blow away PM – but, on the contrary, blew it up into a media event. Academic fury amplified the movement quickly into a brand name. Post-Modernism joined the list of originally insulting labels that came to identify a period or movement or group – Romanesque, Gothic, Baroque, Rococo, Impressionism, Fauve, Cubism and many more.[14]

Insults and persecution are highly dangerous when used by the Establishment. Like George Bush creating terrorism in Iraq, through paranoia and attack, the Modernists would have done better to speak softly and carry a big stick. But they preferred to scream.

Modernism as a Protestant crusade

Underlying all the modernisms, as I have mentioned, is the root metaphor of the cultural *movement* experienced as a religion. Usually, these movements do not have unchanging creeds, nor do they have a ritualised practice and a deity to be worshipped – which is why they are called pseudo-religions. Nonetheless, as observed about secular religions such as Marxism, they may posit a future society free from conflict and difference, a type of heaven on earth or in architecture a physical utopia. In this light Modernism can be seen as one of the strongest faiths to be espoused since 1820, perhaps a quasi-religion, but nevertheless the first great flowering of Post-Christianity.

Where did this notion come from? It arose when the artistic avant-gardes were seen to have a priestly role, as spiritual and cultural leaders akin to revolutionaries. After the French Revolution, in the early nineteenth century, the idea of a comprehensive intellectual elite was born, an avant-garde that would be an integration of as many adjectives as one could credibly string together. It would be artistic-, socialistic-, positivistic-, political-, theological and so on. Henri de Saint-Simon, soldier and originator of the concept of the avant-garde, wrote on 'New Christianity' at the end of his life and published his *Nouveau Christianisme* in 1825. Advanced artists were to take the role of priests in leading society into a positivistic future because they, of all the professions, had access to public feelings. Unlike scientists, they could sway the sentiments. This advance guard, like the famous image of *Liberty at the Barricades*, would beckon followers over the hurdles, past religions and traditions that were acting as a drag. As Saint-Simon wrote of this elite mission:

> It is we, artists, who will serve you as the avant-garde: the power of the arts is in fact most immediate and most rapid: when we wish to spread new ideas among men, we inscribe them on marble or canvas … and in that way above all we exert an electric and victorious influence. We address ourselves to the imagination and to the sentiments of mankind … what is lacking to the arts [today] is that which is essential to their energy and to their success, namely, a common drive and a general idea.[15]

The 'common drive and general idea' was socialism tied to a revolutionary aesthetics. Thus in 1825 the myth of a romantic advance guard, setting out before the rest of society to conquer new territory, new states of consciousness and social order, was formulated. In the history of Modernism since then there might be few artists who were really politically active, such as Gustave Courbet, and even fewer who were agitating politically, as did Filippo Marinetti and the Futurists, but the ideal lived on [13]. The combination 'new politics + new art' justified the Constructivist designers; it legitimated virtually every Modern-'ism' until the 1960s. Furthermore, the avant-garde, to be

truly *avant* the *arrière*, had to recognise its mission, its crusade. As again Saint-Simon said, echoing the prophetic nature of his name:

> What a most beautiful destiny for the arts, that of exercising over society a positive power, a truly priestly function, and of marching forcefully in the van of all intellectual faculties, in the epoch of their greatest development! This is the duty of artists, this their mission ...[16]

Thus the avant-garde as the new priesthood, thus progressivist art as the harbinger. Here was a role which was elevating – a mission for a social group that was fast becoming a patronless class. Artists, like architects, were often underemployed and at the mercy of a heartless economic system. Where before they had a defined social relationship to a patron – the state, Church or an individual – now they related to a marketplace that was competitive and agnostic.

In this sense Modernism is the first ideological response to a social crisis and the breakdown of a shared religion. Faced with a Post-Christian society, the creative elite formulated a new role for themselves, a spiritual one directed against the crasser forms of materialism, of conspicuous consumption. It is this resistance to the consumerism of the day that turned the avant-garde towards a crusade that was Protestant.

It protested against the dreaded academic bourgeoisie, the *arrière-garde*; it protested against the ostentatious 'ruling class taste' and attacked the notion of different styles (Le Corbusier characterised them as 'a lie', Frank Lloyd Wright as 'a sham'). The

ABOVE [13] **The avant-garde crusade** uniting a new art and politics was kept alive by the Futurists and Constructivists in the twentieth century. Umberto Boccioni, *Unique Forms of Continuity in Space*, Bronze, 1913, Kröller-Müller Museum, Otterlo. A dynamic spatial continuity, postulated by Relativity Theory, parallels the emphasis on fluid social change of the Futurists, often turned into a frozen high art by Marinetti, Sant'Elia and Boccioni. (C Jencks)

ABOVE [14] Adolf Loos, **White Villas of the 1910s.** Loos' arguments against ornament coupled with his prescient white cubes, ten years before the International Style, set the equations for the next forty years. Le Corbusier also adopted from Loos the terrace housing with flat roof, free plan and asymmetrical volumes. The code of Modern Architecture is set as white abstraction. (C Jencks, Vienna Exhibition on Adolf Loos)

avant-garde characterised cultural expression – such as ornament – as outmoded, criminal and degenerate. These last terms were Adolf Loos' formulation in his famous article published in 1908, *Ornament and Crime*. [14] In a witty assault on degenerate aristocrats and criminals he equated cultural sickness with tattooing the body, or ornamenting the environment.

> The modern man who tattoos himself is either a criminal or a degenerate. There are prisons in which eighty percent of the inmates show tattoos … I have made the following discovery and *pass it on to the world: The evolution of culture is synonymous with the removal of ornament from utilitarian objects.*[17]

With a fine sense of irony, Loos adds, 'I believed that with this discovery I was bringing joy to the world; it has not thanked me. People were sad and hung their heads.' Well, not the Modernists, who were inspired by the idea that cultural evolution should end in abstraction. Primitives and tribal people needed tattoos and ornament whereas advanced people could listen to Beethoven instead. The higher pleasures rendered symbolism and decoration obsolete. In effect, Adolf Loos adopted a specious argument of progress from Darwin and transposed it to the world of culture.

As this argument developed in the 1920s, the Modernists, like sixteenth-century Protestants, aimed for a radical aesthetic purism. Exclusion and purgation became positive; what one avoided became a virtue; they were well on the road to spiritual nothingness. The Futurists advocated throwing out nature; the new machine civilisation was to steam-clean the environment. There is a Frank Lloyd Wright drawing, circa 1904, which he signs as the 'Grammar of the Protestant'. It shows his recently completed Larkin Building, by his own account a machine-age reduction to blank planes, severe lines and abstraction. The Dutch movement of De Stijl, heavily indebted to Wright, opened its manifesto with the proclamation of Mondrian: 'The life of contemporary cultivated man is turning gradually away from nature; it becomes more and more an a-b-s-t-r-a-c-t life.'[18]

The cultural evolution, to which Loos appealed, meant for contemporary society a mechanised culture, and this meant, in turn, abstraction. Early in life Mondrian had practised the Post-Christianity called Theosophy, itself a heady mix of pseudo-evolutionary theory and spirituality. From here it was a short step to the spiritualisation of machine evolution. Theo Van Doesburg, also with a Dutch Calvinist background (and considerably more pseudonyms than Lenin and Le Corbusier) took the whole worship of mechanical evolution to a preposterous level: 'Every machine is the spiritualisation of an organism.'[19] Nature and representation were out and spiritualised mechanisms were in. [15] So many of De Stijl's manifestos proclaim this credo, and the beginning of their First Manifesto shows why, after 1917, it became the doctrine of the new age:

'1 There is an old and a new spirit of the times …

2 The War is destroying the old world and its contents'.[20]

The First World War is thus understood as the origin and first legitimisation of the Protestant Crusade (just as, ironically, for Post-Modernists, it is often seen as the setting for the first 'death' of Modernism). According to the Modernist version, the global war was caused by a civilisation thoroughly corrupt, overdecorated and class-ridden. It justified total eradication. The Protestant Crusade, with the aid of the machine and its flat Protestant grammar, would wipe out decadence. Le Corbusier called the new age 'the vacuum cleaning period': it stripped Beaux-Arts architecture of its corrupt decor, it cleansed the *anciens régimes* of ethnicity, it washed everything white (or at least a primary, Bauhaus colour). The crusade would be fought as a cultural war on history, ornament, nature and a litany of '*Decadences*' (thankfully, with fewer theses than Luther's ninety-five).

By the 1920s the Modern *Movement* crystallised out of Modernism and proclaimed a new faith in the future. Nietzsche had invented that avant-garde character who would usher it in, the 'Superman', his 'Future Man', who overcomes the present. Marxists had formulated their eschatology, the future rule of the proletariat; Futurists,

ABOVE [15] Gerrit Thomas Rietveld, **Schroeder Residence**, Utrecht, 1924. The canonic Modern building – white, abstract, overlapping planes with primary-coloured accents. 'Every machine is the spiritualization of an organism' – with brilliant buildings like this, the Dutch Calvinists made one believe it. (C Jencks)

RIGHT [16a, b] Le Corbusier, **Villa Savoye**, Poissy, France, 1929–33. Pure white forms, according to Le Corbusier's description of the building, are elevated above an unhealthy ground plane that may give you a disease. Like Shaker furniture, also pure, reduced and elevated above the contaminated ground, cleanliness is next to godliness. Adolf Loos argued that evolutionary superiority could be measured by the degree to which ornament (cultural dirt) is removed. Protestant scrubbing was thus closer to God and Darwinian superiority at the same time. (C Jencks)

since the French Revolution, had written books on the Year 2000, forecasting a social transformation, the secular version of the New Jerusalem, the Second Coming. Lenin, under a pseudonym, plotted his communist revolution and Charles-Edouard Jeanneret, under his nom de guerre Le Corbusier, cooked up the architectural one. [16]

In 1921 he started what he called a 'crusade' for the new architecture, guided by *L'Esprit Nouveau*, his monthly magazine. Basically this was an instalment-plan Bible, where the new spirit appeared regularly in every field, from bodily health to mechanised design to abstract painting (he wrote much of it, under other pseudonyms). Today, his ringing words continue to echo in every student's ear:

> A great epoch has begun …There exists a new spirit …There exists a mass of work conceived in the new spirit; it is to be met with particularly in industrial production … We must create the mass-production spirit. The spirit of constructing mass-

production houses.[21] The spirit of living in mass-production houses. The spirit of conceiving mass-production houses.

Spirit … spirit – the biblical repetition and cadence say it all. So convinced is he of the beneficent effects of a well-designed environment that he ends his Bible, *Towards a New Architecture*, with a madcap claim: 'Architecture or Revolution … It is a question of building which is at the root of the social unrest of today: Architecture or Revolution. Revolution can be avoided.'

Lenin would have laughed. But Walter Gropius, another militant saint of the Design Reformation, founded the Bauhaus as a 'cathedral of the future', and in 1923 declared with the standard creed – 'art and technology: a new unity' – that society could be transformed through culture. [17] Mies van der Rohe made any number of similar pleas to the Spirit of the Age, the Zeitgeist of industrialisation and gave, in 1924, a formulation of the faith that is even more naïve than Le Corbusier's: 'If we succeed in carrying out this industrialization [of the building process] then the social, economic, technical, and also artistic problems will be readily solved'.[22] In effect, architectural determinism has been replaced by industrial predestination.

After 1927, and their joint exhibition of the new architecture at Stuttgart, the religion of Modernism spread around the globe to be disseminated by the apostles, and knighted saints, Sir Nikolaus Pevsner, Sir James Richards, Sir Leslie Martin. The orthodox Bible of the movement was *Space, Time and Architecture* by Sigfried Giedion.

LEFT [17] **Walter Gropius, The Bauhaus**, Dessau, 1926. A pinwheel plan spins over a road, while the black and white graphics give the dynamism a crisp elegance. The white International Style, always denied as a style by the Pioneers of Modernism, was made to be photographed and reproduced at reduced size. Like a slogan or good advertisement, the result was highly expressive and triumphed because of it. (Oliver Radford)

Modern seminaries were formed at the major universities such as Cambridge and Harvard and from there the Purist doctrines were dispersed: of John Calvin Corbusier, Martin Luther Gropius and John Knox van der Rohe. Their white cathedrals, the black and white boxes of the International Style, were soon built in every land, and for a while (until 1960) the people kept the faith. Ornament, polychromy, metaphor, humour, symbolism, place, cultural identity, urban context and convention were put on the Index of Proscribed Taboos and all forms of decoration and historical reference were declared verboten. We are well acquainted with the results, as Colin Rowe termed them, 'the architecture of good intentions'. There are a lot of pleasant white housing estates, and machine-aesthetic hospitals, [18] to prove that the intentions were not altogether misguided.[23] An underlying assumption of this faith could be called pragmatic amelioration; that is, the belief that by 'doing more with less', as Buckminster Fuller put it, social problems would slowly disappear. Indeed, technical progress in limited spheres such as the increasing speed of movement, seems to bear this out, though air travel today is a major cause of global pollution. Nevertheless, the idea that technical progress is inevitable, still dominates *Late*-Modernists.

Before continuing with this little parable, we might formulate a definition of the mother of all Modernisms, at least in architecture. This typifies attitudes in many fields. In brief, it might go as follows: *Modern architecture is the faith in industrial progress and its translation into the pure,*

RIGHT [18] Alvar Aalto, **Tuberculosis Sanatorium**, Paimio, Finland, 1933. The most appropriate and successful application of the International Style was on hospitals and, occasionally, in Germany, Finland and Switzerland, on workers' housing. With its open-air communal block set amid the pine trees giving the patients salubrious views of nature, and its careful detailing and construction, the Paimio Sanatorium has turned institutional imagery into a heroic reality. (© D Porphyrios)

white International Style (or at least the Machine Aesthetic) with the goal of
positively transforming society both in its sensibility and social make-up.

Put thus baldly, the striking oddity of architecture stands out. Its progressivism is quite different from Modernism in the other arts, notably in literature, painting and philosophy. These fields are characteristically not optimistic and progressive. Think of the writings of Nietzsche, Heisenberg, Heidegger, Gödel and Sartre – their views might be close to Social Darwinism, the doctrine of 'might makes right'; or perhaps nihilism; or maybe the uncertainty principle. Or recall the occasionally right-wing politics of modern writers, of Yeats, Pound, TS Eliot; or think of the anti-social antics of Picasso, Duchamp and Grosz. Most of these characters were hardly liberal, not very socialist and certainly not confident, bright and cheery. Whereas Modernism in architecture often furthered the ideology of industrialisation and progress, Modernism in many other fields has either fought these trends or lamented them.

In two key areas, however, the various Modernisms agree, and that is over the value of abstraction and the overriding importance of aesthetics. Why abstraction? For the same reason that iconoclasts have always preferred white architecture. It is why the Cistercians liked the tabula rasa, the Calvinists resisted imagery and the Puritans rejected the pleasures of the senses. Similar psychological motives are widely shared across history and as such, at a professional level are the reason why engineers are attuned to rationality and why technicians eschew history. Psychological types are reinforced through training and practice, and consistently the Protestant sensibility favours elimination. Beyond all this is the great truth of advertising: life is simpler when it is reduced; simple slogans sell.

As for the role of aesthetics in Modernism, it concerns the obsession with form as specific to each art, with style as the primary substance. Its exponent in the 1950s, Clement Greenberg, defined Modernism as having that fundamental goal of focusing on the essence of each art language as the subject of the work. This aesthetic intention became even more exaggerated with Late-Modernism. [19] By focusing on the means of art, in an age where there are few shared values, Greenberg argued that standards can be kept high. What one can do in this agnostic age of consumer pluralism, he averred, is to sharpen the tools of one's trade or, as both Mallarmé and TS Eliot defined the poet's role, 'purify the language of the tribe'. Thus contemporary art comes down to a stark choice, on one side of an equation or the other. As Greenberg put it, in a key Modernist credo of 1939, 'the alternative is between *Avant-Garde and Kitsch*'.

RIGHT [19] Sol LeWitt, *Serial Project (A, B, C, D)*, **1966**, white stove enamel on aluminium, 92.9 x 574.5 x 575cm. The aesthetic intention focused exclusively on the art proposition, here as if it were a mathematical abstraction. Late-Modern art took such self-referential work to lengths that Early Modernism implied but had not reached. An aspect of this reduction, brought out by Post-Modernists, is the unintended semantic meaning – here a relation to a city of towers. (Courtesy of Saatchi Collection, London)

Post-Modernists will soon contest such vicious alternatives, just as the rabbi is supposed to have advised his son: 'Son, whenever faced with two extremes, always pick a third.'

There was another motive, beyond abstraction and aesthetics, which played a role in giving Modernism its Protestant sensibility, and it takes us back to the 1820s and the spiritual function of the avant-garde. This is the primary place of nullity, a poetics of absence, which is not without its humorous side. Like a fourteenth-century Zen Buddhist, the intelligent believer has a strong faith that, in the end, the great cosmic message is nothing else than nothingness. This view is known in the academies, where it is most prevalent, as Negative Theology and it evolves, in Post-Christianity, from Christ's despairing cry on the cross, 'Father, Father, why hast thou forsaken me?' Renunciation and elimination as a style flourish within this metaphysics of absence, where the missing God is taken as the primary truth.

Thus, the purifying function of the artist, which TS Eliot and Wittgenstein had made dominant in Anglo-American literature and philosophy, was slowly understood to have a crypto-religious function that mirrored the void rather well. Mark Rothko gave it a numinous presence. As Modernism developed into Late-Modernism and further stripped itself bare, Mondrian's Minimalism turned into Mies' slogan 'less is more'. [20] The critic Lewis Mumford was one of the few who attacked this trend in 'The Case against "Modern Architecture"'. Mies' buildings, he stated, were 'elegant monuments to nothingness … [having] no relation to site, climate, insulation, function, or internal activity … [they were] the apotheosis of the compulsive, bureaucratic spirit'. Such critiques did little to stem the nothing cult.

By the 1960s, with further evolution, the white on white canvases that Alexander Rodchenko had painted in 1918, had become, as the advertisement for Ivory Soap has it, 'whiter than white', and the black ones, by Ad Reinhardt, almost totally black. Each Late-Modernist out-abstracted their predecessor. The blank whiteness reached an unseeable perfection with such paintings as

LEFT [20] Mies van der Rohe, **Federal Center, Chicago, 1964–5**. 'Less is more', the phrase of Aquinas and Flaubert, was borrowed by Mies who took the credit for this eliminative philosophy. The problem for civic buildings such as this, is that reduced abstraction tells you nothing about entry or use, where to pay a parking ticket, where to get married, or how to feel about it. Ironically, the Chicago Seven were tried here, and as Abbie Hoffmann ran around the courtroom, Judge Hoffmann demanded, 'Get back in your place, where Mies van der Rohe designed you to stand.' Under global corporatism minimalism became the architecture of control. (C Jencks)

Ellsworth Kelly's *White Curve over White 2004* (whose increased subtleties are illustrated in the white margin here). 'Less is more' was also ratcheted up to become 'less than less is more than more is nearly nothing'. Silence became cosmic. It was a religious hush, as the mystics said, emptiness, degree zero. 'Whereof one cannot speak', Wittgenstein said, uttering the ultimate Modernist truth, 'thereof one must be silent'. Amen.

However, for the avant-garde silence speaks for only so long and it takes more and more effort for the acolytes to hear the quiet. Thus, by the 1960s, to keep the faithful in line, a new enemy had to be created, Pop Art and what was damned as 'Neo-Dada', plus a host of other heretical regressions. [21] They arrived on demand, to be chastised even by Duchamp himself. By the 1970s these movements grew ever more heads, marked Neo-Expressionism, radical eclecticism, feminist art, Hyperrealism; *La Pittura Colta* and *La Transavanguardia* – a Medusa-swarm of new styles and national conventions. Here was opportunity for more elimination, for expulsions and excommunications to encourage the orthodox.

Success tames the avant-garde

At this point Modernism encountered an identity problem that had not been foreseen: success. Movements in the art and architectural worlds are usually short-lived, two to five years is not uncommon, but they are not presented as the mainstream culture. Thus, when Modernism became the dominant assumption of the *Pax Americana* in the 1960s, when Jackson Pollock and the avant-garde were lionised by society and featured in *Life* magazine, when the style and attitudes were used by the West in the Cold War against the Soviet bloc, the underlying logic of the whole agenda inverted. It became impossible to believe in a heroic avant-garde, leading society over the barricades. No longer was it an idealist and oppressed minority, as it had styled itself for one hundred and forty years, no longer did it have Saint-Simon's elevated goal of changing the world. It had become the world, the establishment, the reigning taste, the leading edge of the academy (even in London's Royal

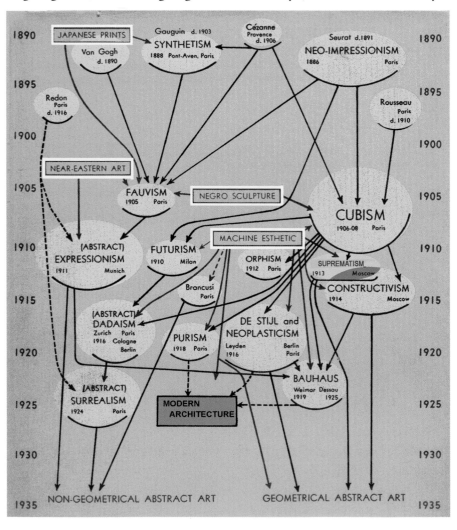

LEFT [22] Alfred H Barr, **Evolutionary Diagram. The arrows imply a teleology leading to MODERN ARCHITECTURE and ABSTRACT ART.** This became the canonic view of modern art leading to abstraction and modern architecture, and the basis for the collection at the Museum of Modern Art. Here I have accentuated the different movements as blobs, to bring out the pluralism of competing 'isms'. My argument for this irreducible critical view is continued, below, from page 172 and following.

Academy). By a strange inversion, it was sold on Madison Avenue and at Sothebys, absorbed into the heart of the bourgeoisie and began to resemble the *arrière-garde*. Impossible, panic, what to do? This did not fit the biblical account, Saint-Simon's 'New Christianity'.

The reasons for the success were manifold. Modernism, with its progressive and libertarian overtones, had all the right associations for Late-Capitalism. With its simplifications and abstraction, it appeared to be easier to teach and understand than movements with a complex iconography. With its freedom from the complications of histories and local culture it became a good style for what Gore Vidal called 'the United States of Amnesia'. By 1980, much of the First World and its youth had been brought up in Academies of the New or, as the critic Harold Rosenberg called it, the Tradition of the New (led, he noted, by a 'herd of independent minds'). The Sunday supplements featured the epigones of De Stijl and 'good design'; Terence Conran with downtown Habitats turned the formula into a lifestyle for young marrieds; forty thousand PhDs appeared on Picasso's minor sketches and love life; Le Corbusier's 'spirit of mass production' came true in a surprising way, as *Corbusieriana* became a mass-production industry. In architecture, the new saints were the big three, the Masters of the Modern Movement, known to every student as brand names like Coca Cola – Corb, Mies and Grope.

Most of all MoMA, the Museum of Modern Art in New York, became the Vatican of the New, as it presided over the canon of who was orthodox. This institution, with its impeccable collection, laid out the main argument of apostolic succession, which Alfred Barr had formulated in 1936, with his *Cubism and Abstract Art*, and the building on 53rd Street in New York displayed in its layout this carefully ordered bloodline. [22] But how could one be loyal to the heart of Modernism, continual revolution, and the High Church at the same time? How could one be avant-garde *and* the main bloodline of the Establishment? Gertrude Stein posited the alternative: 'A museum can be either a museum or it can be modern, but it can't be both.' Or can it? I asked Philip Johnson in 1988, who with Barr was in on the foundation and development of MoMA, about this paradox.[24]

CJ: The *Salon des Refusés* is the archetypal avant-garde institution, and yet in the 1960s with Late-Modernism, Abstract Expressionism and MoMA accepting the avant-garde – suddenly Modernism has triumphed against its traditional adversary, the bourgeoisie.

PJ: Right.

CJ: And become its official reigning culture. So the question is, 'Can Modernism survive its own triumph?' Can it be both adversary and mainstream, both High Church and out of the Church?

PJ: Yes … Well, the 'permanent revolution' – it's a good question. Can you go on being avant-garde, after Albert Barr in the art world. What would your position be?

CJ: If it's a 'museum' then it's to do with the past; if it's 'Modern' then it's attacking history – as many writers have said. There can't be a Museum of Modern Art.

PJ: There can, if you restrict the dates – sure.

CJ: But then shouldn't it be called the Museum of Contemporary Art? MoMA can't be both adversarial and the Establishment.

PJ: Well, the fact is that it was both and *did* succeed as an institution, ideologically as well as popularly – and it's still going on. We'll have to start over with the definition – the avant-garde must mean something else. The Museum of Modern Art worked as an avant-garde institution, and as far as I'm concerned, it's still working.

CJ: But from 1960 to recently, it's been very reactionary.

PJ: Stodgy [23]

ABOVE [23] **MoMA Today,** redesign by Yoshio Taniguchi, 2001–4. This elegant background building is a perfect expression of Modernism as a conservative project – part bankable collection, part mass cult spectacle. The building actually mixes several building types but, by being so determinedly abstract, it smooths over the contradictions in use and content, a good rendition of the complacent cool. The view shows the lobby-atrium and, in the main white cube space, Barnett Newman's *Broken Obelisk*. (C Jencks)

'Backward-looking', I added, as all institutions like the Vatican must be when they try to keep the faith. Yet Johnson was right about the success of MoMA's contradictory stance, no doubt about that. Exactly like the École des Beaux-Arts, which the Modernists attacked one hundred years previously, it fed off its own internalised rebellions, its own marginal differentiation of doctrine and style. Indeed, the history of the Catholic Church is, on one reading, nothing but the mini-revolutions from within its order, reform movements starting with the Benedictine Order. And that may entail the paradox that is hard for the old guard to contemplate. It is this: Post-Modernism is just Modernism in its reformist and reflexive mode, that is, critical modernism.

I started this little parable calling Modernism the first great Post-Christianity, so according to this logic the proposition would be true, and more. Modernism, in its original spiritual upheaval, would be just another Postie! That would explain the screams in the cathedral. To much of the outside world this may not come as a surprise; those claims and counter-claims sound like so many monks squabbling, like theological disputes. Indeed, according to none other than the philosopher Jean-François Lyotard, Post-Modernism is not only in-house Modernism, but by a crazy sexual logic actually gives birth to its parent! He writes:

What space does Cezanne challenge? The Impressionists. What object do Picasso and Braque attack? Cezanne's ... A work can become modern only if it is first postmodern. Postmodernism thus understood is not modernism at its end but in the nascent state, and this state is constant.[25]

This idea, which sounds bizarre at first, accentuates the dialectical nature of the way movements overturn each other and is certainly right insofar as it emphasises the critical element. But there is more than the shock of the new to PM, which Lyotard also claims carries an unutterable otherness.

The postmodern would be that which, in the modern, puts forward the unpresentable in presentation itself ... The rules and categories [of the postmodern work are not pre-established but] are what the work of art is looking for ... Post modern would have to be understood according to the paradox of the future (*post*) anterior (*modo*).[26]

Again, there is crazy insight here. All creative thinking must operate from within pre-established categories and therefore contain unforeseen aspects of these categories that no one knows ahead of time. In this sense, PM would be, partly, a search for the unpresentable. But it is also an *external* critique of the High Church and, to continue the metaphor, a different way of conceiving the spiritual. Instead of the Wittgensteinian silence, or foregrounding the unpresentable, it looks for a richer, more inclusive orientation. Plenitude, not reduction, becomes the goal. Not Mies' 'less is more', but the phrase of post-modern scientists such as the Nobel laureate Philip Anderson. In 1972, he wrote a key article that defined the notion of emergence into plenitude: 'more is different'. Add 'more' to any system and it will suddenly self-organise into something 'different'. This is a liberating and generous insight, and one to which I shall return in the final chapters. With cultural artefacts, however, the question became one of how to achieve the richness of the past, and acknowledge the present pluralism, without succumbing to revivalism or kitsch. Here the strategies of double coding, ironic parody and the heavy use of quotation marks came to the fore.

2. HYBRID CULTURE

Double coding and irony

Post-modern movements vary in each cultural form – economics, politics, dance, psychology, education, geography, etc – and in some areas they have not been defined or perhaps do not even exist. This is important to reiterate, since so much ink has been spilt on the subject: post-modernism is not a totalising category, and only partially defines aspects of contemporary culture. It contests holistic classifications of a period, including those made in its name. (Those who enjoy irony will note that this last proposition itself sounds like a holistic claim.)

In architecture, literature and art, which I will touch on in this and the next two sections, different pm attitudes have developed at different rates, so once again it is the pluralism and Derrida's notion of *différance* that should be stressed (incommensurable difference). Beyond this and complexity, an intense commitment to pluralism is the main value that unites every post-modern movement, and the reason one speaks about post-modernisms with an 's'. Pluralism is also something that marks the tradition as starting in the West, that part of the world where it is most developed.

In architecture the movement grows quite independently of the word, and has to be traced to the early 1960s and the writings of Jane Jacobs and Robert Venturi. Both wrote best-sellers that changed the

OPPOSITE [24] **Plural coding: the locale, the generic and the particular.** Rem Koolhaas' Casa da Musica in Porto combines eighteenth-century tile-work of the locale with abstracted ornament and a generic crystalline structure. (C Jencks)

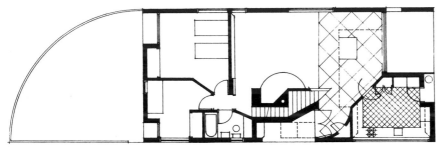

course of architecture and urbanism and both built on early ideas of complexity theory to do it, even employing the word complexity, quite polemically. Venturi flagged up the opposition to the oversimplicity of Modernism in his title, what he called the 'gentle manifesto' *Complexity and Contradiction in Architecture* (1966), while Jacobs left it to the last chapter of her attack – *The Death and Life of Great American Cities* (1961) – to define the key concept, 'organised complexity'. At the time, cities were being eviscerated by a combination of modern planning theories that emphasised purity and functional separation, and an old-time greed that exploited the *tabula rasa*. By contrast, Jacobs' notions of the city as a complex emergent organisation and Venturi's 'obligation towards the difficult whole' were forged to combat this oversimplification and deal with the realities of economic and urban life. [25] Common to both books was also the critical tone, ranging from satire to disgust, from irony to negativity, that we will see in all critical modernisms. Movements that don't catalyse anger don't move. But of course it was not just disgust with the present and changes in theory that created the early pm movement but other changes in mood. Most important was the counter culture of the 1960s, for instance, the Situationists' work in France, and the May Events of 1968, which had grown out of student protests and the anti-war movements in the USA. Black power, feminism, the fight for minority rights; protest against hierarchy in general inspired post-modernists to challenge the reigning power structure. In the 1960s this power was the *Pax Americana*, its style of Madison Avenue Modernism and the Museum of Modern Art.

Corporate Modernism had remodelled the downtown of every global city, and this homogenisation sparked popular protests throughout Europe, Britain and America. It also sparked a new way of understanding the city as an amalgam of urban villagers, and their different ways of perceiving the city. The theories of semiotics and the writings of Umberto Eco, Colin Rowe and Charles Moore all questioned the hegemony of modernism; its elitism and reductivism, its anti-city and anti-history stance. By the mid-1970s much of this was generally known and it was then, in 1975, when I applied the term post-modern to these various departures.[27]

In that first year of lecturing in Europe and America, I used it as a temporising label, to describe where we had left rather than where we were going. The observable fact was that architects as diverse as Ralph Erskine, [26] Robert Venturi, Lucien Kroll, the Krier brothers and Team Ten had all departed from Modernism and set off in different directions which nevertheless retained a trace of their common point of departure. Today I would still partly define Post-Modernism as I did in 1978 as *double coding: the combination of Modern techniques with something else (usually traditional building) in order for architecture to communicate with the public and a concerned minority, usually other architects.* The point of this double coding was itself double. Modern architecture had failed

RIGHT [26] Ralph Erskine, **Byker Wall**, Newcastle, 1974. Some of the first post-modern housing was ad hoc and vernacular in style. Its social pluralism was mirrored in its hybrid style and diverse materials, here green stained wood, brick, corrugated metal and asbestos. The emphasis on participation, with design acknowledging the tastes of the inhabitants, has remained a constant social goal of Post-Modernists. (C Jencks)

to remain credible partly because it did not communicate effectively with its ultimate users – the main argument of my book *The Language of Post-Modern Architecture* – and partly because it did not make effective links with the city and history.

In spite of its democratic intentions, Modernism had become elitist and *the* style of the corporate world. The reason is not hard to find. Architects, as any profession in an advanced civilisation, must keep up with highly technical, fast-changing requirements and their professional peers. This requires some compromise with power and the reigning styles of the moment. In effect, architects are caught between the Scylla of a local society and the Charybdis of a specialised discipline. Each pulls in a different way. An obvious strategy to deal with these contrary forces is to acknowledge the opposition and adopt a corresponding dual approach, a radical schizophrenia. In the 1960s during the Cold War, 'controlled schizophrenia' was suggested as an intelligent strategy for pursuing both nuclear armaments *and* a policy of disarmament. It makes sense when one faces a chronic social problem without a single resolution, as we will see later with the vicious problem of global warming.

Thus the schizophrenic solution I defined as post-modern: an architecture that is professionally based *and* popular, as well as one that is based on new techniques *and* old patterns. To simplify: double coding means elite/popular, accommodating/subversive and new/old. These exaggerated oppositions explain why the pm style is often so ironic. Irony, like parody, can say two different things at the same time; keep a controlled schizophrenia in the mind while one thinks through the contradictions (to echo Venturi's title). As I also stressed in the previous chapter, Post-Modernism has its double meaning as the continuation of Modernism and its transcendence. Another way of looking at the mixture brings out its plural coding, emphasising the variety of languages pulled together rather than the primary two. Double or multiple, it is the way the codes are layered and contrasted that brings the style to consciousness, makes it recognisable.

As also mentioned, the main negative motive for Post-Modern architecture is the visible failure of Modern architecture, its mythical 'death' announced repeatedly throughout the 1970s. In 1968 an English tower block of public housing, Ronan Point, suffered 'cumulative collapse' as its floors gave way in the wake of a gas explosion. After Pruitt-Igoe was dynamited in 1972, these controlled explosions became a frequent method of dealing with the failures of cheap prefabrication, lack of personal 'defensible' space, and the alienating housing estate.

Poignantly, the solution by dynamite became so ritualised that it might create schizophrenic reactions in the same person. A British television programme in 2006 featured one more careful deconstruction watched by inhabitants who had spent forty years in their Modern estate. As their homes blew up, they cried and laughed, at once relieved that their prison was destroyed, yet at the same time horrified to see their home explode. This schizophrenia is of course an analogue of what the pm architect goes through when creating a work.

Although there is no corresponding 'death of modern literature' (the 'death of the author' is another thing), there are literary parallels with architecture, and also social motives for using past forms in an ironic way. Umberto Eco produced the classic formulation of this double coding:

> I think of the postmodern attitude as that of a man who loves a very cultivated woman and knows he cannot say to her, 'I love you madly', because he knows that she knows (and that she knows that he knows) that these words have already been written by Barbara Cartland. Still, there is a solution. He can say, 'As Barbara Cartland would put it, I love you madly'. At this point, having avoided false innocence, having said clearly that it is no longer possible to speak innocently, he will nevertheless have said what he wanted to say to the woman: that he loves her; but he loves her in an age of lost innocence. If the woman goes along with this, she will have received a declaration of love all the same. Neither of the two speakers will feel innocent, both will have accepted the challenge of the past, of the already said which cannot be eliminated; both will consciously and with pleasure play the game of irony ... But both will have succeeded, once again, in speaking of love.[28]

Lost innocence is an inescapable condition of the present. We cannot not know the degradation of the modern psyche, the fact of the Holocaust, and the way Freud, Marx and sociology overturn the flattering side of human motives. However one-sided their interpretation, they make straightforward consciousness difficult. Acknowledging the fabricated nature of self-construction is like a Christian admitting to original sin, it puts scare quotes around contentious statements and ironic marks on deeply felt passions. Thus Eco underlines the lover's use of double coding and extends it to the writer's use of previous forms. Whereas the Futurists declared a war on memory, and Modernists generally outlawed symbolism in the arts, Eco takes a tougher stance by asserting that 'the already said' cannot be avoided however much we try; nor taking an ironic distance from it.

When, in the 1950s, Late-Modernists started to confront the Holocaust, their response in the arts tended towards the minimalism of Samuel Beckett, the abstraction of Mark Rothko and the 'literature of silence', one that insisted a writer could not express the inexpressible, nor should they try. Opposed to this withdrawal and quiescence, John Barth (1980) and Umberto Eco (1983) defined a post-modern literature that employed a panoply of literary devices. Their own novels – Eco's *The Name of the Rose* is typical – cut across literary genres combining such types as the historical romance, comedy, detective story and philosophical treatise. Inherent in the pm agenda is the injunction to cross territories, break down specialisation, hybridise discourses, attack false boundaries. As Linda Hutcheon has so exhaustively shown, post-modern fiction inscribes itself within conventional discourses in order to subvert them. It incorporates cultural realities in order to challenge them: again, double coding is the strategy.[29]

John Barth sees the 'postmodern' as a search for a wider audience, yet one that does not deny the insights of modernity:

> My ideal postmodernist author neither merely repudiates nor merely imitates either his twentieth-century Modernist parents or his nineteenth-century premodernist grandparents. He has the first half of our century under his belt, but not on his back. Without lapsing into moral or artistic simplism, shoddy craftsmanship, Madison Avenue venality, or either false or real naiveté, he nevertheless aspires to a fiction more democratic in its appeal than such late-modernist marvels (by my definition and in my judgement) as Beckett's *Stories and Texts for Nothing* or Nabokov's *Pale Fire*. He may not hope to reach and move the devotees of James Michener and Irving Wallace – not to mention the lobotomized mass-media illiterates. But he should hope to reach and delight, at least part of the time, beyond the circle of what Mann used to call the Early Christians: professional devotees of high art.[30]

The injunction is to go beyond the restricted audience of the Early Christians without sacrificing quality or the valid insights of modernists such as Darwin, Marx and Ford. Faced with an exclusivist modernism, a minimalism of means and ends, Barth and other writers have felt just as hemmed in as architects forced to build in the International Style.

By the mid-1980s, the most convincing use of this double coding in architecture was James Stirling's addition to the Neue Staatsgalerie in Stuttgart. [27] Here one can find the fabric of the city and the existing museum extended in amusing and ironic ways. The U-shaped palazzo form of the old gallery is echoed and placed on a high plinth, or 'Acropolis', above the traffic. But this classical base contains a very real and necessary parking garage, one that is indicated ironically by stones which have 'fallen', like ruins, to the ground. [28] The resultant holes reveal the actual construction – not the thick marble blocks of the real Acropolis, but a steel frame supporting stone cladding that permits the air ventilation required by law. One can sit on these false ruins and ponder the truth of our lost innocence: that we live in an age which can build with beautiful, expressive masonry as long as we make it skin-deep and hang it on a steel skeleton. A Modernist would deny himself this pleasure for a number of reasons: 'truth to materials', 'logical consistency', and the ever present drive to purge and purify.

By contrast Stirling, like the post-modern lovers posited by

RIGHT [27] **Neue Staatsgalerie.** 'Ruins in the Garden', classical blocks which have fallen about in a contrived eighteenth-century manner, reveal the reality of post-modern construction: a steel frame holds up the slabs of masonry, and there is no cement between the blocks, but rather air. These holes in the walls, which are ironic vents to the parking garage, dramatise the difference between truth and illusion, and allow Stirling to assert continuity with the existing classical fabric while also showing the differences. Paradox and double coding exist throughout this scheme, which is more an articulation of urban tissue than a conventional building. (C Jencks)

Umberto Eco, wants to communicate more and different values. To signify the permanent nature of the museum, he has used traditional rustication and classical forms including an Egyptian cornice, an open-air Pantheon, and segmental arches. These are beautiful in an understated way but, with their distortions and modern technology, they distinguish themselves from the straight revivalism advocated by Prince Charles. They say, 'We are beautiful like the Acropolis or Pantheon, but we are also based on concrete technology and deceit.'

The extreme form of this double coding is visible at the entry points: the outline of a steel temple that announces the drop-off point, and the Modernist steel canopies that tell the public where to enter. [29] These forms and colours are reminiscent of De Stijl, that quintessentially modern language, but they are collaged onto the traditional background. Thus Modernism confronts Classicism to an extent likely to annoy adherents of both traditions. There is not the simple harmony and consistency either of language or world-view. In effect Stirling is saying that we live in a complex world where we cannot deny either the past and conventional beauty, or the present and current technical and social realities. Caught between this past and present, unwilling to oversimplify the situation, Stirling produced a hypertext that related to many languages and tastes at once.

At Stuttgart the vibrant polychromy fits in with the youth that frequent the museum – it resembles their Dayglo hair and anoraks – while the Classicism appeals to lovers of Schinkel. [30] This building was popular with both young and old, and when I interviewed a wide range of visitors a group of *plein air* painters, schoolchildren and businessmen – I found their different tastes both acknowledged and stretched. Because of its inclusive pluralism, and the way it confronts one language game with another, the Neue Staatsgalerie became canonic to pm architecture or, should one say, another 'pm classic'.

By 1980, identity politics was framed as multiculturalism, the right of every minority to have their culture acknowledged if not empowered. Juxtaposing tastes was a formal way of recognising this political difference. For Lyotard, modern universalism could be challenged by the 'play of different language games'. For architectural writers such as Robert Venturi, Denise Scott Brown and Christian Norberg-Schulz, it meant designing for opposing 'taste cultures' (in the words of the sociologist Herbert Gans). In any large city building such as an office, varying tastes and functions have to be articulated and these may lead, so the argument of multiculturalism went, towards a radical eclecticism.

At the level of the city, identity politics supported the notion of 'urban villagers' and a corresponding interest in city context, one that acknowledged the local inhabitants and the existing fabric. By the mid-1980s, contextualism had become standard and replaced the previous dogma of totalistic urban renewal, or the sweeping *tabula rasa* approach. Three urban interventions stand out. The great city plan of San Francisco was passed in 1986 mandating many of Jane Jacobs' ideas, including mixed development and legislation controlling the car. Throughout the 1980s West Berlin was rebuilt, under the guidance of an institute known as IBA. This official body adopted all sorts of post-modern strategies including perimeter block planning and figure/ground composition, where the public space became the figure and the private realm the background. [31] Aldo Rossi was the seminal figure behind this movement. His famous book, *L'Architettura della Città* (1966) defined the way a city's identity can remain the same, in spite of constant change, if its genetic code is respected, its infrastructure and monuments reinforced. In his buildings Rossi carried out this agenda, typically with the construction of monumental hybrids of the local language and generic industry. IBA involvement resulted in some of the most dignified and sensible social housing ever produced.

Barcelona, under its self-styled post-modern mayor Pasqual Maragall, was by the end of the 1990s *the* exemplary model of pluralist planning. Each of the city's sectors was treated differently, over 100 mini-parks were created and the nineteenth-century plan was

ABOVE [31 a, b] Aldo Rossi (with G Braghieri) **Social Housing**, South Friedrichstadt, Berlin, 1981–8. Throughout the 1980s, the IBA building programme in Berlin introduced many positive urban ideas of Post-Modernism such as the perimeter block that creates, on the outside, a positive street architecture and, on the inside, a positive, contained green space. Aldo Rossi was the poet and exponent of this form of city memory and architecture. Here his modest social housing mixes traditional Berlin brick and Jaguar-green industrial elements with the northern steep roof, marking the entry towers. (C Jencks)

ABOVE [32] Beverly Pepper,
**Landscape Parc de l'Estacio
del Nord**, Barcelona, Spain,
1991. The decentralisation of
Barcelona into districts and many
parks was a post-modern policy of
renewal brought in by the mayor,
Pasqual Maragall, later a leader of
Catalonian autonomy. (C Jencks)

completed with new building. [32] All this transformation was helped
by the 1992 Olympics, which provided the catalyst and the speculative
finance necessary. But it depended on more than this economic and
social injection. Behind it all was a strong architectural community, led
by such firms as MBM, with a philosophy of pluralism and a strategy for
developing each district of the city according to its history and
possibility. Both a developing pm tradition and preparation for the
propitious moment were the preconditions for success. In 1999
Barcelona won the RIBA Royal Gold Medal for architecture, the first
time anyone or anything other than an architect was so awarded. It was
a good indication that post-modern ideas, first stressed by Jane Jacobs
and Herbert Gans in the 1960s, had become mainstream and were to
now influence strategy in Britain and Europe.

The way pluralism is represented and included in what Venturi
had called 'the difficult whole' then became the focus for debate, and
created another departure of post-modernism. Three distinct
strategies were current and they competed with each other. The
architect might pull the heterogeneous city together with the methods
of collage and eclecticism, as in the 1960s with Venturi's house, above,
or they might adopt a Free-Style Classicism, as did Stirling or Isozaki
or Rossi, as just mentioned. The third strategy, discussed below, was
developed ten years later led by young theorists, as well as older
architects such as Peter Eisenman [33] and Rem Koolhaas [34]: the
idea of 'folding in difference'.[31] Folding was a more pliant way of

pulling together a variety of opposite forces, so supple and integrated that it might look to the untutored eye as if it were reductionist, even modern. But the intentions were again to deal with variety and complexity, the twin concerns that had dominated pm practice for twenty years.

Not even pastiche

This third strategy was also a reaction from within post-modernism to its excesses of the 1980s. These included a debased version of historical styles that was characteristic of commercial culture under Thatcher and Reagan, one not produced by architects so much as by hacks. So stereotyped and craven was this work that it did not even reach the level of pastiche, a genre that, as Mozart shows, requires a great deal of skill. The building boom of the 1980s led to the kind of overproduction that Modernism suffered in the 1960s. It was quickly damned as 'PoMo'. The insult, with its vaguely sexist overtones, was aimed particularly at Philip Johnson who had $2.5 billion worth of work in 1985. He was stereotyping every style he could lay his hands on, just as Jeff Koons was camping it up in the art world, to his everlasting profit. This inflationary period of architecture, which lasted about five years, was also typified by the kitsch work of Michael Graves for the Disney Corporation. This monolithic organisation, hiring the best global

ABOVE LEFT [33] Peter Eisenman, **Max Reinhardt Haus**, project for Berlin, 1992. Folding in difference became a harmonious way of handling heterogeneity in the 1990s. This project mixed the skyscraper, omnicentre, triumphal arch and various conflicting city functions in a resolved fractal geometry of self-similar facets. (© Eisenman Architects)

ABOVE [34] Rem Koolhaas, **CCTV**, Beijing, 2002–8. Functionally this hybrid form – triumphal arch and 70-storey skyscraper – is a continuous loop of all the departments that make up the state TV system, a huge centralised institution. In the competition the client called for an iconic building and this one characteristically mixes its understated metaphors: Chinese puzzle and moon-gate; Moebius strip; spider's-web construction etc. Folding here is semantic and functional, not formal, but the similarity to Eisenman's proposal is apparent. (© OMA/Ole Scheeren, Rem Koolhaas)

[35a, b, c] Arata Isozaki, **Disney Headquarters**, Lake Buena Vista, Florida, 1989–91. One of the few examples of Entertainment Architecture that managed to be creative pastiche and highly entertaining. One entered the Imagineers' Head Office under Mickey Mouse ears to arrive in a central open dome, a cosmic sundial and Zen rock garden – post-modern themes of resistance through humour. (C Jencks)

architects to do their worst work, christened their approach 'Entertainment Architecture'. James Stirling declined the invitation, while Arata Isozaki managed to make something interesting out of corporate Mickey Mouse. [35] Like corporate Modernism, commercial PoMo was loathed for its ersatz and criticised for its inflation. The tendency for giant-sized architecture to approach the condition of the one-liner, the empty icon, was all too evident. I pointed out how the deep causes of this mirrored the faults of modernism, the very ones that had brought about its downfall: that is, overproduction, giant size and elitist control.[32] Consumerism and industrial replication, which had exacted their revenge on every successful movement since 1800, predictably took their toll. PoMo was, like MoMo and LateMo, just another victim.

The negative dialectic seems almost a law of cultural entropy. Every modern movement strives to overcome the corruption of the one preceding it, only to succumb to success in turn. I will discuss this negative dialectic in the conclusion as a force driving critical modernism. Suffice it to say here that PoMo revealed a deep and systemic problem for post-modernism. It is conceived as a minority approach, an oppositional movement, not a ruling style. Once it makes peace with the dominant powers, it loses direction. Thus the reflexive turn within post-modernism against its own ersatz.

Complexity and the enigmatic signifier

One can see this self-criticism at work with the rise of the iconic building, a genre of overblown monuments that dominated the profession around the year 2000. It grew, not surprisingly, with the demand for the Millennium landmark building. Britain alone produced twenty-eight such projects, and they have continued to sprout in all developing countries, from Dubai to China. In the age of electronic reproduction, the notion of an icon, coming from the Greek word for a religious image and copy, took on specific digital meanings. By the Millennium it had come to mean '*reduced* as an image', like the icon on a computer, a visual one-liner that explains its function without words. Thus, when such symbolism became too obvious post-modernists veered away from the one-liner and forged a new form of sign, *implicit* allusion. This, the 'enigmatic signifier', soon became the conventional approach for the iconic building, as strange structures started to look like everything – and nothing in particular.

Post-modernists also developed the third way of dealing with cultural pluralism as they embraced an explicit complexity theory, one that Jacobs and Venturi had only adumbrated. The new complexity theory, stemming from the Santa Fe Institute and Ilya Prigogine's study of dissipative structures, underpinned what these scientists called 'the sciences of the 21st century'. In effect, complex systems work holistically through feedback and thus, from a conceptual point of view, they complement the modern, reductive sciences that have dominated since the time of Newton. The computer's development in the 1970s reached a point where it became possible to simulate these non-linear systems of growth, and soon thereafter the complex, emergent

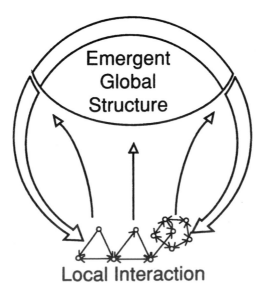

LEFT [36] Chris Langton, **Emergence diagram**, 1992. Global structures emerge (above), with different qualities than their component parts (below) and interact through feedback. Life, consciousness, society and culture are all emergent qualities that cannot be explained just in terms of their component parts. They are dissipative structures that are pushed far from equilibrium, and live off free energy.

structures that typify city growth. [36] Now one could begin to see and understand emergence per se, within self-organising systems, and how complexity arose over time.[33] A convincing example of this is DNA, molecules of memory that have taken more than three billion years to build up organisations complex enough to produce us, among other creatures. Architectural memory and complexity are also the work of long periods of destruction and restructuring. Thus for pm architecture, the 1970s' methods of collage and juxtaposition were supplemented by further ways of dealing with pluralism and history.

Folding theory, mentioned above, stemmed from the writings of the philosopher Gilles Deleuze, more particularly his book *Le Pli*, *The Fold*. The emphasis was not only on the way the Baroque arts used formal folds and curves, but captured through their methods such as calculus a continually changing set of differences. Greg Lynn and Jeffrey Kipnis found in these strategies a way beyond the discordant collage of Stirling and the ironies of Venturi. For the younger architects the strategies of the older Post-Modernists were too oppositional and blatant, so they fashioned a method of 'folding in difference'. Here variety and pluralism are allowed but subsumed into a supple, continuously changing whole. As Kipnis argues, it is coherent and congruent, able to handle multiple variables and yet still inclusive of difference.

The work of Frank Gehry since 1987 epitomises both the folding and complexity theories without being based directly on either. Gehry is aware of these ideas – I once came upon him surreptitiously reading Deleuze's book – but his approach is led by sculptural investigation through making models at many scales. Yet, in spite of his reluctance to philosophise, the new Guggenheim Museum in Bilbao is characteristic of the supple, pliant, moving quality of folding theory and the notions of emergence and fractals, the staple of complexity theory. For instance, the all-over titanium panels of the museum repeat endlessly as they fold into self-similar shapes of natural forms. The two most obvious relations to nature are in the flower-like petals and the shimmering water of the Nervión River, with which the building carries on a dialogue. [37] Pools adjacent to the building merge it with the larger river as both parties to the dialogue carry on reflecting each other.

Into these continuously changing curves many types of space are poured – Gehry's pluralism is typological more than semantic. The interior galleries run the gamut through museum types: spaces that are long, thin, white, curved and high; spaces that are small, squashed, square, coloured, and low; and are both abstract spaces and art-specific

FOLLOWING PAGES [37] Frank Gehry, **new Guggenheim Museum, Bilbao** , 1993–7. A dialogue with nature and the city. The architecture of the new complexity, an extension of Venturi's notion of complexity, is partly based on folding theory, fractals and production by computer. (C Jencks)

LEFT [38 a, b] **Folding theory.** In Gehry's Guggenheim Museum in Bilbao it is most evident in the way various functions are wrapped into a single undulating skin. Note here the way the long gallery and its north-facing skylights move above a lower curved space. The skin is a seamless white or titanium, broken and folded at points of structure and light. (C Jencks)

rooms. Furthermore, the hills, streets and river of Bilbao are very much pulled into the museum and framed through vast warped windows. [38]

The pluralism is most apparent in Gehry's handling of the industrial site. The building slides under an existing highway to one side, and then with its metallic surfaces relates to the buses, trains and the railroad station to the other side. Following the reaction against a pm symbolism that was too explicit, these references are understated and oblique. But, as the reaction of critics and the public made plain, the implicit metaphors provoked an enormous positive response, created the 'Bilbao Effect', put the city on the map, and confirmed the new convention for iconic buildings: the enigmatic signifier. [39]

The way Gehry's Guggenheim helped revive the fortunes of a waning rust-belt city ties together two main themes of this book, post-modernism and post-modernisation. Here a quaternary industry (tourism: the city of culture as destination) was created to replace

RIGHT [39] **Implicit metaphors.** The popular and critical success of Gehry's Guggenheim Museum in Bilbao confirmed the enigmatic signifier as the convention for the contemporary monument. Although critics mentioned some of the suggested overtones of this building – 'Constructivist artichoke' (lower right), 'fish', 'mermaid' and 'boat' – it is the capacity to mean many more things that makes the enigmatic signifier a multivalent symbol. (Metaphors drawn by Madelon Vriesendorp)

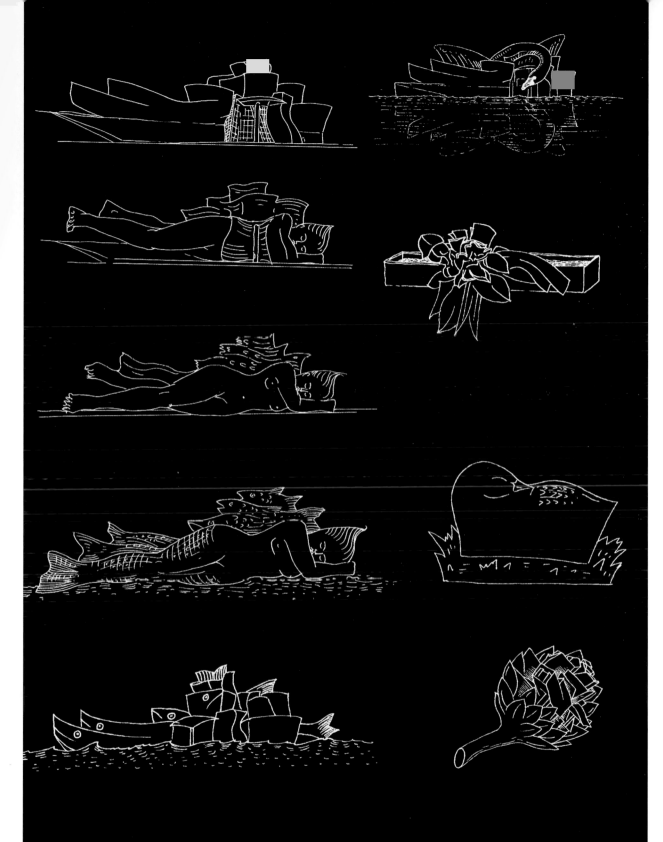

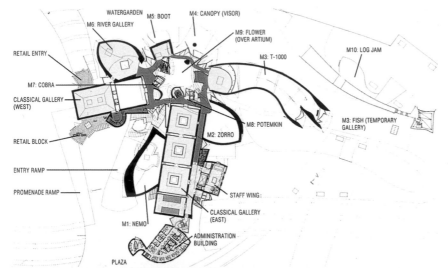

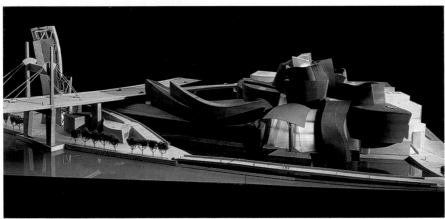

modern manufacturing, Bilbao's dying ship-building industry. The culture industry has, through this and other creations such as a new opera house, revived Bilbao's economy. The particular economic 'effect' of Gehry's museum on the city was measured as $400 million in its first two years, slowly declining thereafter.[34]

Beyond its imagery that appeals to a diverse audience, its multiple-coding and warped curves, its revival of a post-industrial economy, what makes Gehry's Guggenheim particularly post-modern is the fact that, as for other Gehry buildings, its complex organisation was facilitated by computer production. [40–1] This point should be emphasised. As mentioned, the computer is the instrument for understanding emergence in the natural and human worlds; it is to post-modernity what the telescope and microscope were to modernity. For twenty years many predicted a new crafted architecture that would be just as cheaply produced as the mass-produced elements of Modern architecture. This became possible in the 1970s when, in the

automobile industry, robots programmed with variable software manufactured differently shaped elements as quickly and easily as identical ones. Yet it was not until the early 1990s that the goal was generally available in architecture, a fact that Gehry's Bilbao announced to the world. It was as visible a shift in architecture as the blowing up of Pruitt-Igoe in 1972.[35]

By the mid-1990s, Post-Modernism was on the wane as an architectural movement. The term lived on as it had been used before, as one of abuse, but now, adding to the obloquy, it also became démodé. Nevertheless, its truths had been largely accepted, at least the non-political and easy aspects of its agenda: the pluralism, symbolism and stylistic heterogeneity. Late-Modernists, such as Norman Foster, absorbed the major lessons of iconic architecture; Richard Rogers, another self-styled Modernist, adopted most of its urban programme. So pervasive had the basic ideas become that elements of the movement could even be found in the work of those who disliked the new paradigm.[36] As Terry Farrell said at the time, 'everyone is now a post-modernist'. Indeed, to point up the irony, often the less it was mentioned, the more it was practised.

Many different kinds of iconic building, completed early in the twenty-first century, show this pervasive influence of Post-Modernism. Some, like the Museum of American Indians in Washington DC, are straightforward essays in historicist reference. Others, like the Wales Millennium Centre in Cardiff, are oblique versions of identity architecture. More abstract and typical of such understated symbolism is the new Library of Alexandria. This stylises solar and natural iconography from ancient Egyptian practice and marries it, appropriately, with the ecological agenda. [42]

Most complex and fascinating of these iconic buildings is Rem Koolhaas' Casa da Musica in Porto, Portugal. [43–4] On the outside and much of the inside it is an essay in severe and uncanny shapes. These are reminiscent of older Iberian monasteries, the architecture of absolutism and elimination. But, like an eighteenth-century rococo church, the rigorous exterior is contrasted with warmer interior rooms, or spaces that adopt local signs and conventions. One is filled out in eighteenth-century tile-work, another in rotated black and white squares. Like other recent iconic buildings, the 'House of Music' makes extensive use of the enigmatic signifier, and was accordingly perceived through all sorts of metaphors, some more plausible than others. During the competition, which it won, the local press dubbed it 'the diamond that fell from the sky'. In model form, the crystalline

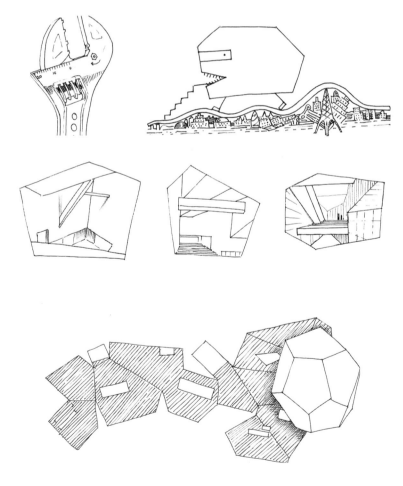

LEFT AND BELOW [43–4] Rem Koolhaas, **Casa da Musica**, Porto, 2005. Opaque 'milky quartz', a seven-sided polygon, made in creamy-white concrete. Metaphorical drawings by Madelon Vriesendorp. (C Jencks)

facets were more apparent, and transparent. However, when built as opaque, it is now known as 'the meteorite from heaven', a white-creamy polygon made from rectangles plus oblique triangles. Because of its seven-sided geometry and repetitive rhomboids, it is more like milky quartz than a meteor or diamond; but the point of such metaphors is not, primarily, denotation. It is the overall, natural connotations that matter, ones that are fresh here, slightly hostile and severe as nature can be and, importantly, ones that are transformed throughout the building.

The carrying over of the metaphor into the plan, section and detail makes it feel more convincing, more inevitable. Even the play of voided space, on the inside, turns the major theme of the crystal outside-in. A meandering route takes one through this cavernous quartz, up and around the musical halls that are slung into the space. [45–6] A consistent geometry is at work everywhere along the route but, in certain places, it is finished in an entirely different code. The rhomboid rooms, or angled facets that jut into the main hall, are faced either in local tiles or an ornamental system in another taste – Pop, traditional or Baroque. We are here back with the strategy of collage, with the multiple coding of post-modernism, a building that speaks in several voices some of which relate to the past and some to nature.

Indeed, if post-modernism has a message that cuts across the arts and different cultures, it may lie in such a natural iconography, codes that are suggested more than forced or explicit. We will return to such large and cosmic issues and see how they stem, negatively, from the ecological imperative and, positively, from an emergent metaphysics.

BELOW [45–6] **Interior polygons.** Within the geometric structure, the free section allows for concert halls to be slung and the space to billow around them. Thus one has a vertical route, up stairs and ramps, all the way to the roof. The abstract crystal metaphor is often double-coded with local or Pop graphics, here by traditional Portuguese patterns used in an optical way. Their rhythms pick up the undulating glass wall. (C Jencks)

 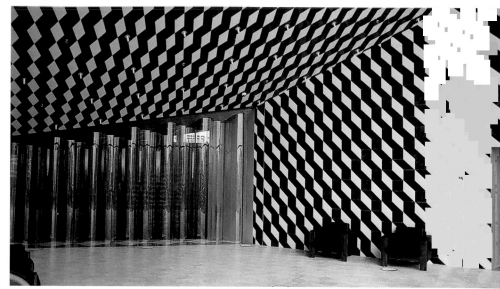

Post-modern art – cross-coding with content

In the most general sense, the post-modern movement has an intense concern with content. This may vary from straightforward narrative to historical metafiction where the storyline and author enter, on different levels, to comment on the action. In art, the subject matter is also of primary interest and likely to be layered, as in architecture, through a mixture of codes. This concern with content carries forward modern preoccupations and may approach abstraction, as in the case of Land Art. But here it combines these languages with issues outside the purely aesthetic – for instance, the green agenda – and in this sense is part of the wide movement.

Like pm architecture, the pm art movements also began in the 1960s as a succession of departures from Modernism. The plethora of labels conveys a message – Pop Art, Hyperrealism, Photo Realism, Allegorical and Political Realism, New Image Painting, Land or Earth Art, *La Transavanguardia*, Neo-Expressionism, the London School and so forth. Each was a more or less fabricated movement creating 'the difference that makes a difference', to use a phrase applied equally to evolution and the art market. Pressure from global competition to produce new brands and synthetic schools no doubt increased the tempo of change. The influence of the international media, so emphasised as a defining aspect of post-industrial society, forced these movements to cross national boundaries.

The global network, and the sensibility that comes with this, also pushed post-modern art towards an ironic cosmopolitanism. If one looks at three Italian post-modernists, Carlo Maria Mariani, Sandro Chia and Mimmo Paladino, one sees their 'Italianness' always in quotation marks, an ironic fabrication of their roots contrived as much for the New York they occasionally inhabit as from inner necessity. [47] Whereas in the past a mythology was given to the artist by tradition and patron, in the pm world it is chosen and constructed.

Mariani, in the mid-1970s, created his fictional academy of eighteenth-century peers – Goethe, Winckelmann, Mengs, and so on – and then painted some 'missing' canvases to flesh out a mythic history. In the early 1980s, he transferred this mythology to the present day and painted an allegory of contemporary Parnassus, with friends, enemies, critics and dealers gathered around him. [48] This is the typical pm trope, an ironic comment on a comment on a comment that signals the long distance from reality; a new myth thrice removed from its originating ritual. The painting is a contemporary rendition of Raphael

ABOVE [47] Carlo Maria Mariani, *La Mano Ubbidisce all'Inteletto*, 1983, oil on canvas, 78½ x 69in. For Modernists the subject of art was often the process of art; for Post-Modernists it is often the history of art producing itself from within. Hence 'The Hand Submits to the Intellect' recalls the Greek origins of painting and suggests that today it is self-generated from within a hermetic space, the history of art and Modernism. 'Painting painting itself', while seated atop the pure white spheres of Classicism and Modernism, is an allegory about the primary place of feedback and recursive structure in post-modern art. (© Sperone Westwater Gallery, New York)

ABOVE [48] Carlo Maria Mariani, *Costellazioni del Leone (La Scuola di Roma)*, 1980–1. Mariani, solemn and supercilious, sits below Ganymede who is being abducted to heaven by Zeus. Ganymede is not only the beautiful boy of Greek mythology being captured in the erotic embrace of the eagle Zeus, but a portrait of the performance artist Luigi Ontani (hence the hoop and stick). To the right, Francesco Clemente gazes past a canvas held by Sandro Chia. Mario Merz is cast as Hercules in an understated bathtub. A turtle personifying a well-known New York art dealer waddles to the water; critics scribble while admiring their own profiles. (© Westwater Gallery, New York)

and Meng's versions of the traditional subject. The texts are layered on top of one another as quixotic commentary. Like the structure of traditional myth there is reiteration, but unlike this structure there is also self-conscious irony.

The work uses pastiche to parody the New York art market and its pretensions, especially those successful friends of Mariani who have ingratiated themselves with the top dealer. All this is accomplished in the mock-heroic style of the late eighteenth century, the style of *la pittura colta* which Mariani has made his own. No one who gives this 'cultured painting' a second look would confuse it with the real thing, or take it as straightforwardly revivalist. Although some critics did brand the work as 'fascist', what they saw was their own stereotype reflected in the mirror, not the parody underlying the style.

If Mariani constructs a personal mythology, then so do many Post-Modernists who are involved with identity politics. This concern for local content is comparable to renewed interest by architects in particular communities. Whereas Modernism, and particularly Late-

Modernism, concentrated on the autonomy and expression of the particular art language – the formal dimension – Post-Modernists focus on the semantic aspect. This generalisation is true of such diverse artists as David Hockney, Malcolm Morley and Eric Fischl, some of whom have painted enigmatic allegories and others a combination of sexual and classical narratives. [49] The so-called 'return to painting' of the 1980s is also a return to a traditional concern with content, although it is a content that differs from pre-modern art. The subject matter of Fischl, for instance, contrasts social class and ethnic identity and thereby sets up the kind of tensions that David Lynch exploits in his films. [50] Suburban situations are cheerfully sunny and yet there is always something nasty about to appear – something suggested, yet never named. And that is very much the question, the latent threat lurking below the surface of everyday life. Ominous ambiguity, and the exaggeratedly constructed nature of identity, give this work its recognisable double coding.

One of the most accomplished pm artists, Ron Kitaj, goes beyond the easy irony of those such as Mariani, to address the more pressing issues of contemporary life, especially the way one deals with

BELOW [49] Eric Fischl, *A Brief History of North Africa*, oil on linen, 88 x 120in, 1985. Like David Lynch, Fischl explores archetypal scenes – the beach, the suburban backyard, the bedroom – to uncover their latent violence and sexuality. The atmosphere is often charged with a dissociated passion that reveals the vulnerability of character and the ambiguity of political and social roles. (Courtesy of Mary Boone Gallery, New York)

mass killing under the modern paradigm. Kitaj, the Jewish-American émigré who lived in London, is an artist most concerned with cultural subject matter, something for which a few London critics savaged him (leading to his dramatic exit from the city). His 1994 retrospective at the Tate Gallery was attacked by Andrew Graham-Dixon, among others, because of its literary and autobiographical content. With its captions and explicit visual cues, the work was provocatively both new and old. Kitaj confronted modern techniques of collage and flat, graphic composition with Renaissance traditions, just as he places the Holocaust – and its modernist causes – in opposition to a more healthy situation, whether a natural landscape or cityscape.

Kitaj's enigmatic allegory *If Not, Not* is a visual counterpart to TS Eliot's *The Wasteland,* on which it is partly based. [51] Survivors of war crawl through the desert towards an oasis; survivors of civilisation (including Eliot himself) are engaged in quizzical acts, some with representatives of exotic culture. Lamb, crow, palm tree, turquoise lake and a Tuscan landscape consciously adapted from the classical tradition resonate with common overtones. They point towards a Western and

ABOVE [50] David Lynch, **Blue Velvet**, 1986. In this pastiche and parody of the crime thriller, Lynch exploits the innocence of small-town America for its unlikely horrors and black humour. In Lumberton, USA, the hero, Jeffrey Beaumont, suddenly comes upon a severed ear and becomes involved in a mystery – and a thoroughly mixed genre.

RIGHT [51] Ron Kitaj, **If Not, Not**, oil on canvas, 60 x 60in, 1975–6. This post-modern painter uses modernist themes and characters as a departure point for his fractured allegories. They sustain a mood of catastrophe and mystery which is alleviated by small emblems of hope and a haunting beauty. (Courtesy National Galleries of Scotland, © Ron Kitaj)

Christian background overlaid by modernism, the cult of primitivism and disaster. The classical barn/monument at the top, so reminiscent of Aldo Rossi and Post-Modern face buildings, also suggests the death camps (it actually represents Auschwitz). Indeed, the burning inferno of the sky, the corpse and broken pier, the black and truncated trees all suggest life after the Second World War, after the last slaughter perpetrated by mechanised culture – modernity. It is a view of life as plural, confused and tortured on the whole, but containing islands of peace (and a search for wholeness).

The title, with its double negative – *If Not, Not* – was taken from an ancient medieval Catalonian political oath. At about the same time, the Scottish *Declaration of Arbroath* presented a similar idea: in effect, 'if you the King do not uphold our liberties and laws, then we do not uphold you'; not, not. The reciprocity of political power is turned into an allegory, and thus the consequences of broken promises and fragmented culture are the content of this gripping drama, one given a classical gravitas set against a modern rupture. The extreme oppositions are artistic equivalents of Stirling's Stuttgart Neue Staatsgalerie, but at the level of content the work has to be seen as part of a growing attempt to confront, and understand – if that is possible – the Holocaust.

This process of confronting the past has been extremely slow and painful and is still very much under way; and it is made even more complicated by the way it has come to justify the politics of Israel. Many attempts have been made to present and represent the experience of the Nazis' mass killing, most of them dwarfed and rendered senseless by the evidence itself. Nonetheless, for individual nations and a critical modernism, this confrontation with the recent past is necessary, however inadequate.

In the USA, and Germany, a series of Holocaust museums and memorials was created in the 1980s that attempted to convey some of the experience. They did this with parallel narratives, the storylines of a walk and a particular life that was ended. The visitor might walk through partial simulations of a concentration camp and, with a memento of one sort or another in hand, take on the identity of a specific victim. The architect Daniel Libeskind, some of whose family were murdered by the Nazis, wrote about the inadequacy of Holocaust memorials before he had the opportunity to design the Jewish Museum in Berlin. His extensive reflection on, and experience of the subject, led him to a convincing form of abstracting the void and how to represent loss. Of course, this is close to modernist notions of absence and elimination, but now it is rooted in an extended semantics and

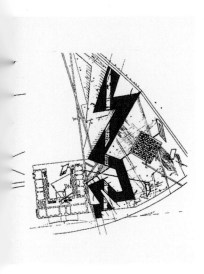

particular event, and it is this content that makes it post-the-modern. It bears comparison with Kitaj's constant return to the same set of subjects, and the whole building itself can be read as a work of art.

Attached to the older museum of Berlin History, the new structure is entered underground from the German building to make the point that both cultures are related, even if darkly so, in a subterranean sense. The history of the Berlin Jews, 240,000 of whom were deported, is integral to German history. Libeskind thus makes architecture by presenting the countless links as broken fragments – lines of connection. [52]

Thus the zigzags are partly generated by lines connecting the points in Berlin where famous Jews and gentiles lived. Some of these references, and lines generating the scheme, are esoteric: those referring, as in previous work, to Mies van der Rohe, Walter Benjamin and Paul Celan, or Modernists who like the Jews were suppressed by the Nazis. [53] But these arcane signs are also set against more accessible ones such as the six-pointed yellow Star of David which the Germans forced the Jews to wear. The same double coding of the esoteric and popular underlies another metaphor, that of Arnold Schoenberg's last opera, the unfinished *Moses and Aaron* that inspired Libeskind. Schoenberg was a quintessential modern twelve-tone composer and the opera breaks off at the point where Moses and Aaron are unable to complete their mission with the people of Israel: 'Oh word, thou word that I lack!' – Moses laments his inability to lead the people to the Promised Land. The building's void expresses this inability to speak the word, whereas the zigzags show Aaron's determination to go forward, nevertheless.

This irregular path is another symbol that has many overtones – lightning bolt, Waffen SS, the dialectical zigzag of history. Libeskind speaks of 'the unfathomable nature of the twentieth century', and looking at these bent forms in plan, elevation and detail one can see the architectural equivalent to chaotic Brownian motion, or at least some randomness. This is a route without a clear destination, the wandering search known in science as 'the drunkard's walk'. The tilts and jagged cuts in the facade are natural metaphors for not knowing precisely where you are going, and a form to be played off against the straight line, the void.

Most symbolic and powerful is the concrete line, or what Libeskind calls 'the voided void', that runs across the crooked forms, to make his basic metaphor: this became a book title, *Between the Lines*. The two lines interact in paradoxical ways. One travels along the zigzag through the galleries always returning to the void down the middle, but

THESE PAGES [53] **Jewish Museum**. Self-similar forms, angles, slashes and lines – a fractal grammar put to symbolic use. A matrix of lines predominates on the faces of the building, connecting places where Berlin Jews lived. 'These are the lines across which one could send a message, a letter, an imaginary thought, an intention towards someone, somewhere.' Libeskind's work, while highly abstract, has a symbolic core. The grey tonalities of the zinc cladding create a twilight ambiguity, a blur, a darkness that on the inside is cut by lines of light, the incomprehensible by clarity. (C Jencks)

ABOVE [54] **Jewish Museum**. The void down the middle. (C Jencks)

RIGHT [55] **The ETA Hoffmann Garden, The Garden of Exile and Emigration** Libeskind also calls it, with willow trees growing out of the top of concrete rectangles. (C Jencks)

this organisational spine cannot be entered, only traversed. [54] The psychological reason for denying access is that the void is a mystery, the presence of an absence, the memory of those who were deported leaving very little, except their names and dates of birth carefully inscribed in two volumes that the Nazis noted down.

Like Kitaj, Libeskind here confronts the dark side of modernity and turns it into an ambivalent, symbolic art, one that is disturbing and pleasurable in equal measure. Indeed, the greatest surprise, given the museum's subject matter and pervasive grey, is the feeling of energy, even exhilaration. [55] It is an oddly hopeful building, the harbinger of a new Europe, one that can acknowledge its past and make an architecture from it. From the most general viewpoint, the slow confrontation with the Holocaust and its meanings is a post-modern process that has to be broadened and deepened in scope to take on its systemic causes. It has to deal with the role of the underdog per se, those minorities always subject to repression.

It is the symbolic and historical reference in Libeskind's abstraction that sets it apart from Late-Modern work, and one can find the same distinction within a single movement, such as Land Art. For instance, the early work of Richard Long in the 1960s has different intentions from the later work of Andy Goldsworthy. They both might use abstract forms, such as circles built from untreated rock, and photography (a quintessential modern art form). However, where Long will take a solitary walk and record it in texts, maps and deadpan commentary, Goldsworthy will dramatise the contrast of culture and nature. Where Long will leave his interventions neutral and minimal, Goldsworthy will heighten nature by exaggerating its qualities, for instance covering rocks in a stream with shiny coats of red maple or yellow elm leaves. The first intervention makes one rock look like a blood-soaked sponge, the other like a giant gold ingot. But these associations are only momentary, achieved with natural means, and vanish after the leaves dry.

The intentions of both Long and Goldsworthy relate to the green agenda, of living lightly on the earth, and it is true that the wider ecological agenda cuts across the stylistic and ideological categories. It is the professed faith of politicians from Thatcher to Blair, of symbolic leaders from Prince Charles to Gorbachev, of all architectural movements of every persuasion. But Goldsworthy, like other Post-Modernists, uses ancient historical forms – arches, ovoids, cairns, sheepfolds – to send unusual messages, to challenge contemporary structures. [56] His nine cairns with voided top circles smash into each

ABOVE [56] Andy Goldsworthy, *Roof*, National Gallery of Art, East Building, Washington DC, 2005–6. Like the Clava Cairns, prehistoric stone domes in Scotland, these nine horizontal structures have an archetypal form open at the top. While they recall these abstract shapes in size and geometry, they have an additional semantic role here, breaking through IM Pei's pristine Late-Modern gallery in a primitive gesture uniting the outside, and a dingy cantilever, to the sacrosanct art interior. (C Jencks)

other, and emphatically through the wall of the National Gallery in Washington, referring at once to the many neoclassical domes of that city and to the Late-Modern purity of the building it violates. In this sense, the content of his work subverts while at the same time inscribing itself within the mainstream.

Examples could be multiplied of this transgressive double coding. During the 1980s, Robert Rauschenberg, David Salle, Hans Haacke, Paula Rego and Ian Hamilton Finlay invoked the Western tradition to indict contemporary culture. [57] Their specific views are widely divergent, but they share a concern to communicate non-artistic content and they adopt multiple languages to do so. The content varies in its political, moral, ecological or cultural reference but, whatever its motive, the result is multiply coded. Contrast this with Modern formalism of the Greenbergian persuasion. This has a reduced focus on the specificity of each art language as the subject of the work. Post-Modernists have an expanded critical agenda, as John Barth notes, one that is evident in other writers such as Umberto Eco, David Lodge, Salman Rushdie and those whom Linda Hutcheon discusses in her study of literature, *A Poetics of Postmodernism*.[37]

In this study, she finds the recurrent post-modern motive of crosscoding: the intention to confront the present with the past, to subvert dominant culture from within its walls, to represent the ironic complexity of contemporary life. This stance is common to the underdog. A certain type of irony characterises minority cultures forced to accommodate themelves to a system not of their choosing: the blacks in

BELOW [57 a, b] Ian Hamilton Finlay, *Nuclear Sail*, 1974, slate (with John Andrew) and **The Goose Hut**, 1982 (with Andrew Townsend). The black 'sail' of a Polaris submarine confronts 'Abbé Laugier's primitive hut' across an artificial lake: the beauty and terror of classicism are often Finlay's themes. (C Jencks)

America, the Poles under the Soviet control, the Jews in racist cultures, or the Palestinians under Israeli law. These situations force a double coding on the subject people, and a sophisticated form of irony that still allows the heretical opinion to be expressed, often with black humour. Such irony also allows minority culture to continue compromising in order to survive, and survive with some integrity and truth. Such are the realities of multiculturalism and its style of ironic hybridisation.

Irony on the verge of cynicism

But there is obviously a point at which this critical post-modern strategy backfires, when the irony becomes predictable and boorish. That moment is reached when, without awareness, the dissenting irony becomes an Establishment voice or, when Post-Modernism becomes a dominant brand. Then the critical view becomes an imposture, and irony turns into cynicism. With the 'new Brit Art' led by Damien Hirst, cynicism actually becomes an important part of the content and makes it hard to distinguish the criticism of mass culture from its exploitation. This alliance of mass media and art is evident in the number of flags that the movement sailed under as it turned itself, in the 1990s, into a highly successful product. The aliases varied around an adolescent centre, from 'Britpop' (Matthew Collings) to 'New Boomers', from 'Brit Pack' to 'Thatcher's Children' ('Saatchi's kids' would have been as pertinent). Most simply this distinctive brand was known as 'young British artists' (abbreviated to YBAs) and most trenchantly and to the point as 'High Art Lite' (Julian Stallabrass).

No discussion of pm art can pass over this perplexing territory in silence. Like Julian Schnabel, and 1980s artists in America, the Brit Pack addresses the big themes of life – death, sex and religion – and, like this overly optimistic painter, many of them have tried their hand at a portrait of God. As with pm scientists, who put the deity in their book titles – *The Mind of God*, *The God Particle*, etc – it is often hard to tell whether the intention is serious, a send-up, or a question of sales. The ambiguity is, no doubt, judiciously calculated. Indeed, with Hirst the neutrality of scientific culture is adopted as a position and, at the same time, lampooned and exploited for its horror.

Brit Art had its official launch in the autumn of 1997 when Charles Saatchi managed to plug a hole in the exhibition calendar of London's Royal Academy that had suddenly opened up. His plug was *Sensation*, the most sensationally marketed show of contemporary art in British history. Having sold off much of his 1980s' collection at a high price, he had been buying up the works of young British artists at a low one. The recession had bitten into the market, the government had stopped funding artists and Thatcherite competition was applied to the culture industry. Saatchi, who with his brother Maurice had made a fortune in advertising promoting the values and image of Thatcher, now had the good fortune to launch his group in the most unlikely of places. The magisterial galleries of the Royal Academy, top-lit and classical, are right in the heart of London. This institution, filled with academicians, is dedicated by charter to good taste, the advancement of taste and the public weal, hence its royal imprimatur. All this was a perfect foil for *Sensation*.

Most lugubrious were Hirst's corpses. Various bodies, floating in formaldehyde, filled his tanks. Most conspicuous was the famous, vulnerable shark displayed under the ironic eighteenth-century title, *The Physical Impossibility of Death in the Mind of Someone Living*. His sectioned cows were placed in white ghost frames, looking like display cases in both a biology class (good) and boutique (bad). Even more adolescent were the mutant bodies of young girls and boys designed by the Chapman brothers, and Tracey Emin's tent, *Everyone I Have Ever Slept With*, stitched in fabric with a short-list of her everyone. Most sensational to the media were Mat Collishaw's *Bullet Hole*, a cibachrome print divided into fifteen neutral squares, the photo of a red hole left in the head by a bullet penetrating the skull (looking altogether like a scatological shot of a vagina) and Marcus Harvey's acrylic portrait of Myra Hindley, the infamous child murderer.

Inevitably, much hypocritical outrage was vented on all sides, by the tabloids, the general public and the defenders of art. They traded insults, and whipped up a media event, fed by the all-too-real, perplexing questions. Was the portrait of the murderer Hindley a shameless exploitation of the original photo and its sexual and religious overtones? Or, was the *Daily Mail's* republication of this image on its front page much worse? The paper had the gall to feature this, just as it damned Harvey's critique. If tabloid culture depended on moralistic outrage to sell its wares, why then couldn't Harvey comment on this commercialisation? Should art be censored where mass culture is not? But what about the victims and their families? Should the relatives of the murdered have no right to stop this double exploitation?

The debate on the *Sensation* exhibition followed the same logic of traded insults, the knowing exploitation of neutral reporting, double-ironies and pseudo-criticism. It never became very sophisticated, but it certainly magnified attendance – over 300,000 visitors, large for a show of contemporary art – and made global, and financial, reputations for half the exhibitors. Post-Modern irony had never been as commercially mined as this, and by all sides except those of the victims. Newspapers, television, critics, curators, the Royal Academy, artists, and Saatchi himself, all gained from the exposure. As far as notoriety was concerned it was the typical win-win situation, a positive-sum game with media and art all coming out ahead, economically that is. Culturally it confirmed the trend towards the ultra-cool presentation of sensational subject matter and critically, except for one or two pieces such as those by Julian Stallabras, it confirmed the way the mainstream press could absorb, with aesthetic pleasure, any nastiness hurled in its face.

Stallabrass' book, analysing *High Art Lite*, was one of the few interesting creations of the movement, especially in the way it pointed up the relationship between the ambiguous approach of the artists and high commerce. As he wrote, the typical work of Brit Art presents a dramatic and often horrific dilemma and then steps back with false innocence and lets the viewer decide what it means. The obligation of the artist, which is to make sense of moral dilemma, is carefully sidestepped. Unflappable coolness is the standard attitude.[38] 'Cool Britannia', the media concoction of Tony Blair, found a fitting expression in this youth cult of ambiguity, of shocking images accompanied by suspended judgement. Cryonic ethics it might be called, frozen way beyond the cool so that morality might never appear. Indeed, if one is looking for comparisons between a shocking life and British Art then the night-time bombing of Iraq is relevant. The policy of 'Shock and Awe' was formulated especially to be seen on prime time television, the aesthetic of *Sensation* applied to global politics. It is not only advertisers who borrow from the world of art.

In such manner, Brit Art became the Establishment, post-modern irony became cynicism and Damien Hirst and his persona became one of the outstanding contradictions of our time. Advertising the 'bad boy' image of his working-class origins, he appeared especially in photographs as a crazed toughie, sporting a shaven head and unshaven face, kiddie trousers and bulging eyeballs. No doubt this image resulted from his manic workload and background in the slums of Brixton. Throughout the 1990s he carefully honed this image of the hard-pressed workaholic as he churned out mass-produced paintings – the spot and spin acrylics – and the factory-made vitrine art. The tabloid and broadsheet press noted each of his triumphs, his escapades and ability to mock – and turn a huge profit at the same time. The poor boy from Brixton managed to make £100 million ($170 million) and remain, ensconced in his country house, the very image of alienated youth. Quite a well-branded contradiction.

'An artist?' an *Independent on Sunday* headline asked rhetorically and answered, 'I'm a brand name, says Hirst'. 'I think becoming a brand name is a really important part of life, it's the world we live in. It's got to be addressed, understood and worked out, as long as you don't become your own idea of yourself, you don't start making Damien Hirsts.'[39] Well, Hirst started 'making Damien Hirsts' and getting away with it on an extraordinary scale. What the critic Robert Hughes damned in another context, the successful avant-garde artist producing 'self-forgeries', was part of the brand. Yet moral and aesthetic failures are not the whole story. The entropy should not blind us to Hirst's several brilliant works that deal with first and last things, among them the early vitrine piece, *A Thousand Years*. [58] Repugnant, *grand guignol*, an example of tabloid and yob culture at the same time? Yes, but more than that the inventive presentation of a work that performs its critique of Darwinian Britain.

BELOW [58] Damien Hirst, ***A Thousand Years***, 1990/2006. A double, black-edged cage surrounds a surreal process, here the birth, growth, consumption and mechanical killing of maggots – a Darwinian experiment given a mordant setting. Vitrine Art draws the viewer on in a mixture of discovery – hunt the drama – and multiple perspectives. Francis Bacon admired the result, and the dialogue continued, below. (© Damien Hirst, photographed by Roger Wooldridge, courtesy of Gagosian Gallery)

It consists of a rotting cow's head and thousands of flies that feed off it, and breed. The upsetting effect is doubled by the buzz of the flyzapper as it attracts the insects to its light, and the horrid smell of decaying flesh (at least when it was first on display at *Sensation*). This closed system of life and death, portrayed neutrally, is an ingenious comment on the way suburbanites routinely deal with flies. At the same time it is a dramatic version of how scientists follow the quick evolution of many generations. The Darwinian world view and our implication in cycles of deathly consumption are condensed in this high-low and smelly art. So too are the nature films of David Attenborough and the horror fantasies of sci-fi. The most convincing, and repugnant, aspect is the way the reality of life and death and decay is used as performance *and* symbol, at one and the same time. If one role of the artist is to reveal repressed realities and turn them into an expressive image, then in several such works Hirst has produced an authentic, critical art.

One of his most convincing and unnerving works is the set of vitrines based on Francis Bacon's three paintings, the triptych dedicated to the suicide of his lover, George Dyer. Bacon's work is his typical mixture of a flat, graphic background and blurred, realistic foreground. Architecture frames the act of suicide, and it also surrounds Damien Hirst's death scene. This houses three flayed sheep, pinioned against the glass in vulnerable poses, poses themselves strangely reminiscent of classical art. [59] Both artists use minimalist devices to set up their theatrical foreground, both focus on the body as the vehicle of violent

ABOVE & OPPOSITE [59a, b, c] Damien Hirst, ***The Tranquillity of Solitude***, 2006. The triptych is best approached from the side so that visual distortions animate the three boxes together. Vitrine Art demands movement, engagement, both distant and close-up views. Here one can experience the generic framing of a religious triptych and the particular splayed corpse of a sheep, the *Guernica* scream and the injecting syringe, the abstract geometry of the vertebrae and its relation to your body. Multiple viewpoints and angled views that double the image. In this sense Vitrine Art is a kind of reverse Cubism. (© Damien Hirst, photographed by Mike Bruce. courtesy of Gagosian Gallery)

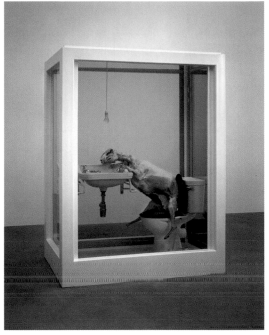

endings. But where Bacon verges on the melodramatic with black splurges of shadow, Hirst lets the carcass and its tender placement convey the message. The arm of one animal rests on a spout; the head of another hovers over the bowl while it seems to turn on the tap. These tiny gestures seem real and frail. One is pulled into their trial by modern hygiene, the humour and the horror of the bathroom as the place of last things, Golgotha. The central lamb as pietà, crucified against the glass, just avoids bathos. Post-modern references also initially escape recognition – Picasso's *Guernica*, Bacon's screaming Popes – because they stem directly from the bodies.

Toilet seat, hanging electric light and washbasin are common to both triptychs, but with Hirst the mechanical fixtures carry more weight. The reason is their reality and size, of course, but also the way they are integrated with the sterilised setting – the whiteness – and contrasted with the white bodies. When you approach these three vitrines from the side, the sheep and fixtures double as an image, they distort and jump about visually. Such theatricality implicates you at the same time that the white abstraction distances the scene. I'm not sure Hirst's vision has grandeur, as one critic has claimed, but it is surely one of the strongest portrayals of suffering and death, in an age that usually avoids the subject. It also shows the way that one artist's work can help another attain balance and confidence in dealing with such difficult content. Placing dead sharks and various cut-up animals in formaldehyde is one thing. Imagine if the triptych were carried out with real, human bodies, or like the embalmed skeletons in Sicilian catacombs, or made of three plastinated people as in Professor Gunther von Hagen's *Body Worlds*. That would have been titillating, ghoulish, a freak show. Here the flayed sheep function as displaced persons and are slightly macabre, but their non-human status allows us to take in the pain and mortality of life, the universal gesture of suffering flesh, without becoming either trite or exhibitionistic.

Chris Ofili, who also achieved global recognition with the *Sensation* exhibition, is equally adept at branding himself with images guaranteed to make a media splash. In his case the logo is not a gruesome vitrine but elephant shit, or dung of several kinds, even elegant and dignified black women and men taking down their pants and leaving a snake of rising gold from their bums. Ofili's work, as this implies, is not without a parodic humour (Rembrandt used the same trope) and, in its sophisticated coding, also plays on the repertoire of high art. Trained at Chelsea School of Art and then the Royal College of Art in London, his decorative paintings allude to the glittering world of Klimt as much as to the all-over action painting of Jackson Pollock, but the primary references are to the brash colour field folk art of Africa and fractal art. These sources are as apparent as the titles are ironic – *Afrobluff* and *Afrodizzia* are dizzy and bluffing paintings, as they say, that exaggerate their Afro origins at the same time as they use them to celebrate purely painterly qualities.

Stereotype versus pattern painting, pretty fractal versus elephant dung, pop photographs versus layered commentary, serious subject matter versus playful evasion – the double coding is as calculated a strategy as it is with Hirst. Because Ofili, the black artist, uses stereotypes adapted from white and black culture to parody both sides of the equation his work is seen as an instance of multiculturalism and 'Hybridity theory'.[40] He is quite open about playing on these sources, about 'blaxploitation' and giving white people what they want – 'voodoo queen ... the drug dealer, the *magicien de la terre* ... but it's packaged slightly differently'. Essentially the dung defuses the prettiness, while the serious dignity of the facial expressions – a recurrent motif – challenges the viewer to face up to reality. This is particularly true of the painting that created such a stir at *Sensation*, the black Madonna surrounded by little fractal bums and crotch shots, entitled *The Holy Virgin Mary*. She stares out at the viewer with furrowed brow, flaring nostrils and an unmistakable, angry '*J'accuse*'. Blasphemy – or a different way of thinking about Christianity in Africa? Britain, with a dearth of missionaries under sixty, is importing a few from the place of Ofili's ancestors, Nigeria.

Ofili may not be a philosopher with an agenda but he certainly confronts some contradictions of global culture, not only racial but religious and epistemological. A case in point is *The Upper Room*, an installation of thirteen paintings inside a dark brown 'chapel' designed by his friend, the black architect David Adjaye. [60–1] One enters this sacred and isolated space via a tight, high, floor-lit corridor – no question about the references to a ritual art experience and 'stations of the cross', the Tate Museum as cathedral manqué. The stained glass of the nave is not overhead but propped on the floor, as usual by dung balls encased in resin – the 'high-low' reference of post-modernism if ever there was one. Each spot-lit rectangle of bright colour buzzes

away like a Jackson Pollock in Dayglo, a psychedelic hallucination of reflecting glitter, gold, map pins and colour tone. The major tones are marked at the base on the dung balls – 'Mono Rojo' for red, 'Mono Verde' for green, 'Mono Blanco' for white etc – as if there were thirteen races of colour. Each 'race' is represented by a seated monkey holding an offering cup as if drinking to the supreme golden monkey at the end, on the high altar as it were, a knock-kneed figure with a silly grin (that can barely be registered). Some have interpreted this figure as Christ, or Buddha, or a Hindu monkey of veneration. Perhaps it is

BELOW [61] Chris Ofili, *The Upper Room*, designed by David Adjaye, clearly alludes to a dark meditative space. Its axial nave is focussed on the 13th golden monkey. Symmetrically set paintings are conceived as radiating stained glass, a critique of the abstract Rothko Chapel and ambiguous comment on nature worship (© Tate, London 2007)

God or perhaps simply an alpha-male rhesus monkey? The questions multiply – a comment on African totemism or the class system; setting for a black mass or a lecture on art history; a serious, layered commentary or kitsch extravaganza?

As so often with Brit Art, the narrative seems cut short to let the viewer decide the question with which the artist refuses to engage. Positively, this agnosticism allows humour and a delight in pattern to take over. The Decorative Sublime dissipates argument but, along with the booklet published on the exhibition, *The Upper Room*, it does raise important questions about our relation to nature and the very intelligent species on display, the rhesus macaque. As conservation biologist Dr Susanna Paisley makes clear in her text, this monkey is extremely creative for a primate, capable of great altruism, clever at fooling us for its own ends, able to communicate via a rudimentary language and bearer of a primitive culture. It can grin and laugh when on top of its very rigid caste system, and it can learn and pass on a set of important traditions, including kindness. Ofili is clearly enjoying the irony that through ethology and art blacks, having once been derided as monkeys, can now contemplate and even celebrate their superior human qualities.

Just as obviously this *Upper Room* makes a comment on our notions of primitiveness and separation from nature. Read as the Last Supper, the way many critics have interpreted it, the installation implies a critique of 'men in groups', the way the twelve apostles mirror the average number of males that bond in a corporate assembly or a fighting platoon. Their conformity, their caricature with a silly grin and turban, comes to the fore as commentary. However, read as a pleasurable celebration of nature's plenitude, of the garden as site of riotous fecundity, of drinking, excreting and laughing, the installation tips the mood in another direction. Now it is the intricacy of nature and art that are the superior mystery. Floral prints, psychedelic whirls and sparkling pins create their brash, jungle honky-tonk. Three basic layers of nature, and painting, interact in this musical ritual – the background forest, the mid-ground tendrils and the foreground profile of the primate. Pantheistic ritual or pre-Christian rite?

At the same time, this installation refers to that modernist icon, Mark Rothko's Chapel in Texas, where sombre abstractions are meant to do the work of iconography. If Rothko's minimalist swaths of colour are illustrations of Negative Theology and meant to induce a feeling of the presence of absence – the sweet void – Ofili's room is much more engaging, and on many levels. The reverence for art is accepted and gently mocked. That cliché of the 1980s, the museum as cathedral, is acknowledged and then turned into a parody of the Garden of Eden.

In this work Ofili confronts some of the basic issues of our time – spiritual, conformist, ecological, political – and, without offering a solution, does give a gentle critique of the customary evasions. As often pointed out in the nineteenth century, art cannot be a substitute for religion or politics, but it can make a pointed comment on them and, as I have argued, perhaps the most effective Post-Modern art comes from a minority position far from the Establishment, as the irritable opposition to modernism.

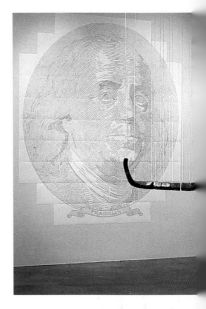

Brian Tolle's commission to celebrate the 300th anniversary of the birth of Benjamin Franklin in Philadelphia is a modest example of this critical position. Three works combine in his installation *Die, or Join*, itself a comment on Franklin's political cartoon and advice to the divided nation, 'Join, or Die'. [62–3] The centrepiece of Tolle's work is captivating and frightening, a two-headed snake that hangs from the ceiling in a series of blue and red undulating sections. Such two-headed reptiles are actually one of nature's sports, and much more sinister signs of mutation than the Chapman brothers' hybrids of male and female genitalia. Here the double heads and segments symbolise the dominance of the red states that voted for George Bush over the blue ones, on the periphery, that supported Kerry in the 2004 presidential election. This idea is underlined by a visual illusion one stumbles over: there, on the floor, is the snake's moving shadow mapping out the shape of America's coastline. It is an ingenious double coding that prepares one for more.

The allegory of divided nation joined at the neck by necessity and the lethal nature of America's foreign policy is presented with a straightforward force. However, what gives this work its shocking aptness is not apparent from a static and silent photograph. The jolt comes from the way the wires, live with Franklin's famous electricity, set up a magnetic attraction. Then the snake twitches and suddenly clicks together making a convulsive SNAP!

This minimalist installation has maximal impact. It's not the most extended comment on Bush's America, and the way he has cut it up, nor is it the most profound work of critical modernism. But it is the kind of exemplary post-modern work that can be found at the periphery while the modernist juggernaut rides on its oblivious and complacent way.

The concern with content, the double and multiple coding, the irony and parody – all the strategies and styles of post-modernism continue to be used by architects, writers and artists. Sometimes these

BELOW [62–3] Brian Tolle, *Die, or Join*, installation ICA, Philadelphia, 2006. A two-headed snake, in segments of blue and red, undulates from its live wires and on occasion clicks together – a dangerous nation divided suddenly snapped together in war. (© Brian Tolle)

methods are coopted to resist the dominant, sometimes to gain entry to the halls of power. Whichever the case, one can find a similar ambivalence throughout global society, visible in daily life as developed nations interact with the rest of the world. Here again the style of post-modernity, its pluralism and hybridisation, becomes the rule as it is in so much contemporary art. Today the old aristocracy of Europe and Britain is as likely to be found adopting the dress and codes of the dispossessed, just as the new elite of India and China is apt to take on the style of a Western businessman. A knowing hybridity and contamination are for many the way to negotiate a fast-changing information world.

3. THE BLURRED SOCIETY

The rise of the cognitariat

In the late nineteenth century the French poet Comte de Lautréamont defined beauty as 'the fortuitous encounter of a sewing machine and an umbrella on a dissection table'. Bizarre, convulsive juxtaposition – sometimes beautiful, always unexpected. In the Middle East today, a traditionally garbed Bedouin can be found riding a camel across the desert while having, beneath his robes, a business suit, mobile phone and laptop computer.

Such cultural hybridisation has been the norm in Japan and China for some time. In a Tokyo tower, designed in the fashionable high tech manner during the 1970s, I came upon seven traditional Japanese weddings going on at once. [64] Colourful kimono smashed into Black Tie on its way to Plastic Curtain. Such incongruities, combining new technologies and old customs, may not be turned into Lautréamont's new form of beauty and they may remain unconscious, but in a globalised world they are the norm. Pure hybrids now dominate the new reality, a strange sounding cognitariat sitting atop the very mixed economy, socitalism.

In his book *Cosmopolitanism*, the Princeton professor Kwame Anthony Appiah describes attending a royal festival in his country of origin, Ghana.[41] It is a traditional ceremony for the king of Asante, focusing on the 'porcupine chief' who sits on his throne listening to

OPPOSITE [64] **Traditional Japanese wedding** on the tenth floor of a Tokyo glass and steel skyscraper, the incongruity that one sees everyday on the newspaper front page. (C Jencks)

songs of praise and flute music. Every bit of the ceremony belongs to the African past but, as Appiah points out, before the king arrived people were taking calls on their mobile phones and discussing such global issues as HIV/Aids, the educational needs of twenty-first-century children, the teaching of science and technology at the local university, and the forthcoming meeting of the king with the World Bank. The moral of this situation for Appiah, typical of the approach to such scenarios by much of the world, is not the preservation of exotic cultures in their pure state but rather a realistic melding. It is neither the unity of a modernising International Style nor the freezing of a homogeneous past. Instead, it is 'The Case for Contamination', as he calls it, for a cosmopolitanism that favours free choice and difference. Preserve the artefacts of authenticity by all means, he avers, but also allow the messy vitality of growth and change (Robert Venturi's 'complexity and contradiction'). It may not be aesthetically pleasing, but hyphenated-culture allows the developing world to develop.

The most visible shift in the post-modern world is towards pluralism and cultural eclecticism, a heterogeneity which is largely unintentional. Pluralism is mostly a by-product of communication and global capitalism, and many nations such as Japan have tried to play down its visibility. But the globe has been irreversibly united by current technologies into an instantaneous, twenty-four-hour information world, the post-industrial successor to the modern world of industrialisation. Karl Marx wrote in the *Communist Manifesto* that capitalist industry was changing every social relationship extremely fast. 'All that is solid melts into air' was his metaphor for dissolution, the landscape and social values that capitalism was transforming. Today, by comparison, there is less traditional society to melt and the global economy is much more effective at liquefaction.

Some nations are dissolving into 'failed-nations', and virtually all national identities are hybridising. Cultural boundaries are now easily crossed because of increasing trade, ease of travel and immediate world communication. This has led to 'space-time compression', the 'global village', which miniaturises the earth spatially and temporally, equivalent in size to a small town – perhaps even to a computer console.[42] The space and time necessary for a transaction, meeting, or media event have imploded drastically while, at the same time, the speed with which the global economy forces styles to change and product innovation has also modified our taste for change in schizophrenic ways. Media cultures are at once more stereotyping – and in that sense conservative – and hooked on constant, marginal variation. Image politics, spinning and the commodification of culture become the ruling taste in Blair's Britain.

Such combustible change has created what Fredric Jameson and others call the post-modern condition with its typical mix of opportunities and problems. This duality means the only intelligent attitude is one of critical selection, to choose or 'eclect' the positive elements and try to suppress the negative ones (that is what eclecticism really means). It is more easily said than done. For instance, the much-proclaimed 'end of work', which the post-industrial society brings, shows the typical Janus face. There is more leisure time *and* job insecurity, more work variety *and* exploitation. But no country has yet been able to have the former goals without the latter by-products. In fact, in many developed countries, save France for a short time, the new technology has not led to more leisure but rather its reverse: longer working hours for the fully employed.

With its 'flexi-time' and outsourcing, the post-modern condition has eroded job security. The overseas call-centres in India and the Philippines do work that used to be handled in the USA and UK. Since the year 2001, three of the largest US call-centres have closed down. Protectionist labour laws are contemplated as multinationals seek to minimise their costs. The Princeton economist Alan Binder calls this 'offshoring' and sees it as the third industrial revolution. It will, he predicts, lead to 40 million jobs going offshore, not only the usual manufacturing (of heavy industry) but many more service jobs than previously imagined, from healthcare (laboratory work) to education (exam marking). If the second and third industrial revolutions (automation and offshoring) are defining aspects of the post-modern condition, they typically lead to lower costs and increased competition, cheaper goods and the driving down of wages. However, where services have to be culturally specific and tailor-made to a language and context, the process can be reversed – to increased employment in the developed world. So offshoring cuts both ways in a complex feedback of loops within loops, of changing labour markets, and of the mutating laws that seek to regulate them.

What could be called 'inshoring' is even more a political problem, leading to a very democratic hypocrisy, shared by most sides. World mass-migration has reached unprecedented proportions with 200 million people on the move across national borders. Most of this is economic migration, the three billion people living on $2 per day who must run away from chronic poverty, the most able among them being able to run the fastest. For a long time in Britain and America politicians have turned a blind eye to this illegal inshoring, because these motivated workers stimulate the national economy while keeping wages down. This has led both countries to engage in a kind of double-bluff. Whereas Soviet leaders used to joke of their workforce, 'they pretend to work and we pretend to pay them', Anglo-Saxon leaders now practise a new double-think: 'We pretend to enforce borders and they pretend to observe them'. The illegality clearly suits both sides, which is why it has gone on so long. But it will continue only up to a point, and that is reached in an economic crunch when a reaction sets in, and racism with it.

To understand the post-modern condition is to grasp many such contrasts and mediate between them. The mental act is hard because there is no single principle at work. How does one decode a kaleidoscope, or comprehend city traffic, or see how bacteria and snowflakes grow? Not by focusing down, but by panning up to see the general pattern of emergence. [65] The post-modern condition shows a series of simultaneous slides from one situation to another, none of them complete, all of them hybrid.

There is the partial shift from mass production to segmented production, from Fordism to Post-Fordism; the slide from a relatively integrated mass culture to many fragmented taste cultures (minoritisation); from centralised control in government and business to peripheral decision-making; from repetitive manufacture of identical objects to the fast-changing manufacture of varying objects; from broadcasting to narrowcasting; from few styles to many genres; from national identification to both local and global consciousness. In no case is the shift and slide complete, an ambiguity that makes it harder to see and comprehend.

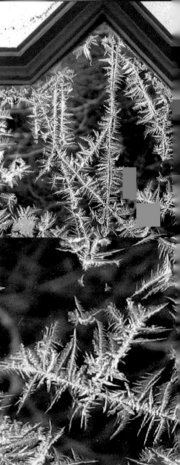

There are many more shifts than this short list implies, but one of the deep causes of change is what Daniel Bell analysed in 1973 as the Post-Industrial Society (sixty years after it had been predicted). If there were a single cause of post-modern society, which there is not, it would be here in post-industrialisation. Others call it the Third Wave, or information society, or media society, or consumer society.[43] Several related events brought it into existence.

Contemplate the kaleidoscope of change. [66] In 1956, in the USA and for the first time, the number of white-collar workers outnumbered blue-collar workers, and by the late 1970s America had made the shift to an information society, with relatively few people – 13 per cent – involved in the manufacture of goods. Most workers – 60 per cent – were engaged in the manufacture of signs and symbols,

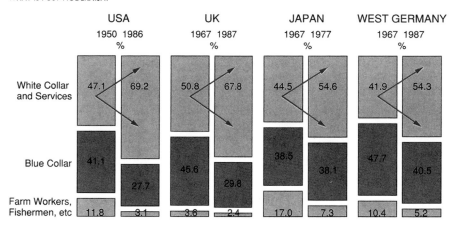

[66] **Sectoral slides**. In the developed world, post-modernism was ushered in by the growth of the white-collar workforce and the accompanying decline of the blue-collar and agricultural sectors.

OPPOSITE [65] **Emergent patterns of growth and movement**. Frost patterns, snowflakes, minerals and bacteria grow along similar fractal lines, each depending on specific temperature and humidity levels. City and pedestrian traffic moves along certain emergent patterns according to speed and density of flow. *Collective behaviour* reveals such patterns of organisation emerging out of chaos, as Philip Ball shows in his study, *Critical Mass, How One Thing Leads to Another*, 2004. Like a controlled experiment the frost patterns (left) grew overnight in eight contiguous panes. They filled out the entire surface in some panes after bifurcating along major and minor routes. (C Jencks)

information and knowledge. Whereas a modernised society depended on most people mass-producing objects in a factory (30 per cent), the post-modernised one depends on the segmented production of ideas and images in an office (by about the same percentage). Very few in the developed world today are farmers; even in 1900 they constituted only 30 per cent of the labour force. In the post-modern world they account for between 3 and 10 per cent of those employed (USA and Japan). The service sector has fluctuated at around 11 to 12 per cent of the workforce – about the same percentage as those unemployed.

In the post-modern world a fundamental social fact is the revolutionary expansion in the number of those who create and pass on information. Put another way, it is the sudden emergence of a new class, the numerical domination of the proletariat by the cognitariat. These new workers are neither working class nor middle class, but rather paraclass. They cut across customary boundaries and make for volatile political allegiances. Who can predict how the electorate will feel next week? Statistically most of the paraclass are clerks, secretaries, insurance people, stockbrokers, teachers, managers, government bureaucrats, lawyers, writers, bankers, technicians, computer programmers, accountants and ad-men.

Indeed, in the developed world there is a plague of public relations agents and those manipulating the 'consciousness industry'. Why has this happened? Because, given the near infinite demand for prime time television and prime space in the quality media, both are in short supply. You can mine gold in many countries, but there is only one *New York Times*, BBC, and *Le Monde*. In the post-modern world the fierce competition is for media validation and this multiplies another part of the cognitariat – the chattering classes, the opinion-formers and the opinionated. It has also hybridised news casting into 'infotainment' and, like the post-modern novel, obscured differences between reporting fact, editorialising and creating fiction. Reality television wins the pm honours in this category for creating the silliest lies, with its celebrities who are not celebrated, and its reality that is totally unreal. [67]

Salaries among the cognitariat differ as much as their ways of life, and shifting status follows media attention. The fundamental fact of the post-industrial society is that, as Daniel Bell made clear, knowledge, not ownership, is power. To navigate through the burgeoning information world takes social skills, a certain intelligence and applied knowledge. This is why, in spite of all the new labour-saving devices, the work done by the cognicrats at the top has not diminished. As John Kenneth Galbraith has shown, with his concept of the 'technostructure', it now takes a small army of experts to launch any advanced industrial product such as a new car: teams of accountants, lawyers, ad-men, not to say designers, technicians and inventors. If there is any final control in this situation it is not just decreed by ownership, but rather by the ability to invent and manipulate knowledge and by the possession of the social skills necessary to negotiate the complex network of relationships. Ultimate power is highly dispersed, but if it has a general centre it is within the cognicrats and their teams of experts.

ABOVE [67] **George Galloway**, the British Respect MP, appears on television reality show, *Celebrity Big Brother*, 2006. He dresses as Elvis, wears skin-tight, red leotard and pretends to be a cat, miaowing, purring and cream-licking. (© Endemol UK/Channel 4)

The triumph of the muddle class

Hence, class-analysis of the old type, the proletariat versus the capitalist, does not work. The cognitariat is too big and amorphous to find the previous, sharp divisions. In the 1990s, Will Hutton pointed to a new polarisation in Britain: 'the 30/30/40 society'.[44] The bottom 30 per cent are the unemployed or economically inactive; the top 40 per cent are the full-time employed and self-employed; and the middle 30 per cent are the part-timers and casual workers, the relatively insecure. While these structural facts can be identified throughout the post-modern world they do not relate closely to individual identity as, for instance, did working-class culture. Furthermore, there is some mobility within the cognitariat; certainly lots of job changing. Thus social distinctions dissolve and cultural identifiers, such as accent, dress, social attitudes and values, become fuzzy. This haziness tells us something. When society at large begins to look like those trapped in an airport lounge, you know post-modern hybridisation has become the norm. [68] One result is that politicians try to capture this messy middle ground. Another is that people are lost in the muddle, and suddenly all want to claim they are 'middle class',

ABOVE [68] **Muddle class dress** seen in Sloane Square, London outside Modernist Peter Jones. (Gillian Innes)

This blur is revealed by so many attempts to pin down the present day system. In 2004 a study conducted by the Annenberg Center at the University of Pennsylvania defined the middle class around the median American income of $50,000 per year, plus and minus $25,000. Thus, even with such precise measures as earnings, the families at either end were lumped together as if, say, $28,000 equated with $95,000.[45] Yet money has also lost its ability to mark a place in society. In America the system was always fluid but still recognisably based on a mixture of wealth, power, heredity, culture and status. Until the 1960s the elite of WASP society (White, Anglo-Saxon, Protestant) formed a coherent system of power that reproduced itself, especially on the East Coast. Thus, for instance, the most privileged members attended such elite schools as Groton, invariably went on to the big three Ivy League schools of Harvard, Yale and Princeton, and then on to the most prestigious and powerful jobs. This pattern repeated itself, with exceptions, for generations and produced over the years the richest families in America, such as the Rockefellers and Duponts. They dominated the *Forbes* magazine list of the richest 400, and other registers of social success.

Today these older families, while not poor, have ceded their traditional place. The *Forbes 400* is a constantly churning flywheel spun by new-tech fortunes, by geeks and hedge-fund managers who share little else in terms of background and style. Partly this is a result of a runaway growth in new billionaires and a drop in their taxes. According to the *Forbes 400*, from 1980 to 2002 the number of US billionaires increased almost thirty times, from 13 to 374, and during the past twenty years the average income of those on the list has risen from $390 million (£206 million) to $2.8 billion (£1.48 billion).[46] In America this new class is more insecure than usual and depends on 'life-style consultants' to get them into the best parties in New York, Las Vegas and Los Angeles – each week – to 'curate their wine collections' and, ultimate contradiction, make them into celebrities but keep them out of the news. Equally hard to achieve, these consultants have to get them both on and off the list of the *Forbes 400*. Confusion? Shameless display? In Britain aristocratic restraint has disappeared, royal duchesses have to subscribe to a newsletter for cues on etiquette and what's in and out; indeed, as media appearances by some members of the royal family reveal, slumming and taste-warp are completely democratic. In the *Forbes 400* for the first time there are also several women who have made over a billion, among them Oprah Winfrey, Margaret Whitman and Martha

Stewart, the first as chat show hostess, the last as life-style guru. Whatever else the list of the top four hundred reveals, it does not illustrate the coherence of tribe, taste and assumption of the old WASP hive, either in Britain or America.

In the US past, what were termed 'legacies' guaranteed a route up life's hill, from prep school to Harvard to law firm to Mount Auburn Cemetery. Today sons of the rich who manage to get into their father's school of Groton do not have an automatic place at one of the big three universities; last year only one-seventh made it that far. Furthermore, the old rich are getting poorer, and downward mobility is taking much of the traditional upper class with it. For instance, since the mid-1970s, 62 per cent of those who were in the top quintile of wealth have fallen from their privileged location. One reason for this fall is merely statistical: due to the rise in new wealth and the great rise in the number of the very rich. So the *nouveaux pauvres* are only relatively poor, that is relative to their past. But that is the point; there have been too many changes for the old system of class to work coherently. Because of the shifts since the mid-1970s in wealth, society, taste, power, assumption, tribe and rank, the customary definers of class have become a jungle too tortuous to navigate. People either oversimplify their rank, into the meaningless three segments of 'upper, middle and working class'. Or they imagine a baroque web of status indicators that fine-tune their relationship to others such as the family next door. The problem with the second option is that the neighbours may have two working parents, have a wealth ranking in the top fifth of the nation, yet call themselves 'working class'! This is the kind of crazy warp revealed in a British survey of 2006.[47]

A study by the Future Foundation think-tank showed the same stretching of the concept of the middle class under way in America, except in Britain this self-perception is exaggerated. Since the 1960s the proportion of Britons who regard themselves as middle class has risen from 30 to 43 per cent while that of those who are prepared to admit they are upper class has shrunk to 1 per cent. There are, apparently, no toffs left. A further oddity of this last figure is that the average income of this minuscule group is actually lower than that of the middle classes, leading commentators to wonder whether they are sadly deluded or eccentric aristocrats. But the study finds such class warp in many groups. A typical deformation is the inversion of home builders and bank managers, with just 36 per cent of the former calling themselves working class and 29 per cent of the latter doing so.

To characterise such distortions the report coins some odd categories showing that many people push themselves down a rank. For instance, the ROBs (rich ordinary Britons) are the 2.67 million who regard themselves as working class, even though their wealth puts them in the top quintile of the population. Then there are the HEWs (high-earning workers), the 534,000 people who earn more than £100,000 per year, have a net worth of £53 billion, and also claim to be working class. Probably this self-demotion stems from a British determination to take one's parents' class, the reverse of what most Americans do, but in any case it shows how money and self-image have diverged. The SALs (suburban asset lightweights) are the 1.84 million who call themselves middle class raising their economic status way above its reality, which is at the bottom quintile of wealth. One can think of many more classificatory twists: the UCD (upper-class deniers) and SRD (stinking rich deniers), those top 10 per cent of the population who own 50 per cent of Britain's wealth; or the TEL (Tracey Emin Louts), those working-class artists, like Damien Hirst who brands himself as an alienated drop-out yet at the same time boasts about his £100 million assets and trad country house. Again, the obvious point is that old class markers – taste, income, background, heredity, power, wealth, style and culture – are a contorted thicket. Those scions of the royal family, Princes William and Harry, spend their free time enjoying *Big Brother* and *I'm a Celebrity, Get Me Out of Here*. Where everyone wears jeans and watches the same Unreality-TV, the muddle class has become a universal phenomenon. One can bemoan growing disparities in wealth, but they no longer relate to the old bugbear that was the staple of British and American literature. Jane Austen today would throw up her hands at the gossip-go-round that changed every week, as warped and evanescent as the pages of *Hello!*

The Rise of Socitalism

Towards the end of the 1980s, the world entered a surreal phase as the leaders of Communism lost their faith but kept their power. President Reagan proclaimed his commitment to capitalism, Margaret Thatcher firmly declared, 'We must roll back the frontiers of socialism', while Gorbachev, seeing perestroika on the horizon, defended the Early Communism of his beloved Lenin. The Cold War had kept the world frozen in a kind of low-intensity peace for fifty years, based on these three different 'isms'. They were irreconcilable, believed in or damned, but in the end all of them were nonsensical. By the time these leaders reaffirmed their faith, the reality to which they referred had become obscure. This is not surprising since the terms were coined about one hundred and seventy years ago. We would not expect Stevenson's steam engine to be very efficient today, even if it could move. The three 'isms' are as workable as these old machines, they creak as they are used, and they refer vaguely to a direction in which the driver wants to move, but as to how an advanced economy actually works, they tell us nothing but half-truths.

The correct half is based on what was the staple of the modern world, industrial capitalism. This took off between 1800 and 1870, when Britain and America enjoyed their highest rates of growth, in the factory sector. Then cheap labour markets were created and mechanised production became the main engine of social change. The next stage of growth, monopoly capitalism, consolidated the previous one, produced the great American oligarchies and the quintessential large corporation, the Ford Motor Company. Henry Ford, as its owner and philosopher, broke mass production down into small, discrete parts that were then repeated and combined to give large economies of scale. Fordism became the model for organisation, even among opposite political persuasions, as mass standardisation of a few items became its method. 'You can have any colour Ford,' went the modernist joke, 'as long as it's black.'

This wry truth of the modern period dominated, as we have seen, Modern architecture, the Bauhaus and Le Corbusier, but it was even more persuasive for Stalin and anywhere there was forced collectivisation (which is to say much of the world). All local culture had to dance to the party line of mass production, whether in the West or East. However, as Ford crucially discovered, mass production of necessity entailed mass consumption. To make economies of scale, to put a cheap Ford in everyone's garage, the market had to be guaranteed. This meant one of two things. Either the masses would be enticed and coerced into buying what the producer wanted, through advertisement, or by more totalitarian methods. In the latter case, black Fords would be the only products on offer. In both scenarios, the *massification* of production and consumption was the great truth of the modern world, and its capitalism and socialism were based on it.

In the developed world, this economic and productive situation lasted more or less until the 1970s, when a new productive mode became significant. It was called many things. With its constant rotation of jobs, the phrase 'flexitime' became popular and economists referred to fast-changing, small firms that learned skills very quickly and, in places like Milan, practised 'Flexible Specialisation'. However, in its symbiotic relation to the big corporations on which it depended, it was called 'Post-Fordism'.[48] As a new 'postie', it became just as essential to the post-modern condition as post-industrialisation has been. Gathering momentum after the oil shock of 1973, in ten years it had become the strongest growing sector in the developed world! In Britain, America and Italy during this time, when large corporations were contracting in size, these small concerns created 18 million new jobs.[49] Small, fast-changing companies of less than fifty people, those that were networked by computer and other media, became collectively as strong as the big, sluggish corporations. The new system was characterised not only by flexible specialisation, but also by what the computer facilitated, another phrase of the time: 'just-in-time production'. And this last meant that stockpiles could be small, not like those huge ones at Ford, and change almost as quickly as fashion. A company such as Benetton managed many such dispersed networks and engaged in little, if any, actual production of clothes. 'You could have any colour Benetton,' the post-modern joke became, 'as long as you can specify it.' In terms of differentiation, production was returning to pre-modern craft.

Since the 1980s, Fordist and Post-Fordist enterprises have become tightly interwoven. As a result all advanced economies have become radically hybrid, and no single sector leads them. In the typical case they are interrelated wholes, with one-third of the economy being Fordist, one-third Post-Fordist and the remaining third supported by the state. Such purified types as socialism or capitalism no longer capture this mixture. The unpronounceable compound *socitalism* – socialised capitalism – gets closer to the truth.

This neologism points to the generalisation that advanced economies depend on a dynamic combination of the large corporation, the small Post-Fordist team, the state and the hybrid whole. However, the general point needs an important proviso. As the post-communist world shows, it is much easier to socialise capitalism than capitalise socialism. The more resilient economies recognise the marketplace, but they do not fetishise competition and privatisation. That is why the 'social market' became the catchphrase by the late-1980s, and many European countries tried to settle on the right mixture of socitalism. The problem is that in the global marketplace, this balance changes dynamically. As France and Germany have found to their despair, not even the European Union can insulate their markets from undercutting by India and China.

The idea of 'post-socialism', a phrase of Thatcherism, has been in the air since the early 1980s. For the right wing it meant the end of the nanny state if not of the entire Welfare State. Yet even under Margaret Thatcher's eleven years of market rhetoric state spending as a percentage of GNP only declined from 43 to 38 per cent – before rising back up to 40, and then increasing under Blair to reach 42 per cent in 2006. The many entitlements in the system, an aging population and a host of other commitments have meant that, whatever anyone says, the welfare leviathan rolls on and gobbles up people's money. The same is true in the USA, where Military Keynesianism takes some of the place of welfare. With Bush's war in Iraq, state spending as a percentage of GNP reached ratios that a communist state would regard with extreme jealousy.

In effect, populations in the West are also crypto-socialists, in varying stages of denial. This is obvious in countries such as France where the thirty-five hour week and protectionism are assumed as 'rights'. As the new Prime Minister of France Dominique de Villepin found out to his cost in 2006, any leader who challenges these assumptions will have to face the rough and tumble of the politics of the street, and after many brave words have to swallow them. Even in more market-oriented systems such as Britain, the people want as many entitlements, health services and educational supports as they can possibly squeeze out of the government, without it going broke or raising taxes. In effect, like the leaders of China's new State-Capitalism which took off in the 1990s, they want to square the circle. This is why so-called capitalist systems are really slouching towards the radical hybridisation of socialism. This is the general trend of the times, but one having the divergent outcomes I have mentioned: the regulatory version of the EU, the corporate and CEO version of the Anglo-Americans, and the state version of the Chinese and Singapore. There is no reason to suppose they will converge, or one type will win out over the others.

To reiterate in general terms, socialism is an economy divided between state spending, Fordist and Post-Fordist enterprise. [69] There is no magic to this three-way split, but if state spending rises well over 40 per cent of GNP there will be long-term problems and, if the 'free market' part of the economy shrinks to less than 30 per cent of GNP, it will not generate enough invention and growth to pay for the state. These are the rough bands in which socialism works.

More debatable are the cultural and public goals that unify a polity. Here, modernist systems of capitalism and socialism have proved inadequate; and post-modernising systems of consumer society and socialism are not much better. Socialism has always had a small moral and cultural component – the idealism of community, the spirituality of Ruskin and Morris – but these have always been marginalised in practice.

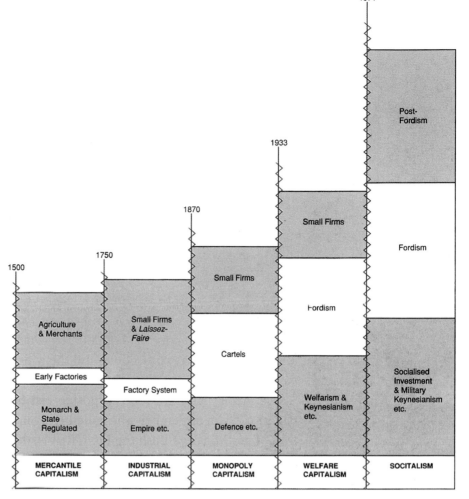

RIGHT [69] **Five stages of economic growth.** To bring out changes in the economic type, this model exaggerates the jump from one stage to the next, and indicates the crisis that brings this on with the red zigzags. Today the socialised capitalism – socialism – is split roughly between government spending, Fordist large corporations, and the most dynamic sector of Post-Fordist small companies networked by computer.

Capitalism has always had a small place for the widely touted ideals of personal freedom and growth, but in practice has made them subordinate to large corporate and national growth. Communitarianism, cultural conservation and the social market, which are all catchwords of the 1990s, are worthy if unexceptional goals of the state. But it is clear, in the developed world at any rate, that the state cannot supply morality and spiritual direction. In Britain, Blair's Third Way and Cool Britannia and Brown's new nationalism were self-inflicted stabs at political branding, not seriously conceived cultural movements.

In spite of these obvious failures, post-modernisation may sound somewhat benevolent for half of the world. It has meant, in the developed world, the end of the working class and the decline of class antagonisms. The 60 to 80 per cent of the population in the paraclass are, in some material ways, better off than were their modern predecessors. But the obvious downside is present in virtually all post-modern societies: a widening gap between rich and poor, those who command an information-society and those who are left behind; the loss of working-class culture and the despair of those now trapped in a new underclass.

Another negative consequence of these fast-moving trends is the confusion of identities and beliefs so that cults and sects and trivial private affairs dominate the news. Is it a surprise that the private lives of Prince Charles and Princess Diana became a staple of the British media for many years? Or that the OJ Simpson trial and 'the Sarin Gas Sect', as it is quaintly known [70] were top of the consciousness industry in America and Japan for a year? Reformed actors such as Ronald Reagan occupied much of the American psyche, in spite of the fact that few may believe in these media-masks very deeply. After Reagan vacated the presidency his followers dropped him with a shrug, when he made a small fortune by featuring in a Japanese advertisement.

Easy belief equals easy disillusion; not even anger sticks to the Teflon President. Indeed, the philosopher Gianni Vattimo insists that 'weak belief' characterises the post-modern condition, a point to which we will return when looking at contemporary convictions and the wider picture of post-modern science in an expanding universe.[50]

The way once effective media-bytes are soon forgotten can be gauged by a series of questions: can you remember who called Reagan's deficit spending 'voodoo economics'? George Bush the First, that is, the man who would continue the voodoo. And who beat the latter with the one-liner: 'It's the economy, stupid'? Yes, the next president, Clinton, whose popularity went *down* when the economy went *up*. Moral? Politicians cannot remember their own slogans that, in any case, have little bearing on the truth. It is no surprise that in this pm media world they are believed in only weakly. Weak thought, weak belief and social insecurities are some of the endemic problems of post-modernisation.

Cyclical, linear and crystalline time

As important as the information society is the organised network of world communication that allows it to function. This started to be joined up at the end of the 1950s, after the launch of Sputnik. The Columbia Space Shuttle of 1981 brackets the period of history when satellite communication was combined with ubiquitous jet travel, computer processing, the old-fashioned telephone and countless world circulation magazines and newspapers, to form an efficient network, a community of world producers and consumers. Since then fax, Internet, e-mail and the world wide web have streamlined global linkage. The significant point is not the invention of this or that technology, but the sudden emergence of an integrated system of communication.

ABOVE [70] **Shoko Asahara as media event**. Japanese television was saturated with coverage of the cult leader for several months in 1995, the terrorist lionised by a media feeding frenzy. The positive feedback of negative news also amplified the affair of Prince Charles, Clinton's sexual hairsplitting with Monica Lewinsky, Blair's supposed departure date and September 11th. Politics became ever more media driven.

OPPOSITE [71] **The World Village**, 19 October 1987. Instant global communication, electronic dealing systems, automated buying and selling programs together exaggerate the market activity as the post-modern world immediately responds to the flow of information.

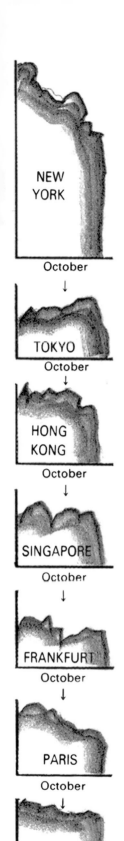

NEW YORK
October
↓
TOKYO
October
↓
HONG KONG
October
↓
SINGAPORE
October
↓
FRANKFURT
October
↓
PARIS
October
↓
LONDON

Sometimes the results of global linkage are catastrophic. On Black Monday, 19 October 1987 the world suddenly lost 5 trillion dollars because of integrated, electronic trading. [71] New York started with a big plummet, next Tokyo picked up the news. Then, as each market woke up in turn – Hong Kong, Singapore, Frankfurt, Paris and London – it collapsed along the same steep profile. The previous modern depression took place over a 10-year period. The electronic meltdown was over in one, and the market returned to its upwards march in two. This is Marxist 'melting into air' at quantum speed. On an economic level the global network gives multinationals greater power to move money and products as they please. On a large scale it unites mass audiences for sporting events and royal weddings and, on a small scale, it puts scientists, artists and individuals with similar interests in touch with each other.

This points to why there is no longer an avant-garde, the artistic stance of Early Modernism. In the world village, there is no identifiable front line to advance, no group or movement that cuts across all the arts, no coherent bourgeoisie to fight, no establishment salon to enter. Rather there are countless individuals in Tokyo, New York, Berlin, Cologne, London, Milan and other world cities all communicating and competing with each other, just as they are in the banking world. As I mentioned, Italian artists such as Sandro Chia who feature their mythical 'roots' are just as likely to work part-time in New York as they are to retreat to the Italian countryside to re-establish their ethnic identity. [72]. Primitiveness and identity are both very real and in need of constant reconstruction. The Nigerian-British artist Chris Ofili shows the mixture. Born in Manchester, educated in London art schools, and from a Nigerian background, he now produces his Brit Identity Art from Trinidad. He picks up one identity marker (the use of map-pins) while on a British Council Travel Scholarship to Zimbabwe; and another, the use of elephant dung, while on another trip in Africa.

Global competition in the art world can, in such examples, lead to unexpected consequences. It produces a slow-changing, identifiable style, in effect the perception of cyclical time. It is one reason that the post-modern world is the age of quotation marks, the 'so-called' this and 'Neo' that, the transformation of the past and recent present into identifiable markers. The negative aspects of this are clear enough in the ersatz creations that have spread everywhere, while the positive aspects are evident in the eclectic work of pm artists and architects.

Globalisation can also lead to its opposite, to very fast innovation and constant change, the characteristics of linear time.

Whether it is slow change and cyclical time, or speedy change and progressive time, or a paradoxical third type of time characteristic of the post-modern, depends on the means of production and communication. Recall the typical classification that anthropologists adopt, the division of historical epochs into ages, based on their fundamental forms of production. This reveals schematic distinctions, and like other diagrams

	production	society	space/time	orientation	culture
PRE-MODERN 10000 BC - AD1450	*Neolithic Revolution* agriculture handwork **dispersed**	*Tribal / Feudal* ruling class of kings, priests and military **peasants**	*Cyclical* slow-changing reversible time **space–time separation**	*Local / City/ Empire* agrarian **closed and integrated**	*Aristocratic* integrated style **rooted cultures**
MODERN 1450 - 1960	*Industrial Revolution* factory mass-production **centralised**	*Capitalist* owning class of bourgeoisie **workers**	*Linear* sequential & progressive **space–time compression**	*Nationalist* rationalisation of business **exclusive**	*Bourgeois* reigning styles mass-culture **machine age**
POST-MODERN 1960 -	*Information Revolution* office segmented-production **decentralised**	*Socitalism* para-class of cognitariat **office workers**	*Cyclical and Linear* fast-changing **space–time implosion**	*Post-National* multinational pluralist eclectic **inclusive and open**	*Taste/ Cultures* many genres knowledge-based **age of signs**

LEFT [73] **Three forms of society, three types of time.** Pre-modern production leads to cyclical time, modern production is characterised by linear time, while post-modern societies exhibit a paradoxical mix of both recurrent and progressive time.

in this book, ones that simplify a situation towards an ideal type. [73] But the diagram does clarify the three kinds of cultural time that operate today, either conjointly or separately.

The first stage of social settlement is the agricultural phase of development, a result of the Neolithic Revolution which occurred roughly 10,000–5,000 BC. Then 95 per cent of the population were farmers and peasants. Many of them were controlled by a priestly class, and later on governed by a king or emperor. In this Pre-modern era, lasting until the birth of capitalism and the Renaissance, production was at a relatively small scale, and individuals controlled most of the property through a hierarchical society. The 'shape of time', to adopt George Kubler's phrase, was slow changing, a horizontal line punctuated fairly regularly with repetitive patterns, the cycles of work and the recurrent seasons. This cyclical situation is also described as *reversible time*, since one year was very like another and returned to an almost identical starting point because of the climate and the calender. Space and time were part of the secure background, the stage on which events occurred. Likewise space and time separated tribes and villages, and were marked by events and boundaries.

With the Renaissance and rise of capitalism in Italy and then the rest of Europe, a sequential time became prevalent. By the nineteenth century, this modern condition of production had come to dominate most of Europe. That is, most of the population was working class, led by a bourgeoisie that owned most of the means of production, though the situation varied among countries. As the diagram also indicates, the modern world tries to *centralise* manufacture, control it for mass production, just as it tries to codify and regularise consumption. *Mass culture* is the ultimate product of this world, the *factory* is its implicit form of organisation, and *rationalisation* its final value. The shape of time is now more vertical and progressive, punctuated by large-scale wars and massive migration. In people's experience, the reversible time of the previous system is countered by the irreversible or *linear* time of history and the conflict leads to the well-known contradictions of the nineteenth century. They emerge spontaneously as the new is slapped onto the old, as technical change is dressed up in revivalist costume, as styles are contrasted or one use collides with another. [74]

Sequential inventions in, say, travel – from horse and bicycle to train and car – become the model for conceiving evolutionary progress, and then Darwinian evolution. Even Charles Darwin himself oscillates between asserting progressive change and denying it. One day he writes of the magnificent hierarchy unfolding as one species supplants the next; the next day, he reminds himself that there is 'no higher or lower'. But because of inventions in communication, spatial and temporal dimensions actually start shrinking, a trend that does not really take off until the post-modern period. On the whole, the nation-state, the great creation of the modern period, manages to remain secure and become the autonomous backdrop for events.

In the post-modern world, since 1960, most of the previous relations of production alter, and the whole value system distorts. Primary products are no longer such things as automobiles, and the main industries in the developed world are no longer interested in heavy equipment and steel production, but rather in information: software as well as computers, such lightweight equipment as that of air and space technology, such discoveries as those in genetics and, above all, the inventions of the gigantic electronics industry, the largest manufacture on the planet. In addition, this information is not 'owned', or at least monopolised, for long. Nor is it consumed by use, or decreased by re-use, as objects tend to be in the capitalist world. Quite the reverse: information tends to *multiply itself through use*, create ever-bigger circles of decision-making. Thus, unlike the previous systems of production, where an aristocracy and bourgeoisie asserted power over a limited resource in order to exploit it effectively, the post-modern world is not owned, or run, or led, by any class or group, unless it is, to reiterate, the vague and amorphous cognitariat. This disappearance of a recognisable class with vested interests has made political polarisation between left and right more problematic, and given birth to new agenda politics. Issues of gender, ecology and distributive justice now dominate debate.

Such kaleidoscopic shifts from a pre-modern to post-modern world are summarised in the comparative diagram and, in this section and the next, I will continue to analyse these emergent patterns. The most paradoxical is the new sense of time.

In the present era, for many in the developed world, the shape of time rises steeply towards the vertical as global events affect each other in a chain reaction. People are so busy they do not have the time to enjoy their leisure and even on holiday take their work along. The marketplace imperative of fast-change and quick obsolescence begins to drive people's psychological life and this is at odds with a deep-seated desire for stasis, for a crystalline society with a clear structure. The anthropologist Claude Levi-Strauss, who has studied many ancient cultures, argues that the recurring message is a longing for social values to be made reciprocal and venerable, not as Marx described them under the capitalist dynamo, 'melting into air'. Let machines and the

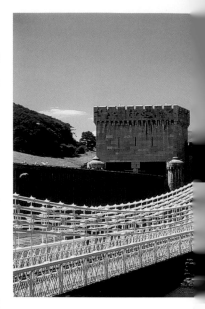

ABOVE [74] **Contradiction embraced**. Thomas Telford, the British engineer, embraced a medieval style for his bridge piers since its heaviness worked well functionally and the towers were adjacent to Conway Castle. One of the first suspension bridges, finished in 1826, it spanned 150 metres with a white filigree of iron so dense as to complement the stone. The beauty of contradiction is more powerful than harmony, because less expected. (C Jencks)

technologies of communication do the quick evolution, the melting, Levi-Strauss advises, and then culture can capture the beauty of eternal return, its cyclical time, its crystalline geometry.

On the level of quick-changing fashion this is an impossible dream. With post-modernisation, one generation follows another much faster than the normal twenty years, as cultural systems fragment into niche markets. The competition evident on any newsstand, of more specialist magazines chasing more articulated sub-cultures, shows the increasing speed of transformation. More information circulates and is processed in ever-smaller periods of time. Andy Warhol exaggerated the speed, and egalitarianism, which the new media were bringing when he predicted: 'in the future everybody will be world-famous for fifteen minutes'. The epigram does have restricted truth, however, especially in the art world where a 'generation', a new 'ism', can last a mere three years. The first is for discovery, the next for promotion, and the third for the movement to be cleared out, declared 'dead stock' like outmoded clothes. This cycle tends to be finished before an individual can develop coherent ideas and mature. No matter how good or bad an artist may be, or how slow or fast he may wish to develop, if he is going to be a player in the world media system, he has to acknowledge the fashion-go-round – if only to reject it. Indeed, much of post-modern art is directed against the exploitation of this fast consumption. In particular, there is the satirical work of Hans Haacke, the wry, commentary art of Barbara Kruger, and that of many artists who use photography and collage to comment on the media and its values. Again, it is subversion from within the dominant culture. [75]

The situation is not promising. But it does contain three positive and paradoxical aspects that, growing from the very speed of change, arrest its velocity. First, there are a good many artists working outside the system, subsidised in one way or another by the state or part-time jobs. They are waiting to be discovered. The pluralism of post-modernism is very real and supports a great deal of talent as well amateur creativity. It is estimated, that in New York City alone there are 45,000 artists, perhaps not a Donatello among them, but nevertheless a population roughly the size of Renaissance Florence.

Second, and most importantly, as cultural change accelerates and the plural movements begin to occupy many potential approaches, a surprising thing occurs: the shape of time becomes suddenly reversible. In effect, trends change so fast that the linear times of development run in sequence, many running together, not just one after another. All possible fashions become in fashion (or, more accurately,

BELOW |75| Barbara Kruger, **Untitled (You are not Yourself)**, Gelatin silver print, 182.9 x 122cm, 1983.

they remain extant, bubbling under the surface). Thus one can predict the cyclical transformation of old into new trends, or their imminent revival in fifteen minutes. For instance, in the art world a previously fashionable artist, who was suddenly rendered obsolete by the three-year swing of taste, does not have long to wait before a new version of the tradition comes round again, in a few years' time. Artistic development and integrity are possible under these conditions, if the artist has the patience to work in obscurity between successive turns in the spotlight. Since the mid-1970s, the architects Isozaki, Hollein and Eisenman have seen their fortunes rise and fall several times, and the same is true of the artists Ron Kitaj and Anselm Kiefer. [76] What occurs in the cultural world has its counterpart in society at large as many social relations carry on in a narrow way from one generation to the next, such as dwindling deference to the Royal Family. These relations no longer show a holistic, integrated pattern. Today the continuities are fragmented into a plenitude of traditions that reveal their crystalline sameness across time, a kaleidoscope of repetitive patterns that only appears fast-changing.

A third positive aspect of post-modernisation is the way ideas and information have become more significant with respect to material things. This point is often made about the relative value of different sectors today, between ideas, extractive industries and ownership. Since knowledge and information are the prime movers of a post-industrial society, the place of science and culture is revalidated as the most important, at least theoretically. One finds this, for instance, with the emergence of the 'Third Culture' in the 1980s, those science writers who are willing to speculate on the wider implications of advances in their fields and write on a popular level about the brain, consciousness and DNA. The implications are, ironically, commercial and spiritual, an issue to which I will return in conclusion. Beyond these points, brought out in the diagram, there are three shifts, all of which increase the post-modern trend towards pluralism.

ABOVE [76] Anselm Kiefer, *The High Priestess – The Land of Two Rivers*, 1985–9. Here as in his other work, the artist highlights the theme of decay and renewal, the constant return of cyclical time. Two hundred lead books are held in two steel bookcases, altogether weighing 30 tonnes. The apocalyptic feel is reinforced by the photographic images inside each huge book, often of ruined or decaying cities seen from afar. The threat of eco-disaster taken up in the corrosion is, however, balanced by *The Land of Two Rivers*. The 'Tigris' and 'Euphrates' are here represented as two sides of the open steel bookcases and given handwritten labels. In his work, Kiefer maximises the contrast of personal label and impersonal products. (© Anselm Kiefer)

From few styles to many genres

The nineteenth century turned the choice of style into a matter of ideology, morality, party politics and the zeitgeist. Either you were for the Gothic Revival, or a hopeless pagan; in favour of progressive engineering, or a reactionary. Fashion, moral arguments and the mental habits of a modernist era all conspired to force you into one camp or another, and if you were idiosyncratic enough to harbour scepticism and a plurality of tastes, you did best to keep them private. Today people are

not noticeably more tolerant, but they do keep changing their tastes, and at such speed, that their successive dogmatisms look particularly weak. Furthermore, with the advent of the global village and the revival of so many competing 'Neo-Styles', the moral claims of each look more and more like wishful thinking. To reiterate: with the breakdown of consensus, with the end of national styles or modernist ideology, we have reached a paradoxical point where any style can be, and is, revived or continued. For instance, there are four kinds of Neo-Modernism still extant: Reactionary Minimalism, all-white Corbusian abstraction, and High-Tech sliding towards Organi-Tech. [77]

The art historian Heinrich Wölfflin once claimed that 'not everything is possible in any period'. As a logical truth this statement is unimpeachable, but it is of little use to us today with our *embarras de richesses*. We need rules, or pointers, to choose among the ten or so reigning styles, rational arguments for dealing with the variety of taste in the heteropolis. Los Angeles, the typical global heteropolis, has thirteen major minority groups, and over one hundred further ethnic divisions. Sweeping this heterogeniety behind an all-white technical abstraction is no longer an adequate response, as it was in the heyday of Modernist universality. In an age when everyone is fast becoming a member of a new minority, architects and designers want to know how to represent significant variety with integrity.

One strategy is to 'choose the right style for the job', a case of serial revivalism. A more ambitious approach is to mix the styles based on the situation as found – the existing tastes, urban conditions and required functions – that is, radical eclecticism. A third method is to

RIGHT [77] **British High-Tech moved towards Organi-Tech** by the year 2000. Under pressure from the ecological imperative and a general movement towards curved architecture realised by the computer, architects previously committed to the machine aesthetic swerved towards the organic. Here Wilkinson and Eyre's *Tilting Bridge* (2001), seen as a winking eye, looks at Norman Foster's *Sage Auditorium* (2004), seen as billowing clouds and human forms. Such imagery, while secondary to use, was clearly intentional. (C Jencks)

fold in variety on the microscale, a recent departure developed from complexity theory. A fourth tactic, often that of Los Angeles architects, is to provide heterogeneous materials and shapes in a language that is fresh and enigmatic. [78] This method can be the most creative, avoiding stereotypes and the conflict of entrenched interests, but it can also produce grotesque mistakes.

ABOVE [78] Frank Gehry, **Chiat-Day Offices**, Los Angeles, 1989. The advertising company given a binocular garage to signal its entrance and ability to spot trends – an iconic form set off by five other styles and building types. The heterogeneity of LA culture finds its apotheosis here. (© Gehry Partners, LLP)

From purist to kaleidoscopic sensibility

The shift in mood that all this variety has brought is, as mentioned with Lautréamont's idea of beauty, a developed taste for juxtaposition, incongruity and paradox. This has grown from the modern world celebrated by Baudelaire, the dynamic life of the Parisian streets, and inevitably it has in turn stimulated the modern poetics of collage and disjunction. As Marshall McLuhan pointed out in the 1960s, nothing is so bizarre as the juxtapositions that occur every day on the front page of a newspaper, and the post-modern sensibility has been subjected to even greater incongruity by television.

A popular film that exploits this is *The Gods Must Be Crazy*. This tells various stories, in parallel, of a Kalahari bushman, a Marxist guerrilla *à la* Castro, a love-sick backwoodsman, and a pretty city teacher lost in the Outback, and it manages to interweave these discontinuous worlds into a lyrical whole. Federico Fellini often turns the mad competition of opposite tastes into a melancholic spectacle of hilarious sadness. [79] Nearly every one of his films contains a scene, a post-modern carnival, where the media force young and old, priests, entertainers and sensualists, into frantic confrontation. The social boundaries are crossed, everyone comes out confused and exhausted. This kaleidoscopic carnival is not to everyone's taste, but it is normal enough in the global village to receive continual representation. Thus many artists such as Rauschenberg and Kitaj and architects such as Gehry and Alsop make an art of incongruity. If much of everyday life is heterodox, then incongruity will continue to form a leading poetics of juxtaposition.

From exclusion to inclusion

Another shift in the pm world is towards openness, tolerance, inclusion. It is not just the taste for heterogeneity that has brought this about, but also the new assertions of minority rights, of 'otherness' as a desirable, category. Now groups like to position themselves on the periphery – 'ex-centrics' as these self-styled outcasts are called. The women's movement is characteristic of many post-modern movements that were taken up in the 1960s and became accepted political forces in the 1970s. No single movement is typical of the new agenda politics, the pluralism of *groupuscles*. If the world village has created the consciousness that everyone belongs to an interdependent minority, then this results in a typical pragmatism of

RIGHT [79] Federico Fellini, **Ginger and Fred**. The story concerns an elderly dance couple, who did take-offs of Fred Astaire and Ginger Rogers, returning for a television celebration to relive their past ersatz creation. The encounter of many such fabrications on a television show creates the carnival of post-modern life, the hilarious and sad juxtapositions of disembodied tastes. (Recorded release)

realpolitik. There is a grudging tolerance of difference in the inner cities, a 'live and let live' (as long as the jobs do not run out). Also, in the West, there is a more cosmopolitan attitude towards conflicting world-views.

The ideology of Modernism was exclusivist at its core, seeking to draw into a single sensibility, and view of history, the plurality of discontinuous cultures. So, one of the benevolent paradoxes of the post-modern situation is that it willingly includes the modern and pre-modern conditions as *essential* parts of its existence. It does not take an aggressive stance with respect to an agricultural civilisation; it has not sought to destroy industrialisation, nor put forward a single totalising ideology. The post-modern sensibility thrives on dispositions different from its own, and recognises that life would be diminished if it all took place in the global city. In effect, it has rediscovered the truth that meaning consists in difference, in relationship more than essence. The insight was especially confirmed by the rise of semiotics, the theory of signs coming from

BELOW & RIGHT [80] Frank Gehry, **'Fred and Ginger', Office Building,** Prague, 1993–6. Like Fellini's film, a comment on a popular icon, with a difference. The city block extends the Prague fabric, and turns the corner with the twirl of a glass skirt. The window units are room-size, designed from the requirements inside and thus they take up the old typology of floors – but in a new way. (© Gehry Partners, LLP)

linguistics. Opposition creates significance in language, the arts, in ideas, styles and life. Oppositions are necessary for establishing identity. Again as the marketplace has it, 'what sells is the difference that makes a difference'.

The enjoyment of difference helps explain why the content of so much post-modernism is the past viewed with irony or displacement. It is the realisation that we can return to a previous era and technology, at the price of finding it slightly different. [80] The post-modern situation cultivates a sensibility that is a compound of previous ones, a palimpsest, just as the information world depends on technologies and energies quite different from its own. The present situation not only includes the previous ones, but benefits from them. We now have the luxury of inhabiting successive worlds as we tire of each one's qualities, a luxury which previous ages, with their lack of opportunity, did not have. There is no dictatorship of the cognitariat, nor is there an exclusive aristocracy or bourgeoisie, but rather the first paraclass to have it all ways.

4. WANING NATIONS, RISING HETERARCHY

Destructive modernity

As mentioned at the outset of this book, among the seventy 'posties' that have changed the scene none is more important than the waning of the nation-state. Or, put positively, nothing since the 1960s is as significant as the slow, but inexorable, emergence of the post-national world. One forgets how intimately modernity and the nation are connected, but as historians such as Paul Kennedy frame it, the nation-state, political overlord of the nation, was the driving force of the modern world for five hundred years, ever since it grew in Renaissance Europe to replace the force of empire. It was also the main engine of mass killing during that epoch. Although new nations are today emerging all the time, with 192 recognised by the United Nations, their individual power is fast diminishing.[51]

OPPOSITE [81] **Babel – or effective pluralism?** As supranational governance grows it faces the conflict between separate identities and common purpose, nowhere more so than in the EU. The European Parliament works in all the official languages, all twenty, soon to be thirty. Nations partly submerge their identity to this heterarchy, but will it produce sclerosis or find common goals? (Apologies to Breughel, C Jencks)

More importantly, when it comes to winning the peace, as the impotence of America in Iraq has shown, firepower can lead one astray. The spectre of US armaments, equal to those in the rest of the world combined, breeds insecurity in places like Iran and North Korea. They create anger, reaction and most recently an alliance across the Shiite crescent, from Iran to Syria to Lebanon – such is the power of paranoia in catalysing opposition. 'Soft power', the influence of culture, laws and heterarchical agreements, is what counts in the post-national world. In this chapter we will look at the most perplexing of all shifts and slides, that from a modern nationalism that has not entirely ended to a post-national system of power that has not entirely emerged. This is a basic post-modern slide and obviously a target for any modernism that calls itself critical. As we will see, even architects get involved in areas outside their discipline, a typical case of the critical temper leading a profession to confront external issues of importance. Critical modernisms always engage the wider landscape beyond their specialisation, sometimes becoming explicitly political, and there is good reason for this extension.

Recall the virulence of the twentieth century, caused by modernity and aided by modern production. The two world wars took a toll of over one hundred million dead, and within that dark fifty-year period the Holocaust and Stalin liquidated a further 40 million people. Inevitably added to this account of recent disasters is the Hiroshima bomb, and the many genocides sanctioned by the nation-state. The list is an indictment of this modern institution, starting in the early part of the century in Armenia and then recurring like a virus since the 1960s, in Vietnam, Cambodia, Bosnia, Kosovo, East Timor, Rwanda, Burundi, Sierra Leone and, in 2005–6, Darfur in the Sudan. That is a short-list. Whatever one thinks of the morality of these acts, bombing from on high or forced starvation, their scale is modern. Their magnitude is only possible after the breakthroughs of modernisation – Fordist centralisation and mass production. Furthermore, as Zygmunt Bauman has argued in *Modernity and the Holocaust* (1989), it is the mind-set of modernity – its instrumental reason and pragmatism – that are indirect but important causes of mass killing. Where efficiency, cost-benefit analysis and functionalism become the dominant values of a culture, there genocide is possible.[52]

As also mentioned, Jean-François Lyotard goes so far as to claim that the Holocaust has 'refuted' the modern project, the emancipation of humanity. He calls this the 'Auschwitz' refutation:

> I would argue that the project of modernity (the realisation of universality) has not been forsaken or forgotten but destroyed, 'liquidated'. There are several modes of destruction, several names that are symbols for them. 'Auschwitz' can be taken as a paradigmatic name for the tragic 'incompletion' of modernity … At 'Auschwitz', a modern sovereign, a whole people was physically destroyed … It is a crime opening postmodernity …[53]

He may have a point in highlighting Auschwitz, but this is hardly the only 'crime opening postmodernity', and they continue. In the 1990s, scientists who studied biodiversity claimed we were entering the sixth period of mass extinction, a trend subsequently confirmed. Because habitats are being destroyed by modernisation some 27,000 species are lost per year; that is, at the rate of 100 a day, three an hour.[54] Since then it has only become worse. Yet, it is only since 1980 that we have begun to understand the mass extinctions of the last 600 million years, and therefore can put the present one into perspective. It is caused not by external forces but, for the first time, by a single species: us.

The transnational heterarchy

Such large and unwelcome truths force a cosmic view on us, and in the next chapter I will consider positive reasons for this view; but they are still just a part of the post-modern picture that leads to the post-national world. On the ambivalent side, there are the 350 largest multinational companies controlling an extraordinary one-third of all world trade. That is what makes the system global. Potentially positive global forces are the exponential growth in communications and the world information network; even the spread of English as a second language to one-sixth of the world, although the French and Chinese might think

BELOW [82] **Map of Freedom 2006**. Every year the independent institute in New York, Freedom House, produces a map and complex measurement of democracy. Here the map shows 89 Free nations in green; the 58 Partly Free nations in yellow; and the 45 Not Free in purple. (© Freedom House)

otherwise. On the obviously negative side there are ecological catastrophes such as runaway pollution.

Two political trends are extremely significant. First is the spread of democracy. Democratisation, as measured by free elections, human rights, a relatively free press, the observance of international law, and other usual criteria, has become more common in the last hundred years. This was especially a trend of the 1970s, reversed only in 1992, to

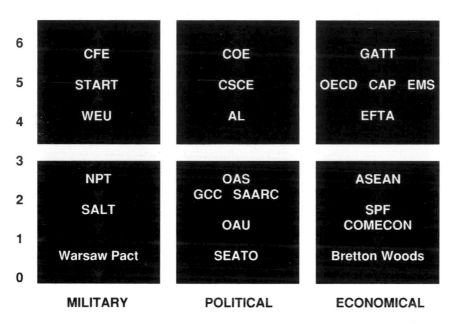

MILITARY   POLITICAL   ECONOMICAL

LEFT [83] **Transnational organisations and the heterarchy of power.** Their relative power on a scale of 1 to 10 and their rise and decline, in 1995, are indicated. Of such organisations, 2,500 have been created since 1945 and they form a binding network that tends to keep nation-states from aggression. Acting in concert they can form a heterarchical power structure of international order. Since 1995, the biggest change has been the disappearance of the Warsaw Pact and the expansion of the EU as the supreme soft power.

GLOSSARY OF TERMS

NATO - North Atlantic Treaty Organisation
UN - United Nations
EU - European Union
G7 - Group of Seven
IMF - International Monetary Fund
CFE - Conventional Forces Europe
START - Strategic Arms Reduction Talks
WEU - Western European Union
COE - Council of Europe
CSCE - Conference on Security and Co-operation in Europe
AL - Arab League
OECD - Organisation for Economic Co-operation and Development
CAP - Common Agricultural Policy
EMS - European Monetary System

EFTA - European Free Trade Area
GATT - General Agreement on Tariffs and Trade
WTO - World Trade Organisation
NPT - Nuclear Non-proliferation Treaty
SALT - Strategic Arms Limitation Talks
OAS - Organisation of American States
GCC - Gulf Co-operation Council
SAARC - South East Asian Treaty Organisation
ASEAN - Association of South East Asian Nations
SPF - South Pacific Forum
COMECON - Council for Mutual Economic Assistance

reemerge again soon thereafter. In 1880 less than one-third of the world's population lived in a democracy, whereas today, in a general sense which the institute Freedom House has defined, [82] about 76 per cent inhabit a democratic state or quasi-democracy.[55] Admittedly, democratic nation-states can act against international law, and very unethically, but the general trend has to be welcomed.

Secondly, transnational organisations, such as NATO, have become more empowered. Since the Second World War more than 2,500 of these have come into being. Bodies such as the UN, ASEAN, IMF, OAU, GATT and AL make nations think twice about starting wars even if, like the US, they continue to disregard the UN and invade other countries. [83] Such institutional and financial networks partly shackle the nation-state within a web of commitments inhibiting, if not altogether stopping, aggression. They can often work in concert forming an heterarchical power structure. It is worth contrasting the two kinds of authority. The usual form, the hierarchy, is that type of top-down order, *de haut en bas*, where power issues from one source and trickles down the grades or ranks. By contrast, 'hetero', meaning 'many different', or 'several kinds' is a typical post-modern prefix referring to pluralism. The heterarchy, then, is that form of organisation where different centres can overrule each other in such a way that no single one has absolute power. The brain, with its different modules (specialised centres) and their interactions, typifies the heterarchy as does the supposed balance of power between the executive, legislature and judiciary (though the British speak of executive dictatorship and the Americans centralise aggressive power in the President).

An easy-to-understand example of the balanced relationship is the game 'Rock, scissors, paper'. In this heterarchy, three or more players use their hands simultaneously to indicate their choice. Winners work as follows: rock, because of its hardness, crushes scissors; scissors beat paper by cutting it; and paper beats stone by wrapping it. [84] By contrast, in a hierarchy, the unilateral system of one superpower, the winner takes all. Formally a heterarchy consists in the distribution of power such that A rules over B, B rules over C, and C rules over A – a circular relationship. Coalitions of power often exhibit these structures, as does the balance of power in some nations, such as that between the executive, judiciary and legislature. Today, those many acronymical bodies that have grown up like a bureaucratic spider's web since 1945, tie the nation-state in knots, a prostrate Gulliver. Some, like the IMF and WTO, are very effective snares.

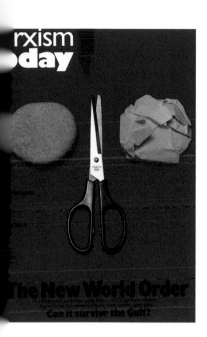

ABOVE [84] **The heterarchy: Rock, Scissors, Paper.** Formally a heterarchy is A>B, B>C, C>A, that is, a circularity of distributed power. This game is a popular example of a heterarchy while the brain, with its multiple modules varying control, is a more complex example. (Magazine cover February 1999, based on Charles Jencks's design)

Also important has been the proliferation of non-government organisations, the NGOs committed to peace and a sustainable ecology – Amnesty International and Oxfam to name but two. Greenpeace's prevention of the multinational Shell Oil Company from dumping its used oil platform in the Atlantic Ocean (1995), illustrates the kind of international activism that is possible. [85] The ecological merits of this particular case may be arguable, but there is no doubt that Greenpeace was successful in mustering support in several nations and bringing this to bear in the boardrooms of both the British government and Shell. The NGOs, as a whole, are creating an emergent tradition of global citizenship, a supranational consciousness and language.

These several trends taken together, in addition to the outbreak of regional ethnic wars (forty-five were under way in the 1990s), have led some theorists to see an empowered United Nations as a future possibility or, perhaps, the creation of an entirely new, more effective, world institution. It sounds unlikely at the moment, but if historical precedent is anything to go by, and we are heading towards global governance, then its character will be determined by the specific events that bring it into being. The particular system of power dominant today – regional 'spheres of influence' led by the USA and other regional powers – was locked-in by the events of the Second World War and the Cold War.

What kind of events might create the mandate for the establishment of an effective world government? A runaway greenhouse effect, which many scientists are predicting? Or, perhaps, a cometary collision, which a few think possible? The destruction of world resources that is now under way – such as the diminishing stocks of wheat, fish and clean water – could justify the creation of an international body and give it the power to control nations. It is not hard to imagine other legitimising catastrophes such as a limited nuclear exchange started by accident. The contestants, as well as the rest of the world, might then suddenly focus their collective mind on creating an impartial super-force. Today there are eleven declared nuclear powers and many are resuming testing. On the horizon are many more, and that means the chances of an accidental exchange will go up, exponentially.

So, the post-national world might produce the leviathan that every nation fears, a world policeman, an empowered UN with the force to impose the will of the majority. But, many would argue, this is as undesirable as it is unlikely. Isaiah Berlin, for instance, claimed that the bureaucracy and arbitrariness of a world government would be so infuriating that it would actually cause more unrest, and civil wars, than

ABOVE [85] **Greenpeace** defeated a multinational, Shell, and a nation, the UK, in its 1995 campaign. (© Greenpeace/SIMS)

it would stop. The argument is that an empowered UN would act slowly, sluggishly and insensitively, enraging all the contesting parties. The question facing the post-national world is, how can *legitimate* global order work? If the UN is fine for peacekeeping and settling disputes where the big powers agree, but is not likely to become the feared and financed leviathan that can do the job, then what effective system can be worked out instead? A small historical digression shows some possibilities.

New world order as heterarchy

In the autumn of 1990, Saddam Hussein's Iraq invaded Kuwait and threatened war in the Middle East. George Bush the First and Gorbachev agreed that this unilateral act was a bad thing, and there followed much talk of a 'New World Order'. Bush proclaimed this vision time and again, since, as he himself put it at the time, he had a long-term deficit 'on the Vision Thing'. Here was a powerful new one, which he and the American Secretary of State, James Baker, cooked up. At first it was backed by his idea of a new order of a united Middle East, one like NATO with the acronym called MEATO. That vision was soon dropped. It was implausible that the Gulf States could agree on anything much, and besides the acronym sounded like aging flesh. Also, there was the fact amplified by the media that Bush was conducting his brinkmanship with Saddam Hussein while he was casually showing off his unconcern at impending war – by playing golf. This gave his MEATO policy the unfortunate new soubriquet, 'GULFO'. George Bush the Second would pursue the same failed policy, announcing to the world what he had in store for Saddam, as he too whacked golf-balls off the tee. He might have learned more from his father's golf diplomacy (but more of that soon).

George the First and his loyal allies in Britain returned to the concept of the New World Order, even with its suspiciously sounding acronym, NWO (pronounced 'New Woe'). Even so named it turned out to be, momentarily, an unexpected success. By organising various Arab states and bringing in the UN, Bush created a functioning heterarchy of powers that reversed Iraq's invasion and looked like being the model for a responsible international force. The mixture of multilateral power, consensus politics and UN sanction together set the precedent. Was a new legal international order in the making?

As the accompanying diagram reveals [86], the US provided the organisation and firepower, **A**. The Japanese and 28 nation coalition supplied the money and, with the Arab states, the local credibility, **B**.

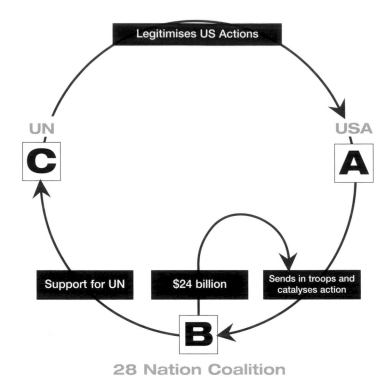

Legitimises US Actions

UN

C

USA

A

Support for UN $24 billion   Sends in troops and catalyses action

B

28 Nation Coalition

LEFT [86] **New World Order 1991 as a heterarchy, operative in the First Gulf War.** A is over B, B is over C, C is over A. Mutual criticism is effectively institutionalised.

And the UN resolutions gave the legal sanctions for Bush's counter-invasion, **C**. The important step here, taken on 10 September at Helsinki, with Gorbachev's necessary blessing, was that the USA agreed to act only when legitimised by the UN vote – Resolution 678. Thus the ethical and military success. The First Gulf War, over in a short time, restored Kuwait's sovereignty and Bush the First obeyed international law by stopping his troops at the gates of Baghdad. Practically, legally and backed by theory, a new critical system had been shown to work. This New World Order, with the countervailing powers each able to hold a critical veto over the other, was a precedent for what could have become a new legitimate system, if the sole superpower had continued to play by the rules.

However, as we know Bush the Second tore up this arrangement, after 11 September 2001. In this he not only went against his country's interest, world opinion and a host of legal judgements, but against the common sense that had been the mainstay of British and American life for a long time. Throughout the nineteenth century, when acts of terrorism (for instance, anarchist bombings and assassinations) were directed against the nation-state, it became apparent to the leaders that the worst response was over reaction. Terrorism, or 'asymmetrical warfare' as it is known, cannot damage national power unless it can leverage that power to create sympathy in a large segment of the population, that is, foment general instability and, by reaction, a new, broader-based insurgency. Leaders such as Theodore Roosevelt understood this theory, that passive aggression, undercover subversion and low level police action are the proper response to terrorism. It was epitomised in his maxim, 'speak softly and carry a big stick'. It was the policy of the British Empire, learned the hard way in India, and the advice of military historians today, such as Michael Howard, who wrote warnings soon after September 11th of what not to do.

Never respond with emotion, avoid all show of hysteria, keep the press in check, work through stealth behind the scenes, declare the killing a criminal act and choke the terrorists of their main source of strength: media oxygen. This was the response of the Indian Prime Minister, Manmohan Singh, after 200 people were blown up in July 2006. Instead of feeding media hysteria, his first act was to denounce the bombing of the trains as 'a shocking attempt to spread a feeling of fear and terror among our citizens'. Instead of treating it as an 'act of war', the response of America and Israel to such events, he labelled it just one more criminal adventure in a long list of assassinations. His reaction was the longstanding policy of how mature nations deal with criminality: 'ice-cool under terror attack' as Anatole Kaletsky frames it.[56] Certainly, the last thing one should do is to declare a general 'war on terrorism'. Like the war on drugs it is the one engagement that cannot be fought because there is no localised enemy, and therefore no conventional battle to win. Bush the Second should have responded to September 11th with measured counter-insurgency, and been content knocking out more golf balls. Instead, he and Tony Blair responded as the terrorists hoped they would and, playing to their tabloid-constituency, whipped up a 'crusade', a nationalism under the slogan, 'you are either for us or against us'. Following this logic was a short step from the bombing of Afghanistan to the invasion of Iraq.

Being wise before the event

One does not have to be a genius to see the folly of this. It is enshrined in such proverbs as, 'Even a paranoid can have real enemies', – their paranoia creates them. This truth is the staple of international relations and war-gaming, and is obvious to anyone who gives it a moment's thought (obviously a precondition of critical modernism). Indeed, it was expressed by a group of prominent architects, whom I helped organise, two months *before* the invasion of Iraq. What they predicted has come about, and what they asserted from a critical perspective has become

LEFT [87] **Bush portrait from US war dead, 2004.** After the first 1,000 American deaths, anonymous portraits of the President were created from photos of the servicemen killed in Iraq, and posted on the Web. The US and UK governments did not bother ever to tally the Iraqi dead, but by 2006 estimates vary from a conservative 50,000 'excess' deaths to 655,000 extra dead, or 2.5% of the Iraq population. (Artist unknown; circulated on the Internet)

generally acknowledged. The letter, signed by three presidents of the RIBA and such luminaries as Frank Gehry, Zaha Hadid and Rem Koolhaas, starts with the forecast that invasion 'will very likely lead to an increase in international terrorism'. By 2006 this prediction was borne out by the US administration, and a CIA report, which acknowledged that 11,111 terrorist incidents had occurred in the three years after the invasion, many of them 'caused' by it.[57] The outcome of war may be unpredictable but many of the political consequences, such as the way repressive regimes would use it, were all too clear before the event.

> The case for a Just War cannot be convincingly made; the link of Saddam Hussein with Al-Qaeda has not been established; a war against Iraq is likely to kill large numbers of civilians and intensify the great suffering there; and unilateral action by the US (with Britain's support) will undermine international law and set a precedent of pre-emption by other nations in places such as

Chechnya, Palestine, Kashmir and Tibet ... A consequence of invasion by the USA and Britain is likely to be the very clash of civilisations sought by terrorist groups such as Al-Qaeda ...[58]

Sadly, these and other predictions of the letter came all too true. It is estimated by the British medical journal the *Lancet*, and other responsible publications, that about 100,000 Iraqis were killed as a consequence of the invasion. [87] Furthermore, several nation-states looked to this US precedent to justify their illegal repression, especially in such places as Chechnya and Palestine. Thus the 'war on terrorism' has led to a predictable Orwellian inversion where 'peace' means 'war', and 'security' means 'aggression'. A powerful nation, with a terrorist incident to hand, has open season on invading a less powerful neighbour. Israel has turned the policy of 'security-aggression' into a way of dividing up Palestine into ever smaller areas ringed by what it calls Security Walls (and the Palestinians term Separation Walls). It bombed Lebanon, killing over 1,000 people, mostly civilians, in the name of the war on terror. Russia and China dominate their minorities and appropriate valuable land under the same pretext. Oil is often the subtext, as it was in Bush's invasion.

As was apparent in the many public demonstrations, much of the world found the war on Iraq unjustified, particularly that part of the world that Bush and Blair wished to persuade: the one billion Muslims. Hard power took the place of soft power and proved inadequate to the task. We know the results at Abu Ghraib, Guantanamo and Fallujah, but leaving aside the morality of bombing and torturing innocent people, there is the effectiveness of a war on terror. As those in the nineteenth century found out, through unhappy experience, it aids the terrorists and creates more instability.

This letter of architects shows that some things are predictable, that history is not just one crazy thing after another. But I bring it up to show the way such general social issues can raise a critical consciousness in specific professions (as the Vietnam War radicalised post-modernists) and also what the letter might have achieved. It was inspired by the British MP Tam Dalyell and his conjecture in early January 2003. He wrote that the decision to invade Iraq was on a knife's edge and that the incipient anti-war movement might just swing Tony Blair against aggression. If that happened it was possible that the US would not act alone, and this would be another example of the restraining force of heterarchical power. A preventive domino effect was imagined in Dalyell's scenario, made from several professions and institutions falling into a collective mass that would become critical (according to the secondary usage of 'critical'). At that time the Archbishop of Canterbury and the Church were tilting against the invasion, the people of Britain were divided; so, if architects came out against war, then other professions might follow – lawyers, doctors, journalists and bankers. The point was that these were the kind of people to whom Blair responds. And if he would back down, then Spain and Italy would probably follow suit, and Bush might put off the invasion until the UN inspectors had finished their work. Such was the reasoning based, admittedly, on a series of 'if-thens'. But at the time it looked possible. A few weeks after our letter was printed, the anti-war movement put on what was called the biggest demonstration in Britain's history. One, or was it two, million people took to London's streets – the figure varied with the political slant of the newspaper and reporter. [88] The mood of the country was sceptical about invasion, as it was in many other nations.

As we now know all these demonstrations and protests had little effect and as we did not know Blair was already committed to war. But the Bush-Blair adventure revealed several more truths of today's political power, besides the impotence of the people and their opinion. It showed that, when faced with security issues and terrorism, the checks and balances of a heterarchy break down and the critical interactions of a democracy fail. When a central government orchestrates national panic, there is no opposition worthy of the name, it vanishes in fear and trembling. The only critical voice to be heard is that of a few lone individuals in the media, or perhaps a marginal party, and even that is not very loud. Yet the Fourth Estate, the media as it used to be called, remains the most audible opposition in orchestrated democracies even if it is muted. This point is worth underlining in the investigation of critical modernism and the possible way the Iraq and Lebanon wars will raise a more self-conscious criticality, as did the Vietnam War before them.

Returning to Iraq and heterarchical power, already at the time of writing events there show the folly of unilateral action by a superpower. The post-national world is too big and interrelated for this to work out positively, and the nation-state is too small relative to the whole. When, after the Second World War, America created 40 per cent of the world national product one could believe it was possible for that nation to dominate the globe economically. But that monopoly has gone for good, while America's relative economic weight has shrunk to 15 per cent. Several conclusions follow. For a superpower to have more armaments than the rest of the world combined does not guarantee victory any more than it brings global peace. Aerial bombardment and occupation of another nation are not a war on terror, but its reverse.

What, then, are the prospects for global stability? If the United Nations is not about to be empowered, there are other alternatives, other post-modern institutions that are growing without much fanfare, working away behind closed doors. They are creating a good part of the post-national world by stealth, and they deserve a modest welcome, suitable to their unproven status.

The post-modern states

The argument is that a new form of international order has started to emerge, most clearly in Europe, and is a model for other regions. This idea is put forward by two authors, the first being the British diplomat Robert Cooper in his *The Breaking of Nations*, a book suitably ambivalently subtitled 'order and chaos in the twenty-first century'.[59] Cooper, who was a foreign policy advisor to Tony Blair and in 2006 worked for the EU's Javier Solana, reveals the tenuous equilibrium that has emerged between three kinds of states. There are what he terms the pre-modern ones of Afghanistan, Somalia and places where the Soviet Union has lost control, such as Chechnya. These may be 'failed states', or ones driven by drugs and crime, and they pose the chronic threat of terrorism. Then there are the typical modern states, in the Cooper trinity, of China, Brazil and India. Finally, the post-modern ones are not nations at all but amalgams, such as the EU.

These last operate on the basis of international law and an openness to enter into each other's domestic affairs, varying from military agreements to the regulation of beer and sausages. Cooper points out such mutual agreement to interfere in national sovereignty is 'an extraordinary revolution'. It is. It has also created a large market of over 460 million people, where goods and capital can flow, somewhat freely, and where there is little need for conflict or expensive armed forces. This is the new Faustian bargain of trade-offs. The nation-states of Europe willingly cede much control over their countries in order to increase their standards, both of living and security. According to this model, the USA is in an undecided space looking two ways. It is a modern/post-modern state in suspension, providing the military shield for Europe and acting unilaterally as it furthers international freedoms (when its suits American goals). Such, in brief, is the new post-modern settlement, operating within the pre-modern and modern worlds.

Many trading blocs are following suit such as ASEAN, the Association of Southeast Asian Nations, or the more informal APEC, uniting some of the same countries in the Asian Pacific area. Japan as an entire country is a post-modern state, entering into multilateral links.

BELOW [88] **London anti-war demonstration.** The biggest political demonstration in British history had no discernible effect on the Bush-Blair Junta. (© Corbis/Steven. E Frischling)

LEFT [89] **European Union** – co-operative empire of 25 nations (orange), candidate countries (light orange), countries to join in 2007 (light brown).

Cooper rightly stresses that the previous modern settlement, the balance of national powers, did not work. Protectionism, the Depression and two world wars proved that, and his idea of 'the breaking of nations' is an attempt to rethink a new type of equilibrium in the wake of these failures. Like other commentators, he shows that, at one level this new arrangement is an ironic slip of nations back into a collective form of empire: but it is voluntary and hidden or cryptic.

America is the most visible imperium, one that is always reluctant to admit its ambitions and take responsibility for them. 'We don't do nation-building, we don't do empire', in the inimitably blunt words of Donald Rumspeak. But the USA extends its economic and military force around the world, as empire-lite. Even more cryptic and hidden from consciousness is the way Cooper characterises the EU, as a 'co-operative voluntary empire'.[60] It is a new form of Commonwealth run by 'an imperial bureaucracy' under which 25 nations huddle for mutual protection. [89] In its defensive mode, known by another metaphor as 'Fortress Europe', it keeps economic migrants at bay and shelters tiny countries like Malta, Slovenia and Latvia. Obviously for them it is a safe haven from Africa, or other crypto-imperial powers such as Russia.

Living under a protective empire also makes sense for minority nations, ethnic groups that lack a nation-state. Armenians, Kurds and

Albanians lived more safely under the Ottoman Empire, Cooper stresses, than under its modern successors. So, the new Faustian bargain makes sense for these people, selling some sovereignty to buy increased security and a rising standard of living. 'The Europeans', he concludes, 'are postmodern states living on a postmodern continent.' As usual, one might add, the pm state depends very much on the support of a modern superpower. Just as Fordism and Post-Fordism are mutually entwined. So, when it comes to armed forces, are the USA and Europe – and Cooper makes the valid point that the latter could not have become post-modern without the shield of the former. That this new arrangement will prove more stable and peaceful than the previous balance of national powers is the hope, but that it is a model for the rest of the world is already apparent.

Another, younger writer, Mark Leonard picks up the story where Cooper leaves off, in his polemic, *Why Europe Will Run the 21st Century*.[61] This best-seller, translated into nine languages, puts the case to a Eurosceptic public, one made more suspicious after the referendums in France and Holland. In a surprising reversal of public sentiment, voters rejected the proposed EU constitution and it was shelved indefinitely. Sensing the change in mood, Leonard admits that there is no bold vision of the future and that Europe is instead driven by a desire to evade the past. He quotes Paul Valery – 'we hope vaguely, we dread precisely' – and says that in spite of the setbacks, he is trying to clarify the large picture, through the eyes of the historian not the journalist. Yet, even with these disclaimers, how could the EU 'run' the twenty-first century? Instead of running the world as the old type of controlling empire, Leonard argues, it will change the globe because the European way of doing things will become the world's. How is this to happen? Again, by becoming a kind of cryptic-empire, a new type of 'hidden hand'. Yet, like Smith's economic regulator, it will be just as compelling because it is imitated by other trading blocs, and it pulls in adjacent countries 'like a magnet'. Leonard's argument depends on several interrelated factors, which I will summarise.

Above all his vision of a successful EU rests on the 'soft power' of laws, networks and an expanding marketplace. This proves more effective than the customary, top-down, hard power. The most obvious attractions are economic, the largest marketplace in the world, one with a growing currency, the Euro. Leonard imagines that soon one-third of the world will be drawn into the Eurosphere. Its strength comes precisely from what Kissinger saw as its weakness, when he asked rhetorically, 'Europe, what's its telephone number?' Instead of a direct line to power and a centralised nation-state, the EU is a network of centres that are united by common goals, traditions that have a long history. Every other trading bloc, all 170 regional bodies with their clumsy acronyms and changing agreements, will finally succumb to this EU logic because it is so interrelated, and has such benefits.

Its 'secret weapon' is the creeping democratic law, the 80,000 pages of rules in thirty-one volumes. Those aspiring countries, such as Bulgaria and Romania, have to read and digest all this. After passing this trial by paperwork, rules on everything from gay rights to food safety, would-be members have to put their own laws and customs into harmony with the thirty-one volumes. This makes for the 'transformative power' that the EU has shown in countries like the Czech Republic and Poland, and is now showing nations aspiring to membership, such as Bulgaria, Romania and Turkey. The last named has had to abolish the death penalty, give rights to minorities such as the Kurds, and grapple with torture in prisons, in the far-off hope of joining the club. It might happen in ten years, or never, but such is the soft power of the EU that anyone in its sphere of influence will be tempted to conform. Leonard claims on his website that the Chinese are fascinated by this notion of 'transformative power' and they hope to mimic it in constructing an equivalent East Asian community, though in what manner they envy the democratic spirit he does not say.

Nonetheless, if all the countries of the EU uphold most of the common laws, and their courts enforce them, the collective drive towards efficiency and democracy is stronger than if they were imposed in the old way, by an occupying force and centralised empire. Look at the trouble with hard power, America imposing its will on Iraq. Civil servants give out EU money, European troops operate under UN flags, common goals are spread through a network, without the member countries having to give up their cultural identity. The EU eschews military threats, so it does not create the ill-will of the classic empire, but instead threatens to close off contracts. Without firing a single shot and by using the contractual form of 'passive aggression', it manages to get its way. 'Worse than the Eurocrats descending on you,' Leonard avers, 'is their not descending on you.'

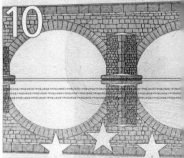

Finally, through economic success, the EU will become the model for the other trading blocs. Already the successful ASEAN, of ten countries, is following its lead. So too is the Arab League, and economic communities set up in Africa, South America and the Pacific Rim. In short, the EU is changing the world through example, the soft transformative power of imitation, and desire of adjacent nations to join

the club. The world, in the future, will not be run by the UN or some supra-global leviathan but by 'overlapping neighbourhood clubs' based on similar laws. This is the logic, and the compelling trend.

One cheer for the EU

As Valery said, 'we hope vaguely', and Mark Leonard's metaphors are not all that precise. 'A neighbourhood club' that 'transforms the neighbours into a law-abiding network' through its 'secret weapon of laws' and 'the hidden hand of the biggest marketplace in the world' – all this sounds plausible, but not entirely convincing. Moreover, suspicion about the EU bureaucracy and its undemocratic imposition of regressive fiscal policy, such as the Common Agricultural Policy, has inspired a whole constituency. They are known as Eurosceptics, and in countries like Britain something like 65 per cent of the population have become doubters.[62] The reason is fraud, corruption, lack of accountability and a £65 billion budget that is dispensed without even the most elementary accounting system in place. This lapse in legality is highlighted by Marta Andreasen, the former chief accounting officer. As if to prove her point, she was suspended from the EU in 2002, after she was told to investigate the shortcomings and report on them. She did, and was sacked, in 2004. Such drawbacks, and there are several chronic problems with the corrupt Eurocracy, dim Cooper and Leonard's bright picture.[63]

One might grant the corruption and ask, how bad is it? How does it compare to similar institutions and to other countries? In the UN corruption is rife. The American superpower is known to have thrown billions at dubious enterprise in Iraq, and the government is often implicated in such scandals as that at Enron. In the 1980s, German investors researched and started publishing a world corruption index, so their overseas traders would know exactly how big a bribe they should offer. The highest bribes went to the poorest countries, in 2005 Chad and Bangladesh, respectively 159th and 158th on the corruption index list.[64] Up the scale of virtue the index climbs, with Italy at 41, just at the point where more bribery and illegality would make the government lose credibility, and create a further downwards spiral. Corruption is both the cause of poverty, as this Berlin institute points out, and a major reason it is endemic. EU nations, such as Spain, score in the middle 20s, which is not too bad. Nonetheless, however benign the EU might be compared to the worst offenders, one cannot get very inspired. Following EM Forster's 'Two cheers for democracy', one might say for the EU that 'one is quite enough'.[90].[65]

ABOVE [90] **The architectural truth**. Why not use the real Pont du Gard? In the interests of not offending twenty-four other nations, the Euro fudges architecture revealing a chronic EU problem. Roman aqueduct, medieval and classical bridges are reduced to generic types – The Culture of Platitude. (Photo of Pont du Gard, C Jencks)

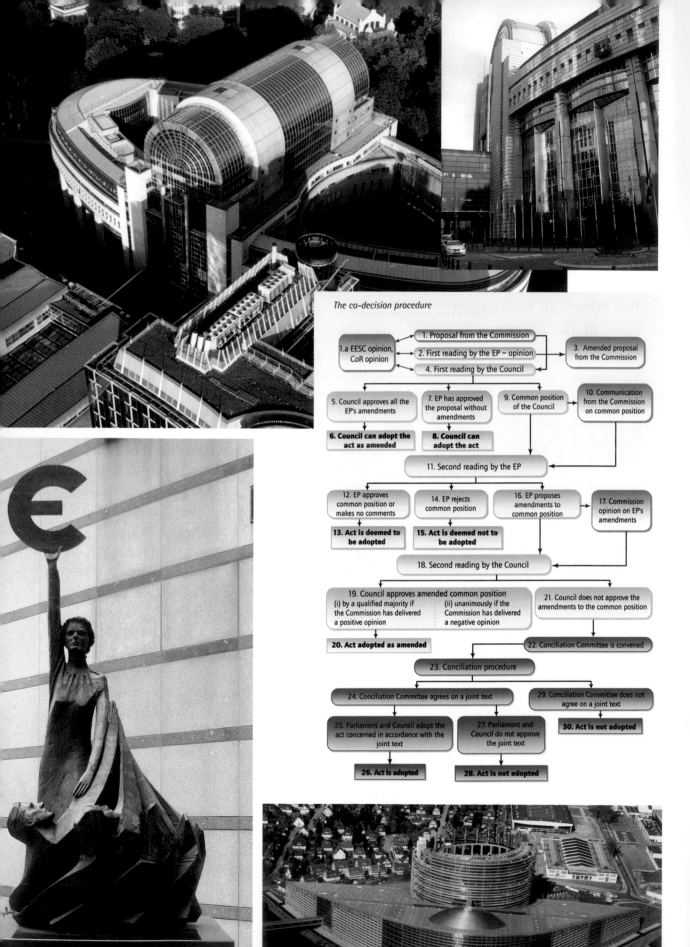

The co-decision procedure

1. Proposal from the Commission

1.a EESC opinion, CoR opinion

2. First reading by the EP – opinion

3. Amended proposal from the Commission

4. First reading by the Council

5. Council approves all the EP's amendments

6. Council can adopt the act as amended

7. EP has approved the proposal without amendments

8. Council can adopt the act

9. Common position of the Council

10. Communication from the Commission on common position

11. Second reading by the EP

12. EP approves common position or makes no comments

13. Act is deemed to be adopted

14. EP rejects common position

15. Act is deemed not to be adopted

16. EP proposes amendments to common position

17. Commission opinion on EP's amendments

18. Second reading by the Council

19. Council approves amended common position
(i) by a qualified majority if the Commission has delivered a positive opinion
(ii) unanimously if the Commission has delivered a negative opinion

20. Act adopted as amended

21. Council does not approve the amendments to the common position

22. Conciliation Committee is convened

23. Conciliation procedure

24. Conciliation Committee agrees on a joint text

29. Conciliation Committee does not agree on a joint text

25. Parliament and Council adopt the act concerned in accordance with the joint text

27. Parliament and Council do not approve the joint text

30. Act is not adopted

26. Act is adopted

28. Act is not adopted

OPPOSITE [91a, b, c, d, e] **The European Parliament in Brussels (above) and Strasbourg (bottom right), 1985 and 1990s.** Architecture reveals the orientation of the EU towards its citizens. A central assembly surrounded by a tissue of proliferating bureaucracy shows the truth of how answerable power dissipates in complicated administration. How can 732 parliamentarians, with only six minutes a year to speak, debate effectively? Iconography betrays the same inadvertent story, bottom left: is it Young Liberty Leading the Charge Over the People? The Sovietesque statue appears to celebrate cadavers struggling under the feet of Currency Triumphant. The official diagram, middle right, thoughtfully explains 'How the EU takes decisions' (or not, as step 30 has the last word). This is taking the heterarchical principle to the point of Byzantine complexity. (Courtesy Gillian Innes, EU, and architects AEL, Association des Architectes du CIC:Vanden Bossche Sprl, C.R.V. SA, GDG Sprl, StudiogroopD, Bontinck; Strasbourg European Parliament photo, Architecture Studio, Paris)

Since architecture is one visible index of civilisation, according to Ruskin and others, I went to Brussels and Strasbourg to have a look at the twin hearts of the EU. There is not one but two centres of the European Parliament. That is in order to satisfy the French desire to have one of them on their land, a corrupting situation in itself. The 732 parliamentarians thus have to move their office back and forth between Brussels and Strasbourg every couple of months, at huge expense, 200 million Euros per year. Furthermore, like the Soviet politburo with which it is compared, the large number of speakers defeats democracy. It allows representatives only six minutes per year to make their voice heard. What I found in this bureaucratic situation did not surprise me. The physical organs were big – bloated with administrative pork-barrel would not be an exaggeration [91a, b, c, d, e]. The style of both parliaments was a mixture of Late-Modern abstraction with the odd window wall stuck on to make the endlessness more 'classical' and 'humane'. Subsidiary buildings, even the Court of Human Rights by Richard Rogers, were not much better and most of them were much worse. The entrance and details to the Brussels European Parliament had written all over it, architecturally speaking, 'here is a plum job for one of the boys' (the architects were Atelier Espace Léopold). The Berlaymont Headquarters in Brussels made up for this heavy symbolism by having no discernible entrance at all – just a sliding wall that, if citizens can find it, visually cuts them in two. Built in the 1960s as a Late-Modern monument in the then fashionable Y-shape, 'Berlaymonster' as it is known, had to be refurbished in the 1990s. It took thirteen years and 'hundreds of millions of pounds' to put it right, get rid of the asbestos and add a few window shades. For Eurosceptics Berlaymonster is the perfect symbol of the triumph of monopoly power over accountability.

Trying to navigate the forty repetitive monoliths in Euroville is likely to bring on a Kafkaesque panic, disorientation by bureaucratic proliferation [92–4]. And so it goes. If architecture is a measure of civilisation, then the EU would have to be placed just above the Pentagon in Washington, DC. Rem Koolhaas, who was asked by Romano Prodi to re-brand the organisation and give the twin hearts a human face, wrote a trenchant critique of the whole EU symbolism, called 'E-conology'. But even he was stumped for an answer to this missing identity, as he came up with his substitute for the 12 gold stars on the blue flag. It was a barcode of the 25 nations, a pluralist sampling of each national flag reduced to something read by machine at a checkout counter [95]. So much for inadvertent symbolism, again a

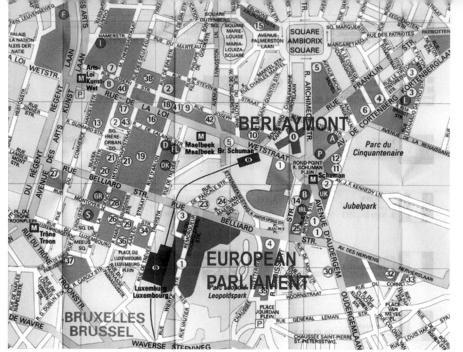

LEFT [92–4] **Site Map and Berlaymont Headquarters in Brussels, 1960s** refurbished 1990s. Small details, such as the invisibility of the entrance at Berlaymont, and the bloated size of forty such blocks in a small area, tell the story. (Photo Gillian Innes)

RIGHT [95] **Rem Koolhaas and AMO, European Barcode for the EU, 2002; EU Flag.** An attempt to be inclusive, open and thorough reduces national colours to the checkout counter. Accidentally, however, when used on the tent in Brussels the barcode loses its former meaning and becomes a fresh sign of ascending pluralism, one aiming toward unity. From false branding to inadvertent breakthrough – is this how symbols emerge? (© AMO/Koolhaas; EU Flag, C Jencks)

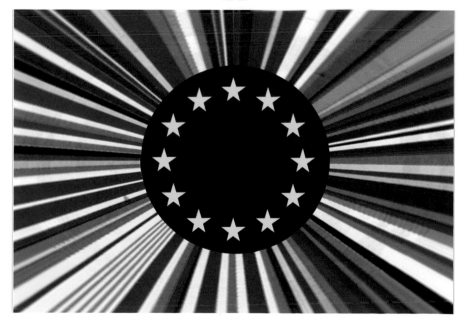

reduction of European identity to the pursuit of money. Just possibly however, his later tent for the EU with the barcode transformed, could be a fitting breakthrough for a flag – we will see.

As often with post-modern reality, there may be a palliative when there is no immediate cure. When there are no other choices on the menu, as classical writers advise, *castigat ridendo mores*, criticise through humour. This is advisable in a world where global governance is clearly a mess and the less bad institutions on offer are still so fallible. Euroscepticism is a realistic orientation, and heavy irony is needed to keep one's sanity when faced by the long-standing corruption of wine-lakes and butter-mounds. At the same time this view has to be accompanied, with a little schizophrenia, by its opposite: the understanding that we have left the world of the nation-state and its destructive balance of power. One only has to recall that the post-national world is the most depressing of the seventy or so aspects that make up the post-modern world, but also the most dangerous. For that very reason one should demand higher standards.

At the very least, the member states should hold the EU to its existing charter of democracy, which is quite noble on paper. Benign concepts, such as that of subsidiarity, where every decision is made at the most local level possible, should be made more of than they are today: pious declarations of intent. The heterarchy of powers within the EU is also positive, except that it is so complex and inward-looking as to be opaque to outside, democratic influence. The E-conology is a mess. Just consider the simplest of sign systems, the names. How many citizens of the community could define the difference between the three bodies, The European Council, The Council of the European Union and The Council of Europe? Or say which is the most powerful? (The first named, with its heads of state that define policy). As the EU expands further east – towards 35 or will it be 50 members? – it will either cut its 'democratic deficit' or be torn apart from within, by further referendums rejecting its elitism. The ideals of regionalism and multiculturalism are also benign in theory, and somewhat operative in practice, but it is an open question as to whether the EU can respond to what is still widely perceived as its chronic deficit.

Cooper reviewing Leonard is hopeful –

> The EU is so difficult to understand because it does not fit into our established categories. It is not a state; it is neither a federation nor a confederation. Leonard makes the striking comparison with the Visa company, whose logo appears on half a billion credit cards though it has only 3,000 employees. Authority, initiative, decision-making and profits belong to the 21,000

financial institutions that own Visa. It is an enabling organisation rather than an old-style corporation. This is not a bad way to imagine the EU: a collective power owned by the members, enhancing their powers rather than appropriating them.[66]

An enabling Visa company, yet another metaphor, is this finally the right one? It sounds benign, like the trusted servant or humble butler who is always silently doing good things for the family – although in the 1963 British film, *The Servant*, he slowly realises and then exploits his expanding powers over his master, and ends up taking over the house. Maybe a little scepticism is healthy?

The search for an effective heterarchy

The EU and all the transnational powers that exist, including the UN, have yet to produce an international relationship of power that is legitimate and therefore stable. The Bush policy of unilateral invasion based on pre-emption is highly unstable and will simply provoke more locally inspired and state sponsored terrorism, as it has already done. At the same time, European and other post-modern states allow themselves to be woefully dependent on the USA, as the world's policeman. The USA is not about to give up its monopoly of power, its declared right to be judge, jury and executioner when it comes to a pre-emptive strike.

Yet, since this policy has gone so badly wrong, and all nations are relatively weak today, it seems likely that an implicit heterarchy may start to operate again. That is, world governance, such as it is, will hobble along as it did in the 1991 Gulf War. A loose multilateral coalition of forces, led by the US superpower, might under many conditions have to get UN and other sanctions before collective actions are taken. The US will be tempted to go it alone, but if Britain and its few allies do not give support, which seems more likely now, then inaction would be the result. With so many nuclear powers around in ten years' time, one can imagine some large nuclear incident occurring but, at the same time, imagine that it would be limited to a place and time. Depending on the particular case, this grim scenario might nevertheless lead to a more formal system of mutual control, of distributed checks and balances, with final sanction resting at the UN, or some other transnational body. This would be far from perfect, but much better than unilateral anarchy and, one can hope, it might set a precedent for a balanced heterarchical system. Repeated enough such action would become common, then perhaps even common international law.

IN THE BEGINNING

"God created the Heaven and the Earth."—Gen. i. 1.   Moses assigns no date to this Creation.   How long after this "beginning" before

LET THERE - אור יהי - BE LIGHT.   "And God created man in His own image . . . . male and female created He them."—Gen. i. 27.

The duration of the period from the Creation to the Flood is variously stated in the Hebrew, the Septuagint, and the Samaritan texts.   The time given is shortest in the
amount by nearly three centuries and a half, making the time 1656 years.   The Septuagint further enlarges it by above six centuries more, estimating the whole period at 2242
of deciding which of the three estimates is preferable; and it cannot be regarded as certain that the numbers set down by the original writer have been preserved
probably estimated the length of the period before the Flood at something between thirteen and twenty-three centuries.   Babylonians estimated it at 4320 centuries.
Modern anthropologists maintain that man must have existed upon the earth for 300 centuries at the least, and some extend the time to 1000 centuries.

The Chronological System of ARCHBISHOP USHER, followed here, and upon which a large
majority of our Histories are founded, enables us to obtain a correct outline of the sequence of
events, and of the relation of one period to another.

IRAD·3rd

ENOCH. 2nd from Adam.

CAIN   The "Firstborn." This "line" is all that is ? known of Cain and his descendants.—See Gen. IV. 16 to 24.
The date of birth and the age of Cain (and his descendants) are unknown.
ABEL   The first Martyr   About 129 A.M., perhaps.

(date unknown)   This mark (?) indicates that the date is
unknown or uncertain.

ADAM (AND EVE) 930 years.

ENOS 905

SETH 912 yrs. Son of Adam.   3769 B.C.   235 A.M.

3874 B.C.   ADAM talked with SETH 800 years, and with ENOS 695 years, and with
130 A.M.

"..And begat

GENESIS embraces 2369 years—from the Creation to the death of Joseph, 1635 B.C.
CHAP. I.—The Creation of the heaven and the earth.   its completion, and the order
CHAP. II.—The Sabbath.   The manner of Creation   (v. 8), The Garden of Ed
Knowledge prohibited.   (vv. 19, 20), Naming the
(v. 21), Woman Created.   Marriage instituted.
CHAP. III.—Adam and Eve's deception, transgression,   and fall
The curse of labor and pain pronounced, and   their expulsion from Pa

100   2   5

80   70   60   50   Century   40   Decades.   30   20   10   50   40   30   20   10   50

04   ADAM 130   Gen. v. 3.   39   SETH 105   38   ENOS 90

This represents the age of Adam when Seth was born, viz., 130—
Seth is 105 when Enos is born.

Difficulties in Egyptian Chronology.

(See bottom of 19th Century Column, B.C.)

1st.   The Egyptians had no ERA from which to date events.
2nd.   They did not distinguish between the years of a SOLE REIGN,
and those of JOINT REIGNS of father and son.
3rd.   They never gave the DURATION of a Dynasty.
4th.   They did not designate CONTEMPORARY DYNASTIES.

Hence the uncertainty of
Dates in Egyptian History.
The Chronology adopted
herein for Egypt is that
of Professor Rawlinson.
(See Letterpress.)

Ancient Egyptian Architecture.

XIIth DYN. OF THEBES (DATE NOT KNOWN)

MIZRAIM OF EGYPT.   XIIth DYN. OF   ANTEF   RENTUHOTEP   ANTEF III.   SANKH-KARA   AMEN-EMHAT I.   USERTASEN   AMEN-EMHAT

Primitive Egyptian
Civilization.
"History knows no
time when the Egyp-
tians were not HIGH-
LY DEVELOPED,
both PHYSICALLY
and INTELLECTU-
ALLY."—Dr. Birch.

WRITING
IN BABYLONIA.

Writing with Cunei-
form characters not
well known and prac-
tised in the time of
rukh; and earliest in
stone.   INSCRIBED
CYLINDRICAL
STONE SEALS of
THAT AGE, are
STILL IN EXIST-
ENCE.—Geo. Smith.

COSTUMES of Priests of Babylon.

CHALDÆA, Capital UR.
LIG-BAGAS   URUKH.
IZDUBAR   THE GREATEST OF BABYLONIAN BUILDERS
(NIMROD)   EXCEPT NEBUCHADNEZZAR.

Temples Built by Lig-Bagas
(Urukh).

At Ur, to the Moon-God; at
Larsa, to the Sun; at Erech,
to Ishtar; at Nipur, to Bel,
and one to his consort, Bel-
tis; at Zurghul, to the King
of the Gods; also a temple
tower (ziggurat) and a palace
at Ur.
DUNGI built a temple at
BABYLON.
Geo. Smith.

DUNGI, SON.   SU-AGU.   AMARAGU.   IBILAGU.   GAMILADAR.
His SEAL is in
BRITISH MUSEUM.   ERECH OR URUK
LARSA   (perhaps the ELLASSAR of Gen. x
NUR-RIMMON.

JUNO, Queen of Heaven;   JUPITER, who was the   NEPTUNE,   VULCAN
Sister and Wife of)   father of Gods and Men.   Brother of
Jupiter.

GREECE (ATTICA, ARCADIA, SPARTA)
JAVAN or ION   JOHN.   GREECE or IONIA.   founded by AEGIALUS   of URANUS in Gree

First Saw Mill at Madeira in 1420

50 feet high, 8 stories
of a mile square at the base

(Right portion — modern history columns)

TOBACCO
found at
ST. DOMINGO
1492.   1492   COLUMBUS crossed the ocean
and discovered San Salvador, Octobe.
continent in 1498; but it was 109 ye
"First Settlement" was made at Jan

1498   CONTINENT
DISCOVERED.

COLUMBUS
& THE EGG.

SAN SALVADOR
Discovered Friday, Oct. 12,
1492.

COPERNICUS, 70   at THORN, PRUSSIA

FIRST POST-OFFICE
IN ENGLAND, 158

1431   FIRST
of ARC   WATCH
at NUREMBERG.

FIRST POST-HORSES
in 1481   BEFORE
1530

PRINTING BY
GUTENBERG.
ABOUT
1440.   WM.
Reading his

SPINNING BY HAND.

1477   MARTIN LUTHER
at
WORMS.   1521

GUTENBERG, JOHN, born   FRENCH NOBLEMAN   GENTLEMAN
in   in 1540.   in 1580.
Inventor of Movable Type   QUEEN
ISABELLA

ERASMUS   1536
CARDINAL THOMAS WOLSEY. 59   1530

JAMES I.   JAMES II.   JAMES III   JAMES IV.   JAMES V.   MARY
Son—Killed.   Son.   29
Branch
LANCAS
TER.   YORK,
WHITE TO
1485   TUDOR to 1603   HEAD of the   TO 1
CHURCH 1534

EDWARD IV.   HENRY VII   HENRY VII
Printing intro-   (Queen Elizabeth,
duced in Eng.1474   Son of Edward IV.
Succeeded by   7 he "Great Harry,"
Edw.V   1498, cost £14,000.

ORLEANS

CHARLES VII.   LOUIS XI   CHARLES   LOUIS XII   FRANCIS
Son.   Son.   VIII.   Great-great-grand-son of   Great-great-gran-dson of
Siege of Orleans raised by   The Tiberius   Son of Duke   Charles V.   Charles V.
Joan of Arc, May 8, 1429.   of France.   of Orleans,   Father of Letters.
"The Victorious."   P.D. in 1483   Great-grandsi   at war with Charles of
son of   Spain.
Charles V.

HOLLAND.   FIRST
 ARGY in   PHILIP   AUGSBURG,
in Bavaria,
1530.

BURGUNDY to FRANCE.
BURGUNDY to FRANCE.   MARGARET of A
GERMANY & AUSTRIA

SIGISMUND.   FREDERICK III. 53   MAXIMILIAN I.   CHARLES V.
Brandenburg sold   King of Austria, 1457.   King of Spain.
to Frederick,   "The Pacific"   Son.
1415.   Son.   37
26

LADISLAUS VII. to   MATTHIAS CORVINUS   SAXONY.   FREDERICK III   LOUIS
JOHN   1445   1450   10
"Ironside"   JOHN III. 23.   JOACHIM I   Son
FREDERICK I.   FREDERICK II. 30.

POLAND

SIGISMUND I
Brother.   The Great.
RUSSIA   1462 CZARS of Muscovy.
BASIL III.   BASIL IV.   IVAN of   JOHN II.   BASIL V.   IVAN IV.
Son.   Title of Czar, 1534.   Called "Emperor."   Promoted Commerce
and celebrated

DENMARK   MICHAEL ANGELO, 89. Architect of St. Peter's
XVIIIth COUNCIL   Denmark and Norway separated from Sweden, 1523.
AT BASLE,   SWEDEN.
ERIC VII.   1439.
of Sweden   GUSTAVUS VASA, 37
CHRISTIAN I.   JOHN.   Son.   DENMARK &
King of Sweden, 1450.   Sought to reign   92
with a crown.   1523   CHRISTIAN

MARGARET,   DENMARK.

The Spinning-Wheel invented.

5. COSMOGENESIS AND THE UNIVERSE PROJECT

Belief in a universe 13.7 billion years big

Fear of war, famine, pestilence and death – the Four Horsemen of the Apocalypse – have their global equivalents today. Terrorism, dirty water, Aids and the mass extinction of species, to name only the prominent candidates, are all already with us. They force a global perspective on us but also the larger one, a cosmic world view. Fortunately, and coincidentally, there is a positive perspective attracting us in the same direction. It is inherent in the paradox of this paragraph heading – how could you believe in the universe 13.7 billion years big? For that matter, after it was announced by astrophysicists in 2003, how could you not? And why big rather than old? Could a universe any younger, and smaller, have given birth to its self-regarding offspring, those like us who are trying to reflect on it? Does the universe have a direction, a purpose, part of which is an inherent code to produce sentient creatures? Does it naturally produce quality? Such are the questions that philosophers, scientists and the general public are asking with greater frequency, questions typical of the post-modern period when professional divides are interrogated, when new hybrids are emerging. After having been brushed aside in the twentieth century as metaphysical and senseless, these questions have returned to the top of the agenda.

The distrust of metaphysics goes back several centuries, to the Modern Settlement. This was negotiated between science and religion sometime in the seventeenth century, when the intellectual landscape was cut in two. Science was given the 'how' and 'what' questions – how the universe works and what is it made from, and religion was given the 'why' questions – for what purpose does it exist, where is it going, and what is its value. After the religious wars and then the conventional divides between the two cultures, the education of scientists versus that of the literary and artistic elite, the opposition became chronic and deep-seated. Darwinism, determinism and materialism were said to be the foundation of the modern paradigm, a rather bleak view. Meanwhile, a creative culture went on its amiable way, oblivious to the fact that its masterworks were, in some scientific way that was never quite specified, supposed to be predetermined.

So the 'two cultures' evolved along different channels, at least according to conventional wisdom and CP Snow, who coined the term in the late 1950s. How much truth this dual reality had may be debatable, but there is no doubt that with the advent of the hybrid 'third culture' during the 1970s, when science writers began to popularise their discoveries, the Modern Settlement broke down. Religion was now interrogated by scientists, ethics by sociobiologists, and a purposeless universe by philosophers. By the 1980s, Richard Dawkins, Stephen Hawking, Paul Davies and then a host of scientists and writers, those collected by the literary agent John Brockman under the title *The Third Culture*, wrote popular books explaining to the general public their emergent ideas.[67] All of a sudden books on chaos theory and fuzzy logic became best-sellers. Most significantly, as we will see, the Institute of Santa Fe, with two Nobel Prize winners, dedicated itself to uncovering what it called the sciences of the twenty-first century, the nonlinear sciences of complexity. Complexity theory, as we noted with architects and planners in the 1960s, was one foundation stone of post-modernism, but in the 1980s it developed into a fully-fledged discipline and acquired scientific respectability. The notions of Complex Adaptive Systems, cellular automata and the Gaia Hypothesis became mainstream theories casting light on the mind and the earth. With writers such as Stephen Jay Gould and Lee Smolin, the notions of a self-organising cosmos became well known. The arcane world of cosmology led to the biggest-seller ever unread, Hawking's, *A Brief History of Time*.

In spring of 1992, NASA announced at a press conference the results of the COBE satellite mission, and showed a picture of the microwave background of the universe. It revealed how the universe looked at about 300,000 years old, when photons uncoupled from matter and the first structures were visible, the seeds of later galaxies.

Some of the scientists, jumping out of their restricted professional compound, claimed it was like seeing the mind of God, and the announcement was carried as a headline in major newspapers around the world. Britain's *Independent* even had the temerity to draw a picture of the evolving cosmos across its front page, accompanied by the provocative headline, 'How the Universe Began'. [97] Contrast this trumpet blast with the era of the Modern Settlement. When Einstein's relativity hypothesis was confirmed, in 1919, the announcement was tucked away deep in *The Times* of London: 'Theory of Universe Proved.' Why the shift from the back page to the front? Yesterday the implications of science were mechanistic, reductive, materialist, depressing and kept from the public. Today they are about self-organising systems, creativity, dynamism and at the forefront of consciousness. It is no longer possible *not* to believe in a universe 13.7 billion years big, whatever other beliefs one ties it to, because that is standard science and such news is frequently on the front page.

This does not mean that the news is assimilated for its implications or yet entirely understood. The view of cosmogenesis has not produced its Plato and Aquinas, its Dante and Michelangelo, its TS Eliot or even its Steven Spielberg. It remains undigested, yet to be fully absorbed into mass and high culture, and go through the mill of Critical Modernism; but that it is at the beginning stage there can be no doubt. A new metanarrative is being formed that will have to be absorbed by

RIGHT [97] **'How the Universe Began',** *The Independent*, Cover 24/4/92. A rather premature announcement stemming from an unfortunate metaphor at the bottom – the Big Bang – criticised in the following chapter. Otherwise this was a fair depiction of the emergent cosmogenesis and the first time it hit the front page. (The Independent.)

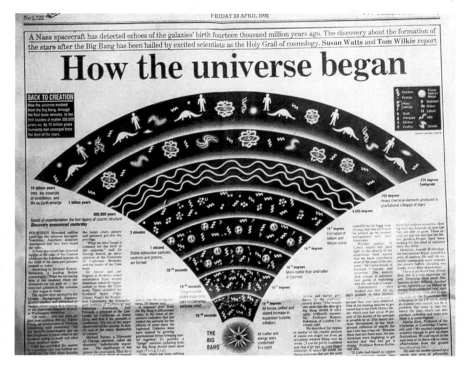

all ideologies and religions, because it is fast becoming standard science. Whether it can be adopted without overturning the traditional views is a deep and perplexing question, because they remain the foundation of civilisation, in East and West. But putting this aside for the moment, one should look at how this shift fits into the post-modern debate.

As mentioned at the outset, an incredulity towards metanarratives – the main explanations of religion, evolution, and social progress – is how Jean-François Lyotard defines the post-modern. To exaggerate, as he does, Auschwitz refutes the idea of universal history and progress, the main thrust of modernism and the Enlightenment Project. One can think of equal refutations of the major religions, but they have not completely destroyed the propensity to believe, nor the long-term power of ideologies and institutions. Rather, I think it more accurate to say, the post-national world has multiplied the plurality of beliefs, making each one less strongly believed in though more firmly held. Incredulity does not mean total scepticism, but more likely a weak belief dogmatically asserted, as with the various Fundamentalisms. Weak belief has strong causes. People worship in traditional ways, but at the same time selectively, with half their heart or *à la carte*, as they try to reconcile, say, Darwinism with a beneficent God.

Slowly, however, another world picture is taking on depth because it is being constructed at different levels, in biology, astrophysics and history, very much a collective effort. A few artists are

[98 a, b, c] Richard Long, **Norfolk Ellipse**, flint and chalk; 710 x 350cm, 2003. Long, with his minimal interventions and primary shapes, usually creates an Indexical Art of traces, signs of a natural process. Here, with an ellipse of darker flint surrounding a flash of white chalk, the result is more characteristic of actual cosmic organisation. Land Artists of all persuasions are probing materials for their natural symbolism. (Kenny Schachter Rove Gallery, London, photos C Jencks)

taking tentative steps. [98] Then there are the writers of the third culture, scientists such as Lynn Margulis and Martin Rees, who are filling out the picture of the earth's dynamics and cosmic evolution, and also the popular writers who are pulling some of this together. One attempt is by the travel writer, Bill Bryson, and his look at the characters that have each added to the picture. *A Short History of Nearly Everything* (2003), invigorates the universal narrative by showing how idiosyncratic and awe-inspiring the discoveries have been. The historian David Christian, an expert on Russian history from San Diego, tells an unbroken story from the Big Bang to the present in his *Maps of Time* aptly given the subtitle of the new genre, *An Introduction to Big History* (2004). 'Big History', the long metanarrative of 13.7 billion years, is becoming standard history and in another ten years may be on the syllabus. Undoubtedly it will be if its meaning is assimilated, its poetry understood, and it is translated into various cultural forms – several crucial 'ifs'.

The idea that the universe story can be told, from the beginning to its present as an unbroken narrative, is itself meaningful. Indeed, considered as an evolutionary explanation it is like the Genesis story, a narrative that provides understanding while it shapes identity. Hence 'cosmogenesis', a nineteenth-century term that means the unfolding of the universe, has gained currency among scientists and philosophers.[68] It necessarily competes with and incorporates the Christian story, and makes it more clearly mythical. It also challenges humanism, man the measure of all things, with the larger picture, the universe as the measure of things, if not all of them.

However, in one surprising way it does not entail the complete end of the human-centred view, and that for a very logical reason. The post-modern account accepts what is called a weak version of the Anthropic Principle, which puts certain requirements on the laws and constants of nature. For obvious reasons, the universe must have a cosmic code such that it allows, after many billions of years, things like us to evolve, and think about it. Thus a new Cartesian *cogito* might be: 'We feel, and think, therefore the universe has to exist within rather strong constraints, and narrow possibilities'. This may be long-winded, and not as poetic as the quintessential modern epigram of Descartes, 'I think therefore I am', but unlike his anthropomorphism it happens to be true. Cosmogenesis raises many such questions that critique the old, three-hundred year view. Among others it asks whether the emergence of quality is inevitable, whether there is some deeper law of cosmic evolution at work that guarantees greater complexity – a New Second Law?

Complexity as a measure of quality

We noted earlier that post-modernism in architecture and urbanism focused on the idea of complexity as a key concept. For Robert Venturi and Jane Jacobs the goal was to recapture the rich mix of meaning that had been lost in contemporary architecture and the modern city. Jacobs used a pointed phrase at the end of her polemic, *The Death and Life of Great American Cities* when she referred to '*organised* complexity' (my italics). This formulation was to become one of the key ideas in science, something she could not have fully appreciated in the 1960s. Complexity theory was not developed at the Santa Fe Institute until the 1980s, nor had the full panoply of post-modern sciences of complexity come on stream. [99] Only later did it become clear that particular organisation is a key to 'effective complexity' and the emergence of quality in the universe.

Since my own writings were very much concerned with this issue, I will digress slightly into the areas of literary and complexity theory to bring out some common themes. They may seem somewhat abstract at first, but they typify the search for structures that could explain the difference between better and worse buildings, or good and bad cities. For that matter they hope to fathom the quality of organisation in general, including such things as evolutionary progress, and in that sense are theories essential to the agenda of post-modernism. For instance, Christopher Alexander argued that a city designed like a semi-lattice, which is rich in linkage, was much better to

BELOW [99] **The Post-Modern Sciences of Complexity** start as a trickle in the nineteenth century with thermodynamics. At the beginning of the twentieth century they deepen with quantum and relativity theories and then, by the end of the century, they become an interconnected river delta with the addition of nonlinear dynamics and chaos theory. These sciences of complexity concern the importance of time, feedback and self-organisation, as opposed to the linear and mechanistic sciences that underlay modernism. Of course, in the end there is only one science, but at various times it develops with different motivations and predispositions.

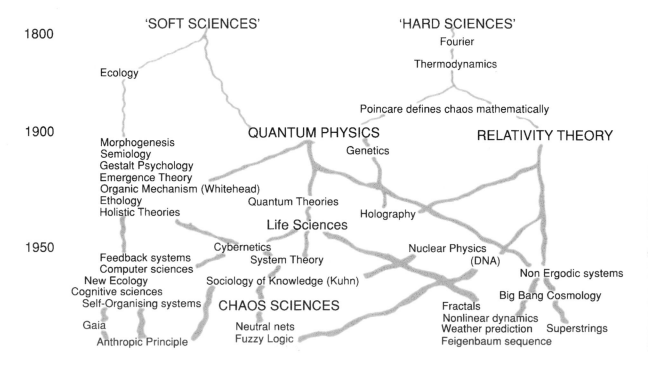

live in than one designed like a tree, a hierarchy poor in linkage. [100] Many others had pointed out the same difference between older organic neighbourhoods that had grown richly connected over time and the British New Towns, where functions were rigidly separated. Again, the point was an intricate complexity versus a reduced simplicity.

In the late 1960s I also criticised the oversimplified building as 'univalent' and later proffered, as the heart of post-modernism, a countervailing 'multivalence'. My evidence came from literary criticism. According to the New Critics of a previous era, the 1950s, there were some objective structures that connected their close reading of a novel to their literary judgement to the long lasting value of the work. The 'organic complexity' of a poem or any work of literature, they averred, was a measure of its quality, and it was this particular organisation that made the work open to constant reinterpretation. Organic complexity explained a puzzle: why it was that the appreciation of Shakespeare, say, was the discovery of new links in a play, meanings that were latent but definitely inside the structure. Different readers could fathom these qualities, different troupes could perform them with opposite slants, yet the structure of the play was strong enough to absorb new interpretations without falling to pieces. What else was the 'judgement of the ages' than this constant reinterpretation? By contrast, a univalent work, weak in imaginative fusion, was vulnerable to different readings, fell apart when looked at with irony or read with an

RIGHT [100] Christopher Alexander, **'Semi Lattice Versus a Tree'** from *City is Not a Tree*, 1964. For instance, a successful city neighbourhood versus an isolated superblock shows structures rich and poor in linkage. Organisational depth partly depends on the sheer number of elements in a work and the linkage between them. Here, the hierarchical tree structure to the right has fewer links than the overlapping semi-lattice to the left. A traditional town with many relationships that have grown up over the years is much richer in linkage than the tree-like structure of the modern New Town. No doubt linkage is one measure of organic unity, the complexity and quality of a work, but it is not a sufficient measure.

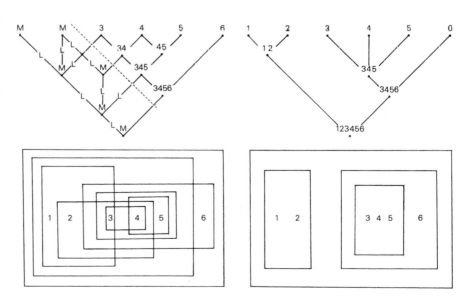

unsympathetic eye. Quality resided in the structure of the work, the linkage between forms, themes and aesthetic ideas. It was real, it concerned the multivalence or relationship of many meanings, and perhaps it could even be measured.

Hopeful that organised complexity was one index of quality, I looked to other writers investigating the subject and eventually came across the polymath Murray Gell-Mann, the Nobel physicist who helped start the Santa Fe Institute. His book *The Quark and the Jaguar* (1994), was subtitled *Adventures in the Simple and Complex* and it did indeed clarify two perplexing issues. It showed that any definition of complexity will be partly context dependent, and to that extent related to the tastes and culture of those measuring the links. For instance, in Alexander's diagram above it would take knowledge about city neighbourhoods and their informal links as well as counting the obvious connections, the street patterns and pathways. Gell-Mann also showed that the sheer number of links was not the only measure.[69] 'Effective complexity', as he termed it, existed between order and chaos, as a rising curve – that was to be expected – but then it suddenly fell away. A work could have too many links, and its quality would decline!

In effect, systems such as large, fast aeroplanes get more complex as they evolve in size and speed, until like the Concord, they become too complicated. The route from simple to complicated is made by adding more elements along the way, rising up a hill until an optimum 'effective complexity' is reached, after which adding more elements makes the system less complex. From this perspective, complication is a type of simplicity, but at the far end of the scale, increasing entropy or chaos (see diagram, 102 below).

This sounds intuitively obvious and accords with the notion that some animals are more highly evolved, more complex, than others. The idea was leading biologists, in the era of computers and genetics, to the measurement of this quality. In theory at least, the complexity of something – the jaguar of Gell-Mann's title is very positively complex – could be calculated by its 'algorithmic information content': ie the length of a concise computer program that it would take to describe the object in question. This would be very long in the case of a beautiful, leaping jaguar and somewhat longer in the case of *Homo sapiens*. But in principle at least, it was measurable. A new branch of mathematics, 'algorithmic complexity theory', had been developed by Charles Bennett of IBM and, so the claim was, it could measure evolutionary complexity.[70] How smart, or developed, or advanced, in short how complex was a species according to one criterion or another.

BELOW [101] **Hox genes of the fruit fly**. The eight basic Hox genes determine the body plan of the embryo (below) and the later adult (above). Each gene regulates the specific region of the fly, or human's, body. Regulatory genes control when and where other genes get turned on, for instance where and when to start building

lab   pb

HEA

an eye, and this sets off a cascade of further interacting genes in the sub-assembly. (Modified from SB Carroll, *Nature* 376, 1995, New York Review of Books, 11 May 2006, The Ulster Medical Society, 2006)

)ULT

| *Antp* | *Ubx* | *abd-A* | *Abd-B* |

BRYO

RAX   ABDOMEN

JMAN

The attempt to pin this down motivated several post-modern scientists. Potentially by measuring the DNA one could see how evolved a species was, how far it had climbed up the epigenetic landscape, the mountain of competition it had to ascend in fighting off the predators and its near relatives. By the Millennium the goal of computing 'effective complexity' seemed in sight. However, when the human genome was finally deciphered in 2002 there were some surprises that underscored the value of organisation in the whole story. It turned out human beings had far fewer genes than previously thought – only about 25,000, and did not even have the most! Mice had about the same number, and the relatively simple nematode worm had 14,000. We might be near the top in terms of numbers, but it was the organisation that mattered, the way regulatory genes, Hox genes, switch the others on and off that was just as important. Again, this was a relatively recent idea only developed since the 1970s.

Hox genes are general purpose ones that lay out the basic body forms of many animals, including flies and humans. They direct the embryo – 'the head goes there, the tail over there'. [101] They are homologous (inherited from a common ancestor) and, being regulatory, can obviously move evolution forward or back in quick jumps. By and large evolution works with similar genes for its sub-assemblies. For instance, we share the Pax 6 gene, the one that regulates the eyes, with virtually every animal. This is in spite of the large differences in structure between our eyes and those, say, of insects. The same goes for genes that control the sub-assemblies of legs, wings, arms, fins and pumping blood through the arteries. The key is in the switching of these Hox genes, they enable the same gene to be used differently in different animals. Complexity is thus created, in part, by nature using old genes in new organisational ways.[71]

The post-modern debate goes on, biologists still dispute how to measure the value of complexity. As mentioned we know it is not just the biological complexity in terms of genome size (minus the Junk DNA) that counts. The morphology of a species has been put forward as another candidate, and also the flexibility of its behaviour, and even its number of cell types. The jury is out, but organised complexity is still the leading candidate in nature. So it is with cosmic evolution, with such inanimate things as crystals, solar systems and galaxies. Cosmic and natural evolution *are* the growth in complexity!

After many books came out on the subject in the early 1990s, post-modernism entered its second phase based on the sciences of complexity (shown on p 150, above). The new paradigm was summarised in such titles as M Mitchell Waldrop's *Complexity, The Emerging Science at the Edge of Order and Chaos* and Roger Lewin's *Complexity, Life on the Edge of Chaos*. As both titles suggested, complexity was to be found at an edge, and this was located somewhere between a simple order and complicated chaos. The question of exactly where this edge happened to be varied for each science and its community, as Gell-Mann had observed, but that it was the place of maximum creativity and 'computability' was clear. To my way of thinking, it was also the place of maximum multivalence, or value.

In *The Architecture of the Jumping Universe* (1995), I put forward a cosmic axiology, a rough measure of organisational complexity of different kinds of object, varying from simple systems, such as a black hole, to very complicated ones, such as the buzzing confusion of white noise, the chatter at a cocktail party. [102] This axiology was a graph measuring value as complexity, and it had that rising and falling shape that Murray Gell-Mann and others at the Sante Fe Institute had derived. It was a *metaphorical* measure of cosmic value, of course, since there is no way one could write a concise program of a rainforest or the brain or paintings by Jackson Pollock (though computer scientists now claim to be able to distinguish his fractal qualities from those of his counterfeiters).[72] The aim of the diagram was to visualise comparative complexity as the basis of value,

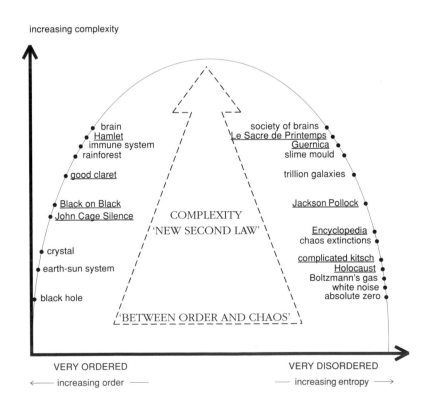

LEFT [102] **Cosmic Axiology – a formal measure of simplicity, complexity and complication.** Illustrated here is a value system that relates to the fundamental processes of the universe. Very simple, ordered systems are to the far left, very complicated systems to the far right, and on the 'edge between order and chaos' are systems which extract higher levels of organisation from both order and chaos. Very simple deterministic systems that repeat themselves again and again were the first to be discovered, such as the earth–sun system that Newton used as his prime example of nature; or the black on black canvases (produced by Modern artists in the 1910s and again in the 1950s). Both natural and cultural systems can be loosely described by concise algorithms, or rules for generating these things. To the far right are those entropic systems, which burn up computer time in description.

or quality, or critical depth. Critics of the arts have often used the metaphor of depth to describe the rich and convincing complexity of a work, and this depth has its counterpart in the diagram.

Between the two extremes of order and chaos, and at right angles to them, are those things which have higher and higher levels of organisation, greater quality: a rainforest, the immune system, and the most complex things we know, the human brain and society of brains. The idea of the diagram was that great works of art are analogues of such cosmic and organic organisation, and that their depth (or height in the drawing) is usually being gauged in critical discourse. Thus a melange of artefacts could be compared to those in the same genre. Here, however, I cut across the disciplines to emphasise that it was the quality of organisation at stake, even that between a good and bad claret. Once again, to capture these distinctions, critics spontaneously resort to mixed metaphors that probe the depth of a work.

To bring out how these differences might be measured, consider three different pavilions designed by a computer: a very regular one, a chaotic one, and one having high organisation. In the first, most ordered program, it might repeat a regular sequence of posts and beams laid out as a row, made of nine identical cubes. Here the program to write is simple and small. It might say 'join cubes flush on side, repeat, and line them up in a row'. Next, imagine nine differently shaped rooms brought to the site, and joined at random however they came off the vehicle. The program specifying this is still relatively simple and short in length, except for the details of how to join the elements where they can be entered. 'Drop each room so that it joins another at the door.' Programmatically speaking, this chaotic layout is another form of simplicity. The third pavilion of this thought experiment has actually been built, and a computer did a great deal of this thought and fabrication. It is the temporary structure for the Serpentine Gallery in London, designed in 2002 by the Japanese architect Toyo Ito and the British engineer Cecil Balmond, a pavilion that is both a good illustration of the post-modern sciences of complexity and a good building in itself. [103] Just as Mies van der Rohe's Barcelona Pavilion of 1929 summarised the Modern Movement, this one epitomises the new paradigm. Toyo Ito describes the method of construction thus:

> The structure is a lattice system made from steel flat bars. Flat bar beams with a depth of 550mm and varying thickness according to the structural stresses were welded in the factory, panellised in a transportable size, and eventually bolted together on site. Although the structure may at first glance seem random, it is defined by an algorithm of an expanding and rotating square.[73]

THESE PAGES [103 a, b, c] Toyo Ito and Cecil Balmond, **Serpentine Pavilion**, London 2002. A clear use of a simple algorithm to generate a beautiful structure. This is modified in colour, size and shape to capture its natural green and blue setting in a striking way. (C Jencks)

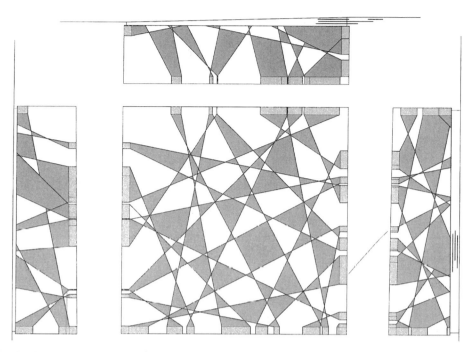

One can see the algorithm most clearly at work in the roof plan, where squares, triangles and rhomboids flare from various points. The result is thus, in one sense, an example of 'deterministic chaos', the repetition of a simple sequence to produce complex results, like the famous Mandelbrot set, which gives infinite complexity with the simple formula, $Z = Z^2 + C$. The algorithm of the expanding square gives the building aesthetic depth, a unity running through variety. This is deepened by the way openings frame bits of green and blue nature and that idea is underscored by various shades of green on the interior. Wall, floor and ceiling march to the same but varied program that, if it were written out in its entirety, would be much longer than those for the two previous pavilions of my thought experiment.

This comparison of the three types of pavilion (illustrating simplicity, chaos and organised complexity) itself oversimplifies the issue of measurement and quality. For instance, it does not bring out the meanings of the fractured white cube, and other key semantic issues such as the way the fractal forms are related to the leaves and branches they frame. Nevertheless, it does show the idea of algorithmic complexity theory, and how the 'effective complexity' of a work in principle might be measured: ie by comparing the lengths of the shortest computer programs that can generate a building, in each case, and understanding that the longest sequence reveals the greatest complexity.

Returning now to the bigger picture of nature, we can also find in the diagram above, [102] the two basic arrows of cosmic time that scientists have contrasted since the nineteenth century. The Second Law of Thermodynamics, which contends that all closed systems tend towards more disorder, is considered one of the most basic laws of the universe, entropy, the law of aging and why increasing chaos leads to dissolution. This, in effect, moves in the diagram to the right. However, at right angles to it, is depicted what some at the Santa Fe Institute are looking for, the 'New Second Law' of organic and cosmic growth. This seems to be building things up in the reverse direction, though really the right angle is a better depiction. For all growth in organisation also pays a price in terms of increasing entropy, in another system. For instance, as Gaia, the self-organising earth system grows towards greater complexity, it does so by living off the sun's energy. This is why it makes sense to conceptualise the two laws as moving not in exactly opposite ways but at some angle to each other. They are interdependent, as the complexity scientist and Nobel laureate Ilya Prigogine observed in his landmark book *Order Out of*

ABOVE [104 a, b] Entropic versus creative use of steel. Jeff Koons' **Diamond (Pink)**, high-chrome stainless steel with transparent colour coating, 1994–5. Blownup and tilted on a clasp, it is not a diamond, and neither pink nor gold. Koons simplifies what already is a cliché taking more from culture than he gives back, while Frank Gehry, in his

Experience Music Project, (ABOVE) Seattle, 1995–2001, explores new effects with coloured steel for their relationship to pop music. Gold, purple, red, silver and black hues rock and roll their way across a palette of silver and pale blue. They are meant to capture Jimi Hendrix's song 'Purple Haze' – architecture as congealed music. (Koons' *Diamond* exhibited at V&A, London, 2006, photos C Jencks)

Chaos.[74] While it is clear that these two different processes are somewhat opposed, it is not clear if there is a single New Second Law or several versions of it. A recent formulation by the astrophysicist Eric Chaisson claims that there is just one, energy. More particularly, he argues that it is the 'energy rate density', that counts, and that this is the universal measure of the growth of complexity, intimately related to the expansion of the universe.[75]

One final point about my diagram and its limitation. While it shows the general value of increasing complexity, it is a truth that is bounded and contextual like all others. There are cases, discussed above, where too much complexity leads to complication and others where simplicity is valued for itself, especially in the case of a Minimalist artist. For instance, Constantin Brancusi claimed he started from complexity, not from simplicity, and then worked until he could find an *apt* reduction of it. Good criticism has always distinguished such intelligent creations from those clichés that start and end in the one-liner. Again they depend on the particular organisation. In an analogous manner, all scientific laws and algorithms are such apt reductions, the ones that do in fact work, and it is obviously the pursuit of science to define them, cogently. Lastly, there have been many artists since the 1930s who have pursued a programme of elimination, consciously producing random signs. Here the Second Law of Thermodynamics, or entropy, is given expression. Dissolution, decay and death are the themes and the results, while never absolutely chaotic (because this is impossible) can be striking. Leonardo advised the artist to look at random elements in nature, decay and cracks in the wall, for inspiration, a method of learning also practised by Chinese artists. The destructive and primitive streak in contemporary art, so evident with the Dadaists and the followers of George Bataille who advocated the *informe* (or formless), continues to be a major tradition of our time. Partly it is a metaphysical position of Late-Modernism, the belief that society itself is destructive and always co-opts anything of value. Partly it is the destructive-creative method of overturning categories and shocking an audience into awareness. Occasionally it produces striking and significant work, as in the case of Ed Kienholz and Damien Hirst, but it is just as likely to result in the kitsch of those such as Jeff Koons. [104] Here the transformation of cliché is minimal. The work exploits cultural value in an entropic way, taking more than it gives back. Clearly there is a place for an art of decay, but like entropy it tends to bore.

Two types of evolution

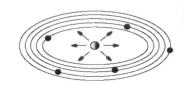

The important idea behind the post-modern sciences of complexity is that the universe has a tendency to be interesting, and grow ever more so with time. This is known most generally as 'symmetry breaking', and the positive arrow of time, the optimistic and benign counterpart to the negative arrow, entropy. Quality, superior organisation and increasing sensitivity are built into the direction of the universe, so the idea goes, even if this general trend has exceptions. This new second law contends that there is a predisposition towards increasing complexity, *not* a predetermination. The view is not Neo-Calvinism, the predestination of John Knox.

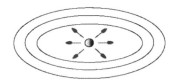

Because of physical laws such as gravity, and the tendency for them to make all matter self-organise, the universe displays ever-increasing organisation. For instance, stars and planets inevitably evolve out of gas and exhibit a limited kind of teleology, or intermittent directional growth. [105]. One can conceive of five basic breaks in symmetry, as the planets emerge from the gas, dust and heat of the early solar system.

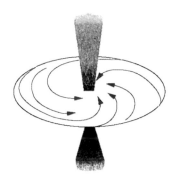

On earth such self-organisation precedes organic evolution by billions of years, and it operates according to different laws than natural selection. This could be called crystallised evolution: the tendency of all material systems, given the input of continuous free energy, to develop towards more crystallised or defined states. This is surprising. We are apt to accord entropy, or the dissipation of energy, the primary place in universal evolution. Everything ages, disorder always increases, heat is always lost when work is done. A cup of hot tea always cools down and, when cream is added to it, coffee turns a muddy light brown. Consider, however, a miracle cup of coffee, one that oscillates between light and dark brown, and generates cream rings while it jumps back and forth. There would have to be something phoney, of course, because this pattern contradicts the Second Law of Thermodynamics. The mixed coffee could not go backwards in time, un-dissolve itself, much less continue to do so several times pulsating into the bargain.

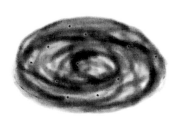

Yet this weird, oscillating behaviour is precisely what happens with chemical clocks and with many systems that are pushed far from equilibrium. They jump back and forth between states, forming beautiful visual patterns as they keep breaking symmetry. The most famous of these is the chemical reaction set up by the Russian scientists Belousov and Zhabotinskii in the early 1960s.[76] In their experiment, now known as the BZ Reaction, one can watch a muddy red mixture of chemicals slowly turn blue, then red, then blue. [106] Moreover, as it does so it produces circular blue wave fronts, the equivalent of our miracle coffee spontaneously growing circles of cream! Ordered spirals emerge from this mixture, one after another, and then turn into more complex whorls of blue and red target-shapes. This reaction takes place in a petri dish and thus the results are flat, like paintings. Indeed, in their way they are as beautiful as the target paintings of the 1960s, those by Jasper Johns or Jules Olitski.

So, one might conclude, completely dead chemicals of the right mix, under autocatalysis can create interesting works of art. Or the kind of patterns one thinks are alive; primitive, circular organisms – pseudo-fossils? Well, these reactions *look like* living works of art, unfolding into super-patterns. One can watch the passage of time; observe simple circles evolve into combined cloud shapes, the kind of thing Chinese artisans carved in the eighteenth century. Ultimately, the BZ reaction will use up its reactants, nature's art will cease and entropy will again assert itself in the petri dish. But, before this point, positive and negative feedback reactions drive the system into higher levels of complexity, just as the sun drives the earth and, all the while, Gaia fends off global warming. Positive and negative feedback, carefully balanced to create sustained quality, is the great idea uniting the post-modern sciences. It can be found at the smallest and largest scale, from the atom to the universe that generates energy as it expands.

Similar patterns of self-organisation can be found in the primitive living organism known as the slime mould, which at once stage in its evolution generates the same kind of spirals. Again, the general notion that development occurs through breaks in symmetry, going from simplicity towards greater complexity, is the principle except with the slime mould the breaks are part of a continuous revolution back to simplicity. Life always merges cyclical with linear time. But, there is at least one, fascinating non-living object that freezes this process at various stages of evolution, and thus makes of symmetry breaking a permanent visual feature. It is called a Liesegang rock, after Raphael Eduard Liesegang who elucidated the process in 1896. [107] Since such rocks are nature's frozen symbol of self-organisation, I have collected and mounted them on a bronze base with variable 'arms'. The flat bronze base, the most perfect state of symmetry, is then broken by various actions – battering, piercing, folding, squeezing – to parallel the symmetry breaking in the rock and underline this all-important principle of nature. In southern Scotland, the Liesegang rock typically is a white or grey stone with red target patterns. These grow as complete spheres throughout the matrix. Like crystals these rings grow as a wave front of atomic reactions. Not surprisingly, such self-organising systems have become the model in the post-modern period for thinking about the universe, sublating the modern model of the machine. While the deterministic world-view lasted from Newton's time up through the 1950s, and the repetitive nature of the machine dominated the architectural world, a more interesting image of reality is beginning to be accepted as standard science.

Organic evolution, like the crystalline variety, also has a general direction towards greater complexity and it is not only propelled by the same self-organising forces but also by natural selection. If we present this progress with a visual metaphor, it would not be the usual Darwinian evolutionary tree of stately growth (much too pleasant an image), but the closely cropped bush with many more dead branches than living shoots. It would be the proverbial leggy shrub hated by the gardener, mostly twigs and only a few leaves. As Stephen Jay Gould argues in *Wonderful Life*, nature is a grim reaper, and natural selection means what he calls natural 'decimation' – killing off nine so that the tenth might survive. Thus the two types of evolution, crystalline and natural, combine to produce more highly organised systems and individuals. This is the main plot of the universe story, but it is a progressive drama that encounters many setbacks.

ABOVE [107] **Liesegang rocks**, like a crystal or the Belousov-Zhabotinskii Reaction, reveal growth in a series of wave forms. Iron deposits, in a matrix of white sand, break the uniform symmetry and pulsate to form a series of rings. Self-organisation and symmetry breaking are the post-modern metaphors and model of the universe. Hence the bronze planes have their smooth symmetry broken and the tentacular arms organise the rock at several points of equilibrium. (C Jencks)

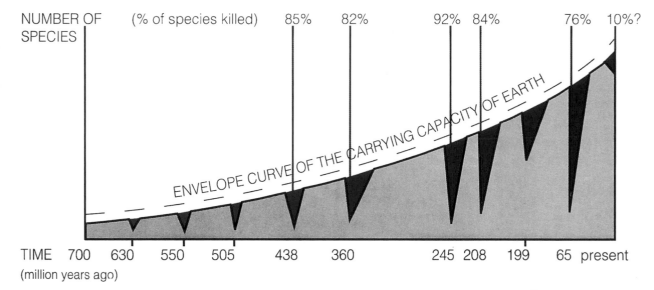

NUMBER OF SPECIES | (% of species killed) 85% 82% 92% 84% 76% 10%?

ENVELOPE CURVE OF THE CARRYING CAPACITY OF EARTH

TIME 700 630 550 505 438 360 245 208 199 65 present
(million years ago)

ABOVE [108] **The general trend of organic evolution** appears to be positive if we concentrate on the envelope curve connecting all the smaller curves. However, five major mass extinctions, which wiped out 70 to 96 per cent of all species, raise a question about the inevitability of progress in species and biomass. The last extinction, 65 million years ago, destroyed the ammonids and dinosaurs and allowed mammals, and us, to flourish. We are at the start of the sixth mass extinction, when one-tenth of all species has already been cut back because we are inadvertently destroying habitat. Even though these mass extinctions occur, the sun is pouring in more free energy, and thereby indirectly creating more biomass. Hence the assumption of an ascending envelope curve that reaches higher and higher ceilings: these would be the carrying capacity of earth at different epochs. There is a general, if not inevitable, direction to organic evolution. (Sources: *Evolutionary Progress*, edited by Matthew Nitecki, University of Chicago Press (Chicago), 1988, pp 42 & 300; Rick Gore, 'The March Toward Extinction', *National Geographic*, June 1989, pp 662–99)

If we adopt another metaphor, and chart the last 650 million years as a whole, we find an increasing slope of progress; that is, an increasing number of species, genera, families and biomass. All of these developments are positive, but they are attended by punctuations and suffering. [108] There is the Permian/Triassic transition, when perhaps 92 per cent of all species were wiped out; or the most recent one 65 million years ago, when 76 per cent of the species became extinct. The story depends on the particular focus and interpretation: the slope and jumps are positive, the catastrophes negative and the overall graph, perhaps optimistic but nonetheless punctuated by infinite tragedy.

The discovery of mass extinctions and their cosmic causes is another part of the post-modern picture that only fully emerged in the 1980s when evidence of cometary collisions began to be collected in many parts of the world. The presence of craters caused by asteroids were obvious signs, but further ones such as the accompanying fractured quartz and iridium helped us to construct a detailed picture of the way life's usual progress could be destroyed. This had conflicting implications. On the one hand, it showed how extraordinarily robust Gaia was, the self-organising system that could survive lethal hits and then after many million years grow back to health. Furthermore, it made clear that positive things could emerge from this mass destruction, that we and other mammals could evolve because the dinosaurs were wiped out 65 million years ago. On the other hand, the evidence also showed the fragility of life, the way over 99 per cent of species that have ever lived are no more, and that the chaotic disturbance of the asteroid belt will hurl another big projectile our way.

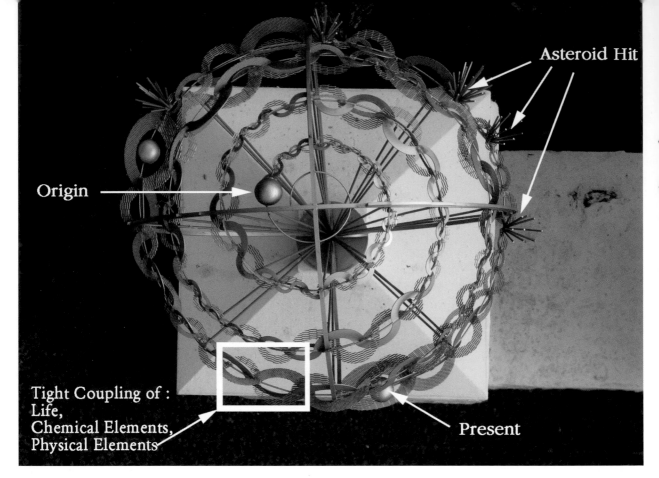

Origin

Asteroid Hit

Tight Coupling of :
Life,
Chemical Elements,
Physical Elements

Present

Much more detailed information on self-organisation and destruction became public by the late 1980s and the significant thing, as far as cosmogenesis was concerned, is that the evidence was both widespread and contradictory.

This led to the mixed metaphysics that is the current universe story. Contrast this with the modern world-view that was necessarily pessimistic, with entropy as the ultimate reality. It finds expression, as we have seen, in Minimalist art, nihilism and Beckett's plays, and is expounded by countless philosophers, such as Bertrand Russell. His classic formulation, as the sun and stars burn up their nuclear fuel, was rather melodramatic but it was based on the then current science:

> all the labours of the ages, all the devotion, all the inspiration, all the noonday brightness of the human genius, are destined to extinction in the vast death of the solar system, and the whole temple of Man's achievement must inevitably be buried beneath the debris of a universe in ruins – all these things, if not quite beyond dispute, are yet so nearly certain that no philosophy which rejects them can hope to stand. Only within the scaffolding of these truths, only on the firm foundation of unyielding despair, can the soul's habitation henceforth be safely built …[77]

Obviously, the danger of reaching metaphysical conclusions based on contemporary science is that the hypotheses and evidence will change. While it is still accepted that the solar system will be burned up by the expanding sun in perhaps 4 billion years, it also turns out the Milky Way and the Andromeda Galaxy will meet up sometime near then producing all sorts of new stars, new planets and unpredictable events. Beyond this, it is likely that human cultures or their successors will long since have colonised other planets. In any case, given the way cosmology today is postulating the universe speeding up in its expansion, perhaps caused by the energy of the quantum vacuum, it is premature to regard entropy as the final word. One theory has the expansion itself creating more energy. Indeed, there are so many contending theories of the origin and fate of the cosmos, from superstrings to branes, so many different plausible theories of ultimate physics, that any metaphysics built upon them cannot, as Russell would put it, 'hope to stand'. What we do know, based on standard science and the 13 billion year history, is more modest.

It leads to what I have just called a mixed metaphysics and this can be put in various ways. The lesson of Gaia, the earth as a self-organising system, shows that there is a certain teleonomy or local purpose that regulates temperature, and gases such as oxygen, in a way that sustains life. [109] In spite of the increase in the sun's temperature by 25 per cent over its history, Gaia has kept the earth relatively cool. Today, global warming threatens that balance, but Gaia is strong enough with its feedback mechanisms to sustain life, even if not ours. Human action thus has a moral dimension that is mirrored by a harmonious interaction of life and the physical rhythms of the planet. Our ethics and global balance are thus analogous and connected, if only loosely. Another implication of standard science concerns our relationship to the cosmos. Since we are so fundamentally built into its laws, as the Anthropic Principle and other discoveries show, we are not as modernists claimed alienated from the universe. If the cosmos is very likely to create sentient creatures such as us, then one view might follow the metaphor of the complexity scientist Stuart Kauffman, and his book *At Home in the Universe*.[78] This is quite different from the Christian view, that we are a chosen species of God, or the humanist position, that we are the measure of all things. Perhaps it is still too anthropomorphic, but it does make us more rooted and less accidental than the alternative, Neo-Darwinian view.

A cultural drive?

There is clearly more than one perspective arising from contemporary science. Indeed, several views of evolution compete with each other and some scientists, like Stephen Jay Gould, deny that there is any overall progress at all. Post-modern pluralism is as real here as elsewhere. Inevitably, because scientists are trained in scepticism, they may not see the narrative of cosmogenesis, nor interpret its various meanings including the importance of the narrative itself. But consider three positive implications in addition to the overall story.

The idea that the universe is a single, unbroken, creative event that is still unfolding from its origin, entails several things. First, that it is dynamic and still creative as a whole relational unit. This is quite different both from the origin event that Christians regard as finished, after God created the world in *Genesis*, and the modern view of a dead and mechanical nature. Cosmogenesis, by contrast, entails agency between beings, and relationship at all levels of the universe. Second, it implies that human beings are an important part of that story as interpreters and celebrants. As we project ourselves onto a cosmic plane, we can also be seen as participants. Global pollution and the understanding of nature's deep laws are two opposite examples of this participation. Lastly, because the cosmos produces surprising, humorous creations of beauty, because it naturally produces the quality of complexity, it looks as a whole rather benign. And there is another positive implication. Within the evidence of growing complexity is the idea that, given enough time, it must even produce culture.

Again this is a fairly recent notion, more characteristic of the post-modern than the modern paradigm. Animals and insects are now appreciated for their ability to learn and pass on various forms of communication. Their social patterns are altogether comparable to human habits, rules and traditions. For instance, the architecture of Bower birds and the mini-skyscrapers of termites, serviced by their ingenious form of air-conditioning, are examples of artistic creativity. They are surprising traditions, in their particularity, yet typical of the shared creativity in general. Primitive forms of thinking, even basic explorative concepts, are apparent in the collective action of ant colonies. The more we study nature, the more we find continuities of culture. Indeed, not surprisingly many members of the Third Culture hold this view and believe that there are also laws of emergence that virtually guarantee increasing organisation. The work of the Nobel laureate Ilya Prigogine and his book *Order Out of Chaos* typify the argument which is coming increasingly from many quarters, the

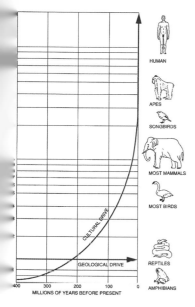

ABOVE [110] **The two basic evolutionary drives**, external and internal to the organism, geological and cultural. As the brain to body size ratio increases, the cultural drive takes over from external pressures and evolution speeds up. Birds, mammals, songbirds and apes can learn and pass on culture, thereby adapting faster. The higher the cultural drive the faster the evolution and the stronger the pressure to evolve. Evolution is always changing its methods, forces and even laws! Today the human species – driven by late capitalism – is the natural selector writ large. Nature, having produced culture, has given way to it. (Source: Allan Wilson, 'The Molecular Basis of Evolution', *Scientific American*, October 1985, pp 164–73, © Joan Starwood)

complexity scientists at the Santa Fe Institute and those who support the anthropic principle: scientists such as Freeman Dyson, Paul Davies and Fred Hoyle; evolutionists such as Allan Wilson.[79]

The last mentioned argues that there is a 'cultural drive' in nature and, the bigger the ratio of brain size to body size of a species, the stronger this drive is and the faster it goes. The more intelligent species we know, birds, dolphins and chimpanzees, have large brain to body size ratios, and their evolution has been concomitantly faster. [110] Brain size itself matters and as a general rule intelligence increases with it. Thus the usual paleontological evidence, showing the growth in cranium size from the first primates through the chimpanzees to human beings, reveals a very crude progress of superior emergent properties at every stage. There are of course exceptions and although we do not know exactly how intelligent the Neanderthals were, their brains were bigger than those of *Homo sapiens*. As with the number of genes, absolute size matters but not absolutely. It is only a partial measure of complexity. Cultural drive and the progress of intelligence have to be treated as crude approximations.

Also the meaning of these concepts can be inverted. With the reductive view of modern science, similar ideas led Behaviourist scientists to explain higher levels of development in terms of lower ones. Thinking was reduced to elaborate sets of conditioned reflexes, cogitation to complex versions of Pavlov's salivating dogs. By extension rats running through a maze, seeking rewards and avoiding punishment, became a paradigm for the human condition. This might seem to work as a model of behaviour on Wall Street, but even here it is reductive. As Arthur Koestler wrote, it substituted for the anthropomorphic view of the rat, the ratomorphic view of man. Indeed, Koestler was right. We can learn as much by elevating a primate towards us as reducing our behaviour to theirs.

I remember watching a film in the 1990s of Bonobo chimpanzees being taught to learn human commands by a group of American ethologists working at Georgia State University. It was a humorous and amazing encounter between ape and human. The chimps could master a vocabulary of two hundred words, and comprehensive skills such as creating their own tools. One had the verbal comprehension of a two and half year old child. The debate with linguists, such as Noam Chomsky, raged over whether they could really understand the 'words' they were taught when used in a new sentence. Understanding is more than the conditioned reflex and fundamentally concerns meaning, the creative and flexible use of language. Hence the battle lines were drawn.

Scientists, who claimed Bonobos could understand language were led by a woman who had a few chimps live at home with her where they could develop a sympathy for the cultural context of speech. She has the unlikely name of Dr Savage-Rumbaugh and her friend, a most intelligent Bonobo, goes by the anthropomorphic sounding Kanzi. [111] This close relationship made for complex interaction, where speaking involves fully comprehending the tone of voice and situation in which words are spoken. Kanzi thereby learned by eavesdropping when his real mother chimp was being taught. Since chimpanzees do not have a larynx, communication from them had to be via a computer keyboard. Otherwise they responded to the human voice.

ABOVE [111] **Kanzi, the Bonobo** that seems to be able to understand complex and creative speech. (Great Ape Trust)

The film demonstrated how Kanzi could master complex sentences, and creative thoughts he had never heard before. One novel command was, 'Give the dog a shot!' The chimp picked up a hypodermic syringe, took off the cap and injected a toy dog nearby. Another surreal demand was: 'Kanzi, go get the ball outdoors and put it in the refrigerator!' This bizarre sentence demanded that he distinguish the ball outside (which he did not see) from the one inside the room (which he did). That takes quite a lot of thought, and will power, because the first temptation, even for a child of three, is to get the ball they see. Kanzi immediately put it in the refrigerator, but – 'without a moment's thought'? No, obviously like the several ambiguous ways he could 'shoot' a dog, the chimp had to string several unusual ideas together and distinguish them from a cliché. According to the experimenters, the chimps responded correctly to 70 per cent of the unfamiliar or novel sentences. In like manner, chimpanzees reveal general creativity and the ability to pass on new habits throughout their society. In effect, they have a primitive form of culture, even if it does not include a developed language capacity that will satisfy all linguists. Ironically, one challenger of this stringent intellectual category was named 'Nim Chimsky'.

More recently a species of monkey from Nigeria has shown similar creativity, the ability to combine alarm signals in new ways that depend on the context.[80] Thus they give the alarm call, 'pyow' warning other animals against a leopard, and 'hack' when an eagle is hovering nearby. But, for instance, when they combine them into a complex sentence of 'pyows' and 'hacks' it can signify, not surprisingly, 'let's get out of here', a meaning that was tested under different conditions. The implication is that these monkeys have a primitive syntax and can choose between the meanings of the same sign depending on the sentence and situation. This capability is on the way to abstract thought, even if it has not yet arrived.

One can generalise from many similar examples the notion that the creative use of tradition and communication runs through the animal world. Those at the Santa Fe Institute term all living creatures 'complex adaptive systems', or CAS for short.[81] The idea behind this abstract formulation is that the universe inevitably creates complex adaptive systems, living creatures like us, that are trying to figure out what is going on. They seek either to adapt their behaviour to the environment, or to change it, or more likely do a bit of both. This intellectual quest is normal and will emerge in evolution as predictably as do other universals of life, such as the means of locomotion. In effect, CAS go all the way down the living realms to the smallest creatures, the one-cell organisms that swim about feeling their way towards light and food, retaining a rudimentary memory of their setting.

Look at this situation from an abstract point of view. It shows that for any living creature the quest to figure out the environment is a deep orientation with a spiritual overtone. What is going on, is the implicit question, where are we going, what does it mean? – such is the logic built into the existential situation for sentient creatures capable of minimum thought. These metaphysical questions, in spite of being asked by modern painters such as Gauguin, were put on the Index, by modern philosophers such as AJ Ayer, for being meaningless. Today they are again on the agenda and conceived as spiritual queries though, as I will mention in the next chapter, in today's metaphysics the distinctions between mind, body and spirit are becoming fuzzy. In any case, the notion of a complex adaptive system, abstract as it is, brings out the logical relationship between a sentient creature and the larger universe.

All living creatures are pulled and pushed by their environment, both attracted by such things as its beauty, and forced to decode its regularities in order to survive. Again, it's a mixed cosmic view with bad taste and humour included in the mix. Woody Allen's metaphysical cry, 'What has the universe ever done for me?' gets an answer from Alan Guth, the scientist who proposed the inflationary period right after the beginning: 'It's given you the ultimate free lunch.' The question and response beg the larger view. At the most abstract level, one could say that if the universe has a cultural drive, then it will naturally produce creatures who have a cosmic passion, the desire to understand and relate to the larger context that has given them birth. This passion precedes religion and science, logically and historically, because it is built into the existential relationship between sentience and the cosmos, between child and parent. The point is that the whole story of the cosmos unfolding to life and culture necessarily takes a lot of time and effort.

There are no short cuts. It takes many billion years of successive creation to give birth to species that can ponder and enjoy its qualities, many offspring that are loved and nurtured in an unending chain of being. Anything that survives, physical or living, is part of this 13 billion year narrative, in the most direct sequence of parent and child. The universe grows in complexity and its offspring grow in culture, as they experience and try to understand it. Of course, the analogy of a familial relationship entails discord as well as love, scepticism as well as desire, criticism as well as understanding. Yet, it is no accident that the leading metanarrative in the post-modern paradigm has become our relationship to the expanding universe, a project that has barely started and is now inescapable.

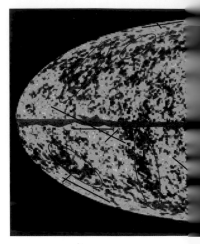

The universe project

Eric Chaisson, the astrophysicist at Tufts University in Boston, Massachusetts, has argued in his book *Cosmic Evolution* that now is the golden age of astrophysics and biochemistry. In terms of discovery and popularity this may be true although, as I have mentioned with the emergence of the Third Culture, science writing has become an essential part of contemporary culture in many other ways. With the end of the Modern Settlement the divisions between science and religion, not to mention the rest of culture, have become blurred. Primitive analogies are found at several levels between cosmic and human processes. For instance, the ecological balance between many species and their environment is perceived as a rudimentary form of ethics with implications for our own morality. The growth of complexity in privileged parts of the universe, such as stars, galaxies and the earth, is understood as being paid for by entropy in other places. Or, a parallel thought mixing these two realms: the increasing world economy, growing at 3 per cent per year, is exporting entropy to the increasing slums and poverty, which are outside the main centres of power. Such analogies between nature and culture may be more or less fitting, but they are normal habits of thought today that arise from the current state of knowledge and global change.

At different levels of reality, the universe is becoming the measure of all things and is wrapped into our daily life. Take the neutral questions of measuring space and time. In traditional cultures the yard, foot and inch systems had an anthropomorphic scale. From the Egyptian pharaoh to the king of England dimensions were taken off the ruler's body, from such members as his finger and outstretched arms. The Roman architect Vitruvius describes how one lays out a harmonious

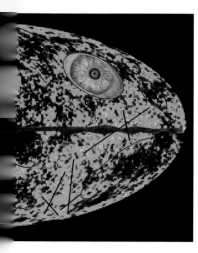

ABOVE [112] The eye of the universe – cosmic dimensions as revealed by the **Microwave Anisotropy Probe, or WMAP**, February 2003. According to this probe, dark matter constitutes 22 per cent of the stuff of the universe, our galactic unconscious that holds these bodies together. Dark energy, at 74 per cent, is much greater and harder to measure, while the visible universe – our tangible reality – is a mere 4 per cent, the atoms and stars etc we can see. Other basic measures were approximated, such as the age of 13.7 billion years, and rate of cosmic expansion, 71 kilometres per second per megaparsec. Colours indicate warmer (red-yellow) and cooler (blue) spots; the central red belt is our galaxy seen from the side. Note the clustering, exaggerated here by my crosses. The eye of consciousness reflects back on the history, its laws and possible cosmic codes.

temple by taking its proportions from a man lying down, moving his arms and legs about to generate a perfect circle. The square, another ideal form, also emerged. In the Renaissance this famous Vitruvian Man was drawn by several artists, particularly Leonardo da Vinci, who shows the figure doing ideal jumping jacks, as it were, for architects to follow. The French, being good modernists, abstracted such measurements and turned them into the metre, absolute units to be kept under lock and key. They were placed in a vacuum in Paris to fix this arbitrary standard for all time, with a French accent of course. Power resides in these weights and measures, as every tax authority has known, and the battle goes on between the Anglo-Saxon yard and the European metre. Since 1967, however, the situation has started to move away from an anthropomorphic and nationalist scale, and irreversibly so.

All fundamental measures, except the kilogram, have been put on a much more exact and universal basis as they are redefined in cosmic terms. Instead of measuring days, hours, minutes and seconds by the wobbly, erratic turns of the earth, it has been put on a regular atomic standard. A caesium clock has, since 1967, redefined the basic measure of the second as the duration of 9,192,631,770 cycles of atomic radiation. Since 1983, the metre has been redefined by international agreement as the distance that light travels through a vacuum, ie, in 1/299,792,458th of a second. Thus the ultimate unit of space is derived from an atomic unit of time – a convergence of space–time universality – and some day soon weight will also fall to the quantum standard. As the physicist Hans Christian von Baeyer states: 'In the twenty-first century the atom will replace man as the measure of all things'.[87] Indeed, now that further probes have been made, and a map has been made back to the first billionth second, the cosmos will become the standard for us, and the rest of nature that emerges from it. [112]

Such new orientation and recent discoveries lead scientists to religious metaphors. For instance, Stephen Hawking, otherwise an atheist, writes in *The Brief History of Time* that uncovering basic aspects of the cosmic code is like 'seeing the mind of God'. It reveals the ultimate laws on which everything is based. As mentioned, when the results of the COBE satellite mission were announced in 1992 scientists used just such a metaphor to describe what they saw. As Paul Davies put it in *The Mind of God*, published in the same year, the laws of nature turn out to have most of the attributes of God. They are universal (apply everywhere in the universe), absolute (do not depend on anything else), eternal (do not change with time), omnipotent (all-powerful), and creative of the universe (cosmogenic).[88] Today, scientists are questioning whether the laws and constants are eternal and unchanging, but in other respects the equation between the cosmic code and God still holds. Of course, if one pursues the metaphor to its limit the main difference between the two becomes pronounced. God, in most religions and metaphysics, is a personal, responsive creator who takes a daily interest in individuals and nations. The universe, while beneficent on the whole and fine-tuned to produce us, is nevertheless impersonal.

These are just metaphors, it is true, but for that very reason all the more crucial for culture, for both our self-image and seeing how we relate to the bigger picture. As Virgil wrote: 'We make our destinies through the gods we choose.' Destiny is partly shaped by ideas and their framing which feeds back onto society. There is a choice and a projective one at that. Knowledge and cultural development are at a point today when the universe story is still emerging as the grand narrative, the cosmogenesis that in the West is sublating *Genesis*. Many attempts are made at telling this account, as I have suggested, all of them partial, none of them capturing the mixture of truth and poetry necessary to be convincing. 'The universe project' is a collective endeavour that includes not only all the scientists and authors I have mentioned above but also artists, craftsmen, historians, archaeologists, intellectuals and interested amateurs (deriving from the Latin *amator*, as in 'lover' of a subject). No group or individual can get a final take on this account, but more and more relevant versions are emerging. If there is one project that is gathering strength across a globalised culture, it is the construction of this common narrative. In the following section, I add my contribution to this endeavour not because it is definitive but because, knowing it well, it allows me to make critical points.

A jumping universe

A naïve, but significant question that arises when pondering the universe is, what does it look like? It appears like itself, might be one answer; or, nothing we can see since there is no outside space from which to take a look; or, a shapeless, edgeless, expanding four-dimensional thing – are also possible answers. Nonetheless one can conceive of a growing shape and time-line, starting from an infinitely small point, which expands during an inflationary period very quickly then with a constant stately speed. In the late 1980s with the help of Paul Davies and others I started working on such ideas, light-cone universes, to see what possible combined shapes might emerge. [113] The result brought together three basic hypotheses, which looked very robust at the time.

OPPOSITE [113] **The Jumping Universe Model**, 1990. The steps show the various jumps in organisation. At the bottom the four forces divided soon after the origin yet they still hold it all together making a universe (not a pluriverse) and the eye, at the top, reflects back on its history and meaning. This model was drawn when the age of the cosmos was approximated at 15 billion years and it shows 30 basic jumps, some of which have been reordered in the intervening years. The extraordinary fact of our time is that we can recount this cosmogenesis back to the first microseconds, even if some of the detail is wrong.

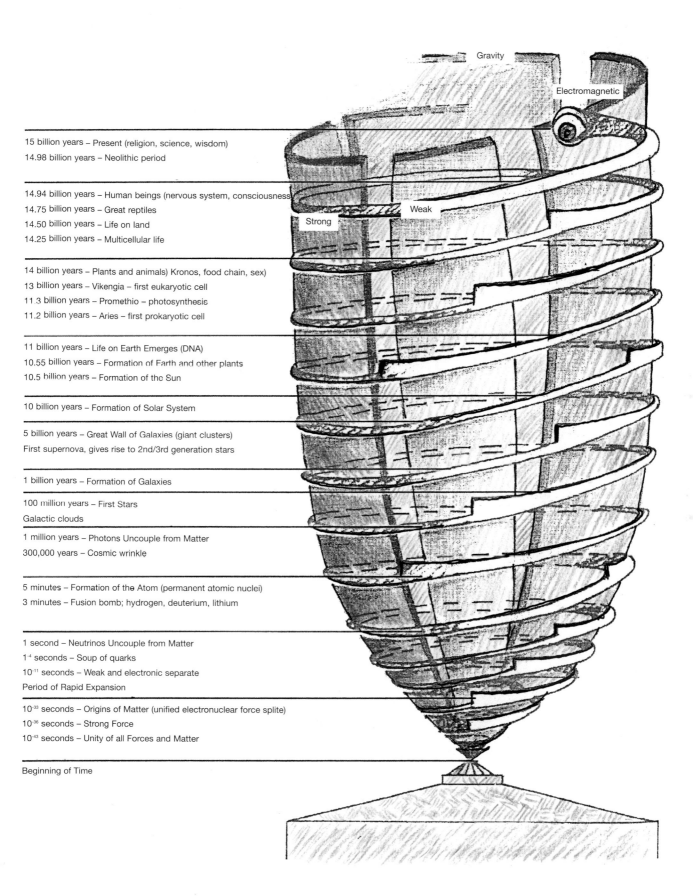

Gravity

Electromagnetic

Weak

Strong

15 billion years – Present (religion, science, wisdom)
14.98 billion years – Neolithic period

14.94 billion years – Human beings (nervous system, consciousness
14.75 billion years – Great reptiles
14.50 billion years – Life on land
14.25 billion years – Multicellular life

14 billion years – Plants and animals) Kronos, food chain, sex)
13 billion years – Vikengia – first eukaryotic cell
11.3 billion years – Promethio – photosynthesis
11.2 billion years – Aries – first prokaryotic cell

11 billion years – Life on Earth Emerges (DNA)
10.55 billion years – Formation of Earth and other plants
10.5 billion years – Formation of the Sun

10 billion years – Formation of Solar System

5 billion years – Great Wall of Galaxies (giant clusters)
First supernova, gives rise to 2nd/3rd generation stars

1 billion years – Formation of Galaxies

100 million years – First Stars
Galactic clouds

1 million years – Photons Uncouple from Matter
300,000 years – Cosmic wrinkle

5 minutes – Formation of the Atom (permanent atomic nuclei)
3 minutes – Fusion bomb; hydrogen, deuterium, lithium

1 second – Neutrinos Uncouple from Matter
1^{-4} seconds – Soup of quarks
10^{-11} seconds – Weak and electronic separate
Period of Rapid Expansion

10^{-33} seconds – Origins of Matter (unified electronuclear force splite)
10^{-36} seconds – Strong Force
10^{-43} seconds – Unity of all Forces and Matter

Beginning of Time

First is a vase or trumpet shape that represents the expansion of space and matter over time, the linear arrow of time which everyone perceives as they grow up, mature and then decline. But at the bottom of this vase is a very steep curve, which signifies the inflationary period when the cosmos expanded faster than the speed of light and tuned the rest of history to its present fine balance. Although not conclusively proven it is still the favoured theory, and most evidence bears it out. Then, going up the sides of the model, are the four forces that make the universe a unity over billions of years. Gravity, electromagnetism, the strong and weak nuclear force, these four are so finely balanced as to be the closest thing to a miracle, something worth celebrating. Finally there is the internal, spiral staircase of development towards more complexity, the story of history, a sequence that moves up and down continuously *and* in jumps. The progress towards complexity, in fitful starts and setbacks, is a key insight of our time. Both cosmic and natural evolutions show the history of gradual change *and* breaks in symmetry, as will be explained. Furthermore, the jumps in organisation are the inherent drama and surprise, the basic metaphor that gives the history a meaning and excitement. A beautiful metaphor of the historian George Kubler is 'the shape of time', the way all experience has a characteristic form over time. A crucial question thus arises, what shape is our space-time? In this model it is the vase shape, punctuated by steps, held together by forces and surveyed at the top, the present, by the quizzical eye of consciousness.

This was my first approximation at modelling the universe according to evidence, but I should also explain the basic metaphor and how this has slowly come about since the mid-1970s. Throughout most of the twentieth century, Darwinians rejected the idea that evolution proceeds in sudden jumps, but by the last decade the notion found renewed favour from an unexpected source, the world of physics and self-organising systems. The idea was framed under different headings, showing how sudden self-organisation is deep in nature. I have mentioned many of these headings: 'emergence', [36] 'phase transitions', 'nonlinear dynamics', 'bifurcation and tipping points', 'the butterfly effect', 'order out of chaos'. The same notion was called all of these things, and most generally [106] 'symmetry breaking'.[84] At one level, a phase transition is a familiar process, like the sudden change from a liquid to a solid or gas. When water freezes to ice, or vapour suddenly condenses to form droplets, there is a break in symmetry and the material suddenly acquires a new structure and complexity. Phase transitions occur throughout nature and are now subject to manipulation, as in the superconducting of electricity (when substances

[114 a, b] **The symmetry break terrace, the universe in four jumps**. Reading from the left, the first jump shows the fast expansion due to energy and the hot stretching of space. Then as the universe cools there is another symmetry break as matter bends space-time. After 9 billion years life emerges, shown as the dip, then in the last 2 million years consciousness emerges (the hedge). The drawing indicates the end of three breaks. (C Jencks)

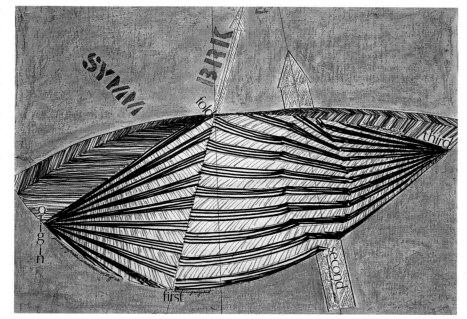

are cooled to near absolute zero) or laser beams (when atoms are pushed 'far from equilibrium' by adding more energy).

This last phrase, employed by Ilya Prigogine to such effect, made the basic point of post-modern science. As Phil Anderson expressed it, 'more is different'. Add more of anything to a system – energy, information, matter – and it is pushed far from equilibrium, so that it suddenly reorganises on a new level of complexity. Atoms, stars, life, consciousness are four such breaks in symmetry, and four major stages of evolution in the universe – surprising, because they cannot be predicted by their constituent parts, and nonlinear, because they are jumps. [114] Again, the point is that the linear sciences of simplicity underlay the modern world-view, since the time of Newton, and the nonlinear sciences of complexity underlie the post-modern world view.

Of course, there is only one universe and one science, but the linear laws were discovered first and mistakenly assumed to be the model of truth. By the 1980s the theory of symmetry breaking was generalised and we could see that, since the universe started off in supersymmetry, its history comprised a series of breaks in each state towards greater organisation. Hence the metaphor of the jumping universe.

Inevitable questions followed when I translated this into a larger garden structure, a cascade on the side of a hill. What breaks in symmetry are the most significant? How to turn a spiral, showing the development and setbacks of history, into a usable staircase? [115-16] Which jumps to include, which to leave out? Fortuitously there is a parallel between a universe developing in stages and our walking up steps and reaching various plateaux, the levels of attainment. Furthermore, one can dramatise the way complexity grows in richness by using ever more intricate sculpture, and underline the increase in meaning by amplifying the size. To accentuate the expansion of the universe, each level flares out further than the one below, and the elements that symbolise each jump, well-shaped rocks, are also bigger in size. In effect, the elements of nature are used to depict nature evolving. The two basic kinds of evolution

ABOVE LEFT [115] **Universe cascade, model in 25 jumps,** 1999. The 13 billion year history ascends in complexity as the universe expands. To indicate the setbacks and dead ends, the path is a zigzag with plateaux showing various stages.

ABOVE [116] **Universe cascade** as built, 2001. Water flows down, time runs up. Rocks and growing nature are used to present the two basic forms of evolution, matter and life. (C Jencks)

discussed above, inanimate and living nature, tell their own story of self-organisation. Twenty-four jumps to the period of modernity are shown, and then several more into the future. Important stages of evolution are not just described, but dramatised. For instance, the point when 65 million years ago an asteroid wiped out the dinosaurs, when perhaps over 70 per cent of species were killed, and the small primates were thereby allowed to evolve in stature and number. [117] Rocks, water, plants and sculpture characterise each of these transitions. The story is hardly neutral, either from our point of view or that of growing complexity and that is why it asks to be told with emphasis and art.

After these several models were designed, Stephen Hawking produced similar diagrams that brought out the key aspect of balance, the way the forces of expansion and contraction are carefully tuned so the universe does not fly apart, or cave in on itself. [118] Those universes where gravity is too strong collapse before life can evolve, those that expand too fast do not produce stars that can cook the heavy elements like carbon, on which life depends. Our cosmos (centre right in the diagram) is in that tight range of 'just right' worlds where the kinetic and gravitational forces together allow a stately expansion. It is balanced within an accuracy of 1^{-59} (.0000000001 with 50 more zeroes in front of the 1), so that for the next 13 billion years it neither contracted into a black hole nor blew apart. A metaphor, sometimes used, conveys how extraordinary this is. Imagine a pencil being thrown through a vacuum to land on its point, and then standing up for eons. This balance of forces is one of the several moments in universal history that is crucial and naturally dramatic, an event entirely worth celebrating. But then so are all the other essential shifts in organisation.

While the cascade was under construction, astrophysics was going through one of its periodic bouts of questioning and hit upon a most unusual discovery. From the observation of distant supernovae, it turned out that the universe, about 5 billion years ago, had started expanding faster again. The prime candidate implicated in this unexpected acceleration was termed 'dark energy', a force that could only be discerned indirectly because of its effects on the supernovae. Dark matter had been discussed for more than twenty years and accepted as a reality because of the way it held galaxies together. Now dark energy, its twin invisible force, implied that the expansion of the universe was speeding up, and just enough to prevent the cosmos from ever collapsing in on itself in the future. Gravity would not overpower the kinetic force, there would be no 'big crunch' but rather an eternal unfolding.

The discovery of the acceleration led to what has now become the standard model of the expanding universe. This is the familiar vase or trumpet shape, but one given a very gentle outward curving lip about three-quarters of the way up. [119] No doubt there will be more surprises and even more radical discoveries, if quantum and relativity theories are reconciled. But the picture of the universe is like the universe itself, irreversible. It goes forward and changes, taking on new shapes, but does not go backwards. In this sense the standard model provides a lasting

BELOW [118] **Multiple universes**, after Stephen Hawking, *The Universe in a Nutshell*, Bantam Press (New York), 2001. Our universe, centre right, has the forces of expansion and contraction balanced to an extraordinary degree.

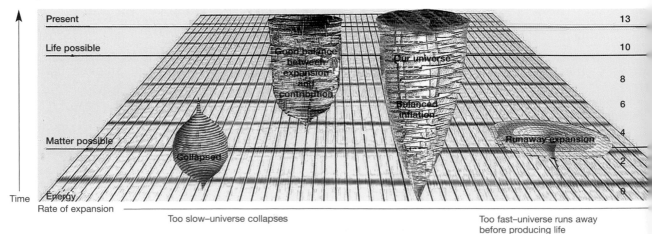

architecture and iconography, a cumulative one. It arrives at the time of other post-modern shifts I have touched on, and becomes an important part of the new intellectual structure. Cosmogenesis is the metaphorical web that penetrates every area of life and matter, tying them together in a partly finished architecture. Perhaps surprisingly, for those so used to fashion as the arbiter of change, in forty years the universe story has grown cumulatively and only been modified in its details. It is here for the long term, maybe eternity.

RIGHT [119] **Expanding universe**, standard model showing the effect of dark energy. Note the small flare at about eight of the thirteen units. The WMAP picture at the base, 380,000 years after the inflationary period, is as far back as we will ever be able to see. I have changed NASA's 'Big Bang' to 'Hot Stretch' for reasons outlined in the text, below. (NASA and the WMAP Science Team)

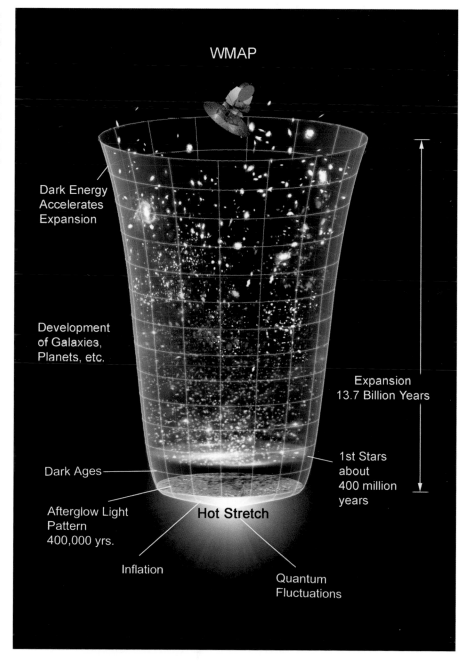

WMAP

Dark Energy
Accelerates
Expansion

Development
of Galaxies,
Planets, etc.

Expansion
13.7 Billion Years

Dark Ages

1st Stars
about
400 million
years

Afterglow Light
Pattern
400,000 yrs.

Hot Stretch

Inflation

Quantum
Fluctuations

6. CRITICAL MODERNISM

Creative to be critical

[120] **Emergent iconography – the dialogue with the cosmos.** Nature sometimes grows in visible forms, such as the spiral, which are decoded over time and transformed into an iconography. The pineapple displays the typical Fibonacci spiral (the red and gold florets here), later seen to generate the growth angle of 137.5 and finally understood as a process leading to the most economical close-packing and the beauty of the golden section (bottom). Le Corbusier (top right) turned such insights into his Modulor Man, while Norman Foster (centre) used the spiral diagrid in several buildings (including the 'Gherkin'). The hurricane, the ammonite and the Whirlpool Galaxy also show different spiral patterns, classics of self-organising growth over time, which become potential icons. The dialogue forges visual metaphors of value. (Galaxy: N Scoville, T Rector et al, Hubble Heritage Team, Nasa; diagrams after G Doczi, *The Power of Limits*, Shambala, Boston, 1994).

In mid-September 2006, five years after 9/11, an independent survey of the British people measured the degree of trust and suspicion pervading the land. At the bottom of the barometer were tabloid journalists trusted by 24 per cent of the population, followed closely by politicians and then estate agents. More than two-thirds of the country, if these figures can be trusted, believes politicians regularly prevaricate or, to put it in their terms, are 'economical with the truth'. Lying, the shorter word, is now wearingly considered routine by a public verging on cynicism, at least in the UK, Europe and USA.[84] The soubriquet for the Prime Minister – Bliar – became current just as the electorate voted him in for the third time in 2005, *faute de mieux* (well, are there any better liars?). As Jean-François Lyotard pointed out, the post-modern directly grew in force with mounting public scepticism, especially during the 1960s. Then scepticism was aroused by the Vietnam War, among other things, while today it is provoked by lies about Iraq and the Middle East.

However such disaffection may be justified it usually amounts to weak negativity. Two thirds of the British may be disillusioned, but they are not yet ready to be fully critical. They may be disgusted, but such feelings are just as likely to beget alienation and disengagement as any deeper commitment. A sophisticated criticality depends on going the next step towards a consistently sceptical point of view, an attitude that has to reach an historical understanding of its place in cultural space and time, today the period of multiple modernisms self-consciously aware of themselves. It is at this moment that a possible bifurcation takes place, a critical turning point is reached (to use the other meaning of the term) and suspicion is generalised from politicians through estate agents to the media and then the whole of society. But it has to be on a nuanced and situational level. Why? It dawns on those who have become sceptical that this orientation can be itself uncritical, especially when it does not encourage the social passions, a sympathy and empathy, a close listening to the other – above all creativity. In the end, one can think critically only because one knows alternatives, has different codes of meaning with which to question the reigning assumptions, and these alternative codes need nurturing and careful timing. Furthermore, they are projective. Literally and especially in such fields as architecture they involve *projects*, liaisons between architect and client. Like a love affair they require a mutual suspension of disbelief, while both sides take creative risks. That is, creativity entails the momentary relaxation of the critical in order to go beyond the present impasse, the customary categories. This point was implied by Rem Koolhaas in a 1994 debate between two groups that were later to style themselves as 'the critical and post-critical'. As he overstated the pragmatic position:

> The problem with the prevailing discourse of architectural criticism is (the) inability to recognise there is in the deepest motivations of architecture something that cannot be critical.[85]

Cannot be? – well, Koolhaas has a point. Projective thinking, in any kind of future project, takes a different talent than the analytical and critical, engages a different part of the personality and the brain. It takes different skills, those which are customarily called romantic, imaginative, chaotic, challenging, overcoming, progressive – in an old word, 'modernist'. Hence the power of the duality critical/modernism, a combination we will explore.

Critical modernism is a continuous and implicit tradition within modernism made more explicit since the mid-1960s with the developments I have outlined in previous chapters. As self-critical it responds to problems of its own making and as generally critical its reacts to the pressing external issues, above all global warming. I will look at such problems here, provocative questions such as that of a different spirituality, and the ways modernisms trump each other, before concluding on a possible conscious movement, *Critical Modernism*. But first one might look at the bigger picture I touched on in the previous chapter, the emergent metanarrative of cosmogenesis. This sets the stage for what is entailed in other global shifts, an iconography of our time.

A critical iconography

For critical modernism the first confrontation is with what I have called the 'mixed metaphysics' of cosmogenesis, its constant creativity and wanton destruction. At the simplest level, this presents a positive opportunity for combining critical doubt with risk-taking invention. How do we frame metaphors to describe and relate to the new view of a threatening *and* benign universe? Take the origin event, usually misnamed the Big Bang. It was neither big (as a quantum fluctuation) nor a bang (no one heard it). Rather it was the hot stretching of space, and the expansion of something smaller than a quark to the size of a grapefruit and, if we are to believe inflation theory, expanding faster than the speed of light! This microsecond fine-tuned the universe to its perfect balance, an extraordinary event very much worth celebrating. But noise was not its virtue. The metaphor Big Bang was invented as a bad joke by the astrophysicist Fred Hoyle, who was out to lampoon and discredit the idea ('like a woman jumping out of a cake'). Yet to his dismay it caught on, just as did the 'Selfish Gene', as a moniker typical of an age wedded to video-nasties and war-games, a propensity to frame things in the manner of James Bond (known in Italy as 'KissKiss – BangBang'). Sadly, most scientists and then the general public adopted Fred Hoyle's joke, unselfconsciously, without giving it much thought. On reflection they may realise it is not very apt and more suitable to the Pentagon than science or a New King James Version of how events came into being ('In the beginning was the firecracker, your mother Shock, your father Awe …').[86] How has this metaphor been translated into art?

The polymath artist Isamu Noguchi created a rock sculpture that now resides in the garden museum dedicated to his work. Called *The Big Bang* it consists of a roughly circular rock of weathered granite that was smashed at various points so that it broke into five pieces. [121] Placed on black ballast, in juxtaposition with other sculpted boulders, it has some presence but as an interpretation of the origin of the universe it is, as they say, underwhelming. I have the highest respect for this designer; not only an inventor of brilliant furniture such as his paper lights, but also of contemporary versions of traditional Japanese Zen gardens. Yet in *The Big Bang* apparently he has made no effort to interpret the content of his title, or respond to it with mood, sensitivity or feeling. No attempt to understand, transform or comment on the basic mystery at the heart of things. This is not for want of talent or commitment to the metaphysical or symbolic plane of art. His other work shows this, indeed very nearby. There *The Illusion of the Fifth Stone* can be seen in dialogue with these

[121] Isamu Noguchi, **The Big Bang**, granite chunks in the foreground (1978) while **The Illusion of the Fifth Stone** can be seen in the background, a much more engaging composition. (Lily Jencks)

broken lumps, but by contrast the illusion leads the viewer on in exploration, round and round the visible boulders in search of the missing stone. In *The Big Bang* there is no imaginative engagement, no wrestling with the physics of the origin, the stretching of space, the miraculous balancing of forces, the mystery of what came before – the big questions. One has the feeling that Noguchi just settled on the metaphor, as physicists did twenty years before him – absentmindedly, pragmatically, perhaps because he had a few nicely broken chunks of granite to hand. Call them The Big Bang – Hoyle's bad joke. Such a vapid attitude is typical of Late Modern abstraction, for instance, Barnet Newman's stripe painting where a single zip down one side of the canvas is called 'the creation of the universe'; or Anish Kapoor's vacuous column of light, based on it.

A critical modernism will obviously have a lot to do when the best artists are approaching content with throwaway titles. It will have to explicate the recent cosmology *and* at the same time reinvent a language for making it poetic but not banal, both verbally and visually. Criticising the language of war and selfishness is one part, and enjoying the challenge of creative substitution, the formation of persuasive metaphors is the other. Perhaps the most exciting aspect of the new paradigm lies in its possibilities for evolving this new iconography. Already we can see some of this new poetics, mentioned in the second chapter, the new fractal architecture with its enigmatic signifiers referring to nature, and an art that takes the major themes of life and death as its subject matter.

But how might a critical modernism frame a cosmogenic subject matter? Here the basic laws of the universe would become the protagonists; the constants of nature and the basic units of cosmic organisation would become particular icons. For instance, one can imagine, as I have done, a landscape and architecture that present such things in new formal codes. For instance, the law of gravity, when the conditions are extreme, bends space and time very tightly into a black hole, and one can use actual gravity, as well as functional elements, in a bodily way to underscore the meaning. [122] Instead of just representing ideas of curved space visually, the black hole can be a presentational symbol that pulls one physically into its space-time. The difference between a denotative sign and a reverberant symbol is that the latter works on several levels at once.

A critical long-term iconography might focus on those things that we know will last. Thus the question becomes, what are the ultimate units of the universe, those that have existed virtually unchanged over its whole existence? Put another way, what are the organisational units that have created complexity, that is quality in the universe? There are two basic forms of quality. When it comes to material self-organisation the constant units are such things as quarks, protons, neutrons and the hydrogen atom, and when it comes to organic self-organisation such things as the DNA molecule. From an artistic point of view, these virtually eternal elements can be interpreted several ways, and in countless forms and materials. One is partially constrained by reality and the science of the time, but open to interpret the reigning metaphors critically. Furthermore, this emergent

LEFT TO RIGHT [122] **Several units of the universe**: quarks, DNA, the atom and black hole. These permanent elements become possible subject matter for a new iconography, to be explored with pertinent metaphors. The **black hole** bends space and time and creates rips in the fabric of the universe. **Quarks** are inferred from the way ultimate particles move in high-energy explosions – the **P** (proton) is made from **uud** (two up quarks and a down). Quarks are at the centre of the Deuterium **atom**, while the basic electron orbits are shown (in wave and particle form) circling in complete waves. The **DNA** double helix interacts with life, here a growing seat, as its RNA arms unfurl and replicate; Clare College, Cambridge, 2005. (C Jencks)

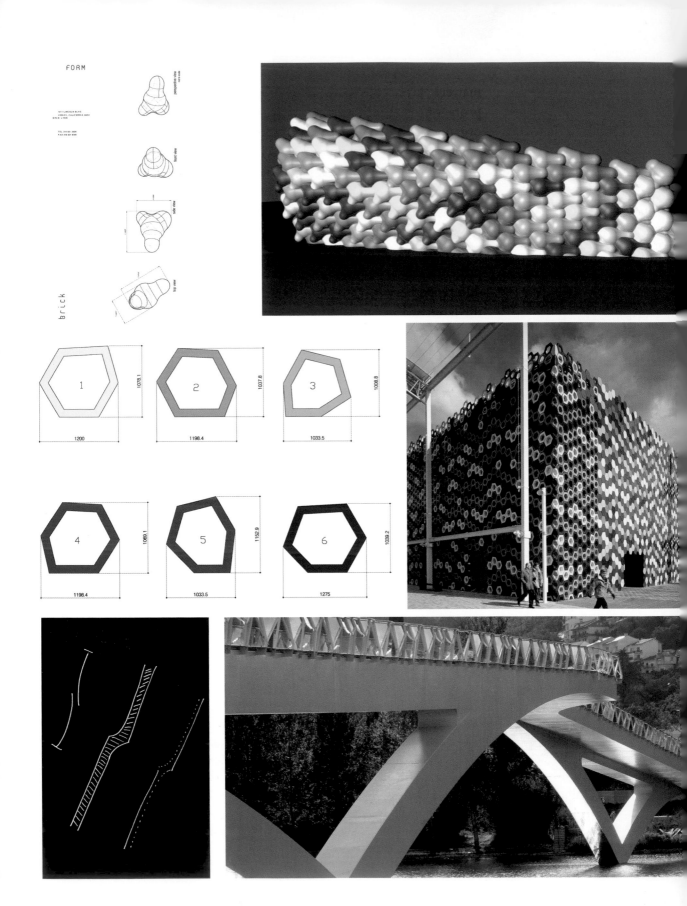

FORM

brick

[123] OPPOSITE **New Ornamental Morphologies.** Architects are revisiting ornament again, as they did in the 1980s, but now as a result of digitalisation beginning to vary their modules. Greg Lynn, for the Slavin House, Venice California, 2007, varies a brick unit across the site in form and colour; FOA, for the Spanish Pavilion at EXPO 2005 Japan, varies three types of hexagonal ceramic with colours of the Spanish flag; Cecil Balmond constructs an anarchist bridge in Coimbra Portugal whose two sides veer away from each other so as not to meet – but do in a central island, thus providing lateral stability. The fractal balustrades also exploit digital production. The next step for ornament will surely be to return to the full symphonic possibilities outlined by Owen Jones. (Top images of Slavin House: © Greg Lynn; middle images of Spanish Pavilion: courtesy FOA, photo © Satoru Mishima; bottom elevation of bridge designed by Cecil Balmond in collaboration with Antonio Fonseca, AFA, courtesy ARUP)

iconography can celebrate some of the most significant conceptual breakthroughs of our time. For instance, the notion of Gaia, the earth as a self-organising system, has moved from being a marginal, contested theory in the 1970s into a central position (see above p 166). It is now one of the most important models for contemplating the interdependence of life and non-living matter, the feedback of organic and material elements to produce a delicate balance of oxygen (among many things). Along with the discovery of DNA, black holes and an expanding universe, it is one of the essential ideas that have changed our world-view, irreversibly so.

Here is an answer to the evanescence of fashion. If one is looking for more permanent icons than those thrown up by the art market, it could be in such distinctive units. As Plato argued, the good carver cuts the chicken at the joints, a bad one bludgeons his way through the bones. The challenge for art is to find the right joints, the key units, the lasting iconic ideas and then transform them into a lasting iconography. There are several architects who might share this view, Ben van Berkel in Europe, Charles Correa in India, Kenneth Yeang in Malaysia and a host of Land Artists and ecologically inspired creators. But it is too early to define a mainstream practice, and attempts to do so necessarily choose mere traces of an approach, not a fully worked out programme and aesthetics.[87]

A critical coding

The second level of a critical modernism concerns a reflective response to the codes of expression. Today this might mean an unusual mixture of science and visual languages, or design codes based on the myriad patterns of organization that the fundamental laws generate. The computer is particularly adept at revealing these patterns of nature, the fractals, strange attractors, complex morphological shapes of folding, and close-packing. This has led to a strong movement especially among the young architects today, groups with exotic sounding acronyms that imply embarking into another universe of architecture – NOX, ASYMPTOTE, dECOI and FOA, or more readable hybrids such as OCEAN. Their watchwords are 'emergence and morphogenetic design', themes deriving most generally from the complexity theory that we have touched on. [123] Their architectural language usually stems from structural or ornamental parameters and curved morphologies, complex elements that are often best explored through digitisation.[88] While much of this work remains on paper, and in computer code, Zaha Hadid has through many years of drawing, painting and modelling a similar set

of codes, managed to build some convincing versions of the new paradigm. This work is often organisationally based and presentational; that is, the new morphological codes are presented as ends in themselves.

Peter Eisenman is also committed to such ideas of coding, though with a twist towards displacing convention and setting up collisions of meaning. Significantly, he has returned again and again to the concept of the critical.[89] For him the idea has many meanings

[124], a.b.c **Peter Eisenman, City of Culture, Santiago de Compostela, Spain**, 1999-2009 aerial view of site, competition model, and tilted coquille. An artificial mountain, the size of old Santiago, with contemporary alleyways that mediate the strong sunlight. A network of markings inflect and deform the organising grammar throughout the whole site, as if geological forces were the architect. Here, instead of placid sedimentary layers, the pressures writhe up in metamorphic angst and hurl their twists skywards as if tectonic plates were pushing from opposite ends. Old Santiago also is built on tilting stone, where one constantly is aware of gravity and being off balance. The warped coquille shell, repeated often in the cathedral at odd angles, is also a symbol of this other reality. (Courtesy of Eisenman Architects)

including the obvious ones of questioning clichés and opposing negative trends. Recently it has meant for him resisting customary conventions, the early modern ones of abstraction and collage, because they have become unquestioned assumptions of everyday practice. But it also means what he calls in one article a 'displacement' from functional and formal origins, a building that 'oscillates' between different readings; or, in another article, 'the becoming unmotivated of the sign'. This latter expression sounds curious, but it refers to linguistic ideas of 'motivation', in architecture that, for instance, function or convention motivates a solution. 'Becoming unmotivated' is essential for Eisenman's notion of the critical because it entails architectural codes that are 'singular' and 'cut off from previous legitimation'; they are 'autonomous and self-regulated'. His definition of the critical emphasises the creative autonomy of the architectural language, its oscillation between readings, and it is this he sets against both the marketplace and the customary understanding of architecture as motivated by its origins.

A case where he sets different codes of architecture in juxtaposition is his city of culture in Santiago de Compostela, a competition Eisenman won in 1999. During the 1990s the northern Spanish city of Santiago was in an expansionist mood and it became the spearhead of a local Galician nationalism. Eisenman read this new cultural temperature more clearly than the other architects. He came up with a project that, in the words of the City's brochure, 'was inspired by Compostela's historical town centre and the five medieval town pilgrim ways that lead to the Cathedral.'[90] Santiago had become the third focus

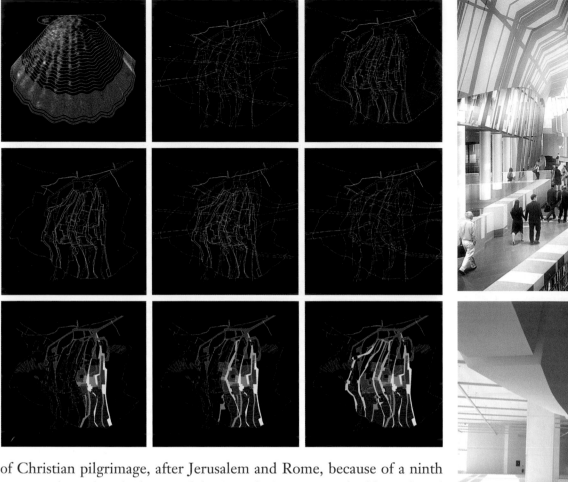

of Christian pilgrimage, after Jerusalem and Rome, because of a ninth century claim that the bones of the Apostle Saint James had been found on a hillside in Northern Spain. These claims have now merged with the foundation stones of the cathedral. Relics, a narrative justifying travel and grand architecture as the culmination of pilgrimage have worked for eleven centuries: "build it and they will come." They still do, in large numbers, some sporting the famous coquille shell as sign of their goal, the city and the Saint.

Eisenman's response to the brief was a parallel city on a hill, but a secular one. With its several Galician signs, and layout recalling the old city, it was a post-modern dart aimed precisely at the nationalist target. All these allusions are, however, oblique and absorbed into his undulating grammar as it worms its way over the brow of the hill. Like Stirling's use of stone at Stuttgart [28] masonry is exaggerated in its artificiality, celebrated as clip-on surface with rough facing and diagonal shifts in geometry. It now serves as weather shield, not structure, and marks various 'flow lines'. In effect, the architecture carries forward the 1980s critique of revivalist work, the pseudo-

[125], a,b,c,d. **City of Culture, computer renditions and views**. Five interacting codes. 1. The coquille shell, wrapped into the plan and section, is a traditional sign of the pilgrimage route. 2. The Cartesian city grid (16x20m), deformed and marked on the roof made of quartzite blocks, is an architectural code. It is also marked on the windows, soffits and floor. 3. The ley lines of pre-historic culture mark the lanes and also the thick tartan grid on the roofscape 4. These last are also related to the medieval city

plan, visible from the site. 5. The curved morphology of the existing hillside into which it is all carved relates, of course, to 'nature.' Having layered these diagrams by computer, a new vermiform grammar is allowed to emerge, which then Eisenman further articulates. The resultant landform is thus biomimetic and cultural, a cross-coding that is richer and metaphysically more convincing than one based on a single discourse. (Courtesy of Eisenman Architects)

classicism that either denies the reality of its underlying steel structure or builds anachronistically with stone all the way though.

As a work of urbanism Eisenman's scheme also responds critically to the normal object-building of our time, the free-standing monument or the iconic skyscraper. It counters these trends by becoming a landform-building, that is the typical hybrid of post-modernism, part undulating hill, part walk-in excavation. [124] The ecological motive is to burrow into the site and avoid excessive heat gain or loss. The naturalistic motive is to let the software programs grow the landform, as if it were an electronic-biological species. Then come the historical motives, including the distinctive emblem of the gastronomic delicacy known to pilgrims, 'Coquille St. Jacques' – the scallop shell of the saint.

Eisenman takes this famous icon and combines it with four further codes, which he then has proliferate on his computer until the result looks sufficiently strange or 'unmotivated'. [125] In effect, it is a layered mixture of landforms, a palimpsest that also looks a bit like the natural hill he has had to excavate. Furthermore, it recalls the tight, shaded streets of medieval Spain, the alleyways that snake between its five linear 'buildings', This is most welcome in the strong southern sunlight, particularly acute now with global warming. The old city's layout is indeed one of the codes that has generated Eisenman's invention. The others are a modernist grid, the topography of the old hill, and the ley lines of pre-history that Eisenman supposes may once have led 'Druids to Santiago'. His pre-history may be way out of whack here (Druids are Northern and three thousand years later than he supposes), but these lines do play an important role in deforming the interior spaces of his landforms and getting their red markers laid down as pavement for his approach roads. No doubt, devout art pilgrims of the twenty-first century will make their climb up to this secular museum city, Santiago-on-the-Hill, with their Eisenman-Codex in hand.[91]

The critical text is a provocation with a codicil attached, an invitation open to everyone but with the proviso that, all the same, one has to work hard at understanding. Through enticements and rewards it tries to transform the naïve reader into the critical one.[92] Double coding, as we have seen, uses popular signs and mixes them with more esoteric ones to further encourage this transformation, a form of non-snobbish elitism. In like manner the critical text of Eisenman's Santiago sets up an opposition of codes to heighten consciousness, for criticism from one angle is nothing else than the interplay of meanings questioning each other in someone's head. The critical is that interior voice that the text elicits, the 'yes-but' one hears as two or more ideas battle in the mind, the interrogation of one set of codes by any other.

In effect, the Santiago project exemplifies the cross-coding of critical modernism, mixing at least the five codes evident in the drawings with material codes related to the site and construction (the quartzite stone roof versus artificial glazing). As a burrowing building it is, of course, responding to the ecological imperative and the fractal languages of nature, but in the pronounced artificiality of its window types it also critiques the current clichés of organic architecture. Thus it is quite a knowing text, positioning itself to engage the moment and history. It is at once a secular art-city on a hill that relates dialectically to the cathedral, and a slippery piece of stoney landscape that is sliced on the sides as it undulates upwards towards its central canyon. It aims towards this culmination. But is it a geological stratum, a version of the Grand Canyon, or a public piazza? Indeed, is the whole thing building or landscape? Foreground waveforms or background hill? Cultural destination or Mother Earth as a place of pilgrimage? Such binary oppositions, or double coding, are the way this project puts several contemporary issues in question. It does not seek to answer or resolve the problems, but rather layers them neutrally into a supple architecture of marks and notation.

Cross-coding is invariably a development of post-modern double coding, in architecture an elaboration made much more possible and rich by the electronic media. Where the previous strategy tended to be confrontational, the subsequent one is more sinuous and congruent. There is a danger with this, of allowing the computer to do too much of the generation, and thereby a tendency for the smoothness and integration to become slickness, as maddeningly evasive as any political cliché. But, on the whole, multiple cross-coding allowed by the computer is an effective way of dealing with the pluralism of many generators. It is an approach gaining more adherents. The basic polarities set cosmogenic themes against cultural ones, the fact that we are simultaneously part of nature and separate from it, subject to gravity, for instance, yet capable of momentarily suspending its effect. It seems to me that in mixing the codes of nature with those of culture, a parity should be sought. One cannot imagine with the mixed metaphysics of cosmogenesis, either nature on a pedestal or man. Moreover, the juxtaposition of these languages heightens consciousness, and is more stimulating than architecture based on restricted codes.

A critical spirituality?

Some of the implications of the new cosmology are clearly religious and while they are much too complex and large to explore in a short survey, one cannot avoid touching on the subject since it pervades every area of life. Just take the shift in the meaning of terms. As others have pointed out, today the various concepts of spirituality have been thrown into question. It is a time when the old dichotomies of body, mind and spirit look overdone because they are now known to be so radically interconnected. Perception, for instance, is recognised to be distributed throughout the body, thinking is thought to have a quantum component and the spirit is conceived as a momentary form of creative inspiration. All such changes in recent understanding throw the old modern dichotomies – body/mind, spirit/soul – into disarray. The oppositions between matter and spirit have been further eroded by the discoveries that the most primitive bacteria have sentience. Indeed, experience is believed, by some post-modern philosophers, to go 'all the way down the hierarchy' to the level of self-organising matter, a theory called 'panpsychism'.[93] Discoveries made since the mid-1970s in neuroscience and quantum physics have completely blurred the old oppositions and it is no longer clear where matter leaves off and mind starts. Perhaps they are extreme parts of a bipolar unity. [126] They may be just different ends of a continuous spectrum, or alternatively two sides of the hardware/software coin. Some physicists even conceive the universe itself as a vast information processor.

[126] **Bipolar unity – the continuous spectrum from matter to mind.** The idea that the mind ultimately controls matter, as the brain directs the hand, is known as downwards causation. Conversely the theory that material states determine society is called upwards causation. The age-old argument between holism and reductivism, or these two opposite causations, is virtually dead. In explaining life, biologists have long accepted the nature/nurture duality, that upwards and downwards causation both have to be acknowledged, and they now also grant a place for self-organisation. The nine fields of specialisation depicted, from physics to aesthetics, show different proportions of 'mind and matter', or freedom and determinism. But the deeper truth of bipolar unity is that pure mind and matter do not exist. There is both an iota of self-determinism in every atom and a physical correlate in every aesthetic decision. (C Jencks, after Augros and Stanciu, The New Biology)

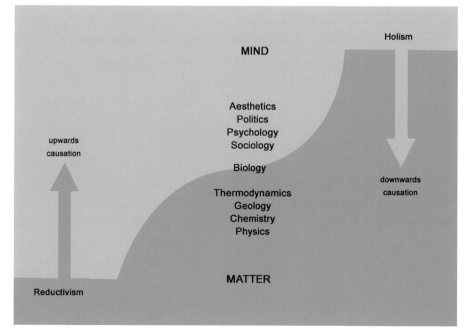

For such thinkers the bipolar unity reverses the major blight of the modern age and materialism, the disenchantment of nature, the way it was reduced to a dead mechanism. For if self-organisation extends into matter and sentience goes back to basic life, then the world has qualities *throughout* the continuous spectrum. It cannot be divided into the old oppositions stemming from Descartes: animals such as dogs were supposed to be purposeless and conditioned automata to be set against free, creative, human beings. But these clear distinctions do not apply. Hence today the notion of 're-enchantment' that is continuously re-invented in one field after another, one that extends all the way up and down the hierarchy. Book titles repeat the mantra – *The Re-Enchantment of Nature, The Re-Enchantment of Art, The Re-Enchantment of Physics, The Re-Enchantment of Science* – and this is just a short list.

Yet why consider these issues at all? Some have argued that the whole question of religion and spirituality is bogus in an age when global commerce has corrupted the words and concepts. They have become kitsch ciphers of their former self, marketable products on the Body & Mind counter of airport checkouts. This objection is to the point. But it is still no reason to cut off discussion when the alternatives are considered. The substitute concepts, most of them psychological, are even worse for dealing with the subject, for discussing significant feelings and the way they continue to relate to the bigger picture. Furthermore, recall the case of 1920s' Modernism, above, and its cryptic spirituality of the void, the presence of the absence of God, the Negative Theology of Wittgenstein. All those white canvases of Minimalism, and those reductionist philosophies that swept away pluralism as troublesome detail. Today this is countered by a more generous, maximalist practice in the arts, one that engages the body, mind and nature – once again in a continuum. [127]

Whether one calls such work critical or spiritual or both or neither is endlessly disputed, and depends largely on the particular case. But there is an identifiable strain of contemporary art that has a spiritual overtone or trace, and it is widely recognised as such. For instance, there is the commissioned work of Anthony Gormley, his installations of human figures standing sentinel in the sea watching the tide come in and out below them; or spreading their arms out like a glider above raw nature – his *Angel of the North*. There is the Video Art by those such as Bill Viola and the spiritually motivated work of Anselm Kiefer, Christian Boltanski and Marina Abramovic. Most Earth Art that engages the processes of nature is perceived as quasi-spiritual. When Andy Goldsworthy throws sticks in the air in beautifully composed

[127] Helen Chadwick, **Oval Court**, 1984–6. Chadwick mixed science and subjectivity to evoke opposites on the continuum. As she said, her work was seen as 'gorgeously repulsive, exquisitely fun, dangerously beautiful'. The contradictions are held in ironic tension, almost becoming oxymoronic in our culture. Here white on blue photocopies of the artist's naked body writhe in ecstasy, dance, eat, etc showing personal pleasures. These are placed in a riotous swirl of animals and contrasted with four platonic balls (planets?) and a larger fifth (sun?). In her work cosmic mathematics and distancing techniques are set against the subjective side of nature, a good illustration of mixed metaphysics and, incidentally, a great influence on Hirst and later YBAs. (© The Helen Chadwick Estate/V&A Images)

patterns, or interacts with the elemental forces of water, ice and rain, these acts are understood as the gestures of a primitive sanctity. [128] It appears that Mother Nature is the pantheist deity invoked. His site specific work is often inspired by the lay of the land and the materials to hand such as the twigs, mud or brightly coloured flowers and leaves. One of his many books was called *A Collaboration with Nature*, 1990, which seems apt, except that his most striking works use nature to *contrast* with the existing site – bright yellow leaves are set off against water, stone optical vibrations are juxtaposed with an old shattered tree, the perennial arch is turned upside down, repeated, and placed against a heroic Scottish hillside. Goldsworthy's father was a professor of applied mathematics at the University of Leeds, and one feels the pull of primary geometrical forms in his work. Yet it is the rhetorical operations that bring these familiar forms to life, make them a non-natural representation of a law of nature – the arch as a structural discovery of man. Thus if it is a pantheistic art it is not a direct collaboration with nature nor a straightforward worship, but one with contrasts and aesthetic twists – in that limited sense, a critical response. And if the movement of Land Art is a pantheism, it has no ritual, beyond the photographic recording, and no doctrine. It makes no demands on belief, collective organisation, scripture or all the directives of religion. Yet people immediately recognise it as a cryptic form of spiritual practice with implicit ecological norms and tacit natural rhythms. Injunctions are suggested by this work but never uttered: 'Live lightly on the earth, interact with its cycles, identify with its growth, decay and death', Perhaps the most religious injunction of all is strongly hinted at: 'become an aesthetic participant in the process of life, identify with the greater whole'. This is a religion that dare not speak its name, and for good reason.

As I have pointed out, the traditional religions have 'lock-in' on collective worship. The two biggest, the Catholics and Muslims, each administer to over a billion followers and they do this by keeping their structure and theology more or less frozen. All attempts at change are thwarted by a power structure that is itself locked into the past. One can see this in the marginal movement from orthodoxy of Vatican II, or today in the vain attempts by Prince Charles and the Archbishop of Canterbury to inch the faithful from their entrenched positions. The Pope, the Chief Rabbi or any mullah or imam – virtually all the religious leaders – face intractable problems when they try to be creative or up to date. This situation, coupled with the way religions have been enlisted for war and mass-cultural politics, means that the traditional faiths no longer have a strong following among the cultural elite (except at Christmas). The result is that organised religion has gone off the creative radar and spirituality has become suspect too. Forced underground, they reappear in bizarre clothes, speaking in strange tongues. Like esoteric sects or ones being persecuted during the religious wars, they are hard to recognise.

There is no mistaking, however, the allusions and traces and hints, most of all in Land Art. A book by Mel Gooding and William Furlong, *Song of the Earth*, *European Artists and the Landscape* (2002), shows that cryptic spirituality is alive, thriving and as conventional as the blush on a nineteenth century virgin. Whether one can go so far as to say it is also 'critical', the question-mark of this section, is a moot point. Certainly, many artists included in *Song of the Earth* make an art, as Goldsworthy does, from enigmatic interventions that celebrate nature and our precarious place on top of it. At the same time much of this work is underdone, weak in expression and symbolism, especially when compared with the earth art of prehistory. Put against stone age artefacts created by communities in 3000 bc, contemporary Land Art can seem thin and lacking in conviction. [129] The comparison is especially relevant because the two genres have become popular at the same time, occupying a similar semantic space and wild landscape. One million visitors to Stonehenge try to fathom the meanings of these enigmatic and expressive rocks just as they do the cryptic signs of Richard Long and herman de vries (embedded in lower case). When one visits the Clava Cairns outside Inverness, in a glade of old trees by

[129] **Balnauran of Clava**, 5 miles from Inverness, c 3000–1500 BC Three Clava Cairns are oriented south-west to the midwinter sunset. Circles of stones ringed by graded kerb-stones and standing stones mark the place of ritual and burial, a religion without scripture and spirituality without political correctness: perhaps a lesson for the present? Although not necessarily conceived as 'land art', it would be wrong to dismiss an aesthetic eye and intention. Indeed, the power of this work becomes the challenge for contemporary artists to meet. (C Jencks)

the River Nairn, the sense of a sad mystery is so overpoweringly strong, in the sun towards which they are oriented, that no contemporary earth art seems its equal. Colin Renfrew, the British archaeologist, has made countless comparisons between contemporary art and prehistory. His book *Figuring It Out* is given the long questioning subtitle – '*What are we? Where do we come from? The parallel visions of artists and archaeologists*' – and it is the questions not answers that dominate the parallel.[93] That seems to me the right, if modest, truth and the same goes for the cryptic tradition of 'critical spirituality'. It is very much present, but what it is exactly is a matter for questioning.

Critical theory carves up doomsday fatigue

A large part of the post-modern movement has been framed under the notion of Critical Theory, a theory of judgement that has two roots. It stems from eighteenth-century philosophy, particularly Immanuel Kant's *Critique of Pure Reason*, and a smouldering social oppression of that time coupled with the desire to get out from under the yoke of those religious orthodoxies I have just mentioned. These double origins ultimately led to the social movements of the 1960s, and the intellectual formation of Critical Theory. The latter found haven in US and UK academia, such disciplines as semiology, post-colonial theory, deconstruction, the close analysis of texts or hermeneutics, feminism, cultural studies, the critique of mass and elite culture and so on. The drive of all these groups and intellectual formations is to unmask repression, reveal hidden bias and, as the originators of Critical Theory put it, criticise society in order to change it. The method differs in each field according to the situation, but as Max Horkheimer framed the strategy it must be simultaneously explanatory, practical and normative. The goals likewise differ, but they do share a commitment to pluralism and the democratic process, two keynotes of the post-modern paradigm. Beyond this is the desire to reduce entrapment or, positively, to liberate thought in order to give creative freedom to the individual and group. How far this creative autonomy can go is a disputed point since there are grave issues facing the globe. If critical theories have relevance, it is in how they deal with reigning assumptions under the extreme pressure of imperative events.[95]

The biggest issue is of course global warming, and what we are going to do about it. It is a universal question, to reiterate, and one that is forcing a cosmic view on the world. For some Green philosophers and those who see Gaia as forming a new focus for collective belief, it will supply the moral equivalent of war. Only if the globe acts in concert, and on a war-footing, is there the chance of reversing the inexorable warming. Yet there is a *cultural* problem with this view that now has to be addressed. We have heard so many prophecies of doom based on the population bomb that, simultaneously, we can well imagine the explosion predicted – of 13 billion people by mid-twenty-first century – and dismiss it as alarmist. 'Hell is other people', as Sartre wrote. Now these 'other people' are tired of hearing about the apocalypse. Ever since the 1980s, runaway global warming has been from twenty to forty years in the future.

Recent information shows that positive feedback effects, such as the sudden melting of Arctic glaciers or the Siberian permafrost, will overcome the usual negative feedback that has balanced the earth's temperature so sweetly for the last thousand years. One British report in early 2006, by the MET office in Exeter, led to the fearful headline in *The Times*, 'World has only 20 years to stop climate disaster'. Sea levels will rise by up to 40 feet. Goodbye London, New York, Bombay and Tokyo. Two weeks later *The Times* carried an even more pressing title, 'Ten Years to prevent catastrophe', This story, written by the former British Environment Minister, Michael Meacher (who ought to know), was based on the American expert Jim Hansen, who models the climate for none other than George W Bush. The grim statistics were the usual ones: the end of coastal cities, the rise in mega-droughts in China and the American West and some unusual horsemen of the apocalypse, such as the fast spread of the world's most dangerous vector-borne disease. Actually, pestilence was one of those four plaguing London in 1666, due to its overcrowding, quickly followed by the others – famine and, of course, the great fire that destroyed 13,000 houses and churches. As today, Londoners predicted catastrophe as a consequence of decadent culture and saw a premonitory sign in a conspicuous cosmic event, a bright comet that lit up the night sky.[96]

Well, what are the predictions for today – is it twenty or ten or five years to apocalypse? Since we have heard this sort of thing for forty years, interspersed with warning cries over Aids, bird flu and Weapons of Mass Destruction, the public is suffering from an advanced case of doomsday fatigue. Ever since 9/11, when Bush put America on a terror footing and Blair amplified the fear, people began to lose their faith in political warnings. Terrorism became the typical media event, to be

THE INDEPENT

FINANCIAL TIMES

Doomsday America

Blair blames Isla as Lond ... **at least 37**

THE ✦✦✦ TIMES

When war ca...

9/11 + 7/7

fabricating a culture of fear

[130] **9/11 and 7/7 – events amplified to create a culture of fear**. Media and politicians work in tandem to exaggerate a danger, each with their venal motives. As insurance statistics reveal, from a survival point of view any number of other risks are far more dangerous to the population than terrorism. Yet for five years the public has been cowed by this fabricated culture of fear. (The Independent, The Times, Time Magazine, The Financial Times – media collage, C Jencks)

fabricated, exaggerated and constantly manipulated by the two leaders. [130] False documents were produced at the UN to justify the Iraq invasion, high alerts went up and down the colour scale of impending catastrophe, Blair massaged the truth so often, as mentioned, he became 'Bliar'. Is it any wonder the polity became cynical and privatised? Global warming is perceived as real, but also against this larger background of apocalyptic politics. Doubts spread. Is the politician crying wolf again? Or, if global warming is so far underway, and now driven to further tipping points by glacial meltdown, what can a family do but try to save itself? These are rational reactions in the culture of fear.

Yet global warming is now very tactile and measurable, for instance in the retreat of the world's glaciers. The fact that ice sheets are melting at unprecedented rates, and one can view from satellites the acceleration of glacial slide, means that political parties are putting it high on the agenda. Call it global meltdown for short, to echo the nuclear version, it has become another mainstream anxiety and for good reason. The fact that global warming leads to more hurricanes, of increased power, was accepted after Hurricane Katrina destroyed a hundred miles of coast along the Gulf of Mexico. The spectre of the Greenland icebergs sinking the Gulf Stream is now taken seriously. [131]

Such predictions are becoming the norm, even for conservative research groups like the UN Intergovernmental Panel on Climate Change (IPCC).[97] This normally cautious body, that reports every five years, forecasts a temperature rise of 3°C about the year 2050. They report that, with positive feedback, the figure could jump by a further 1.5°C. Among many knock-on effects, such rises would put 400 million people at risk of starvation, because of water shortages and loss of arable land. The IPCC noted the 'widespread evidence' that the increase in greenhouse gas since the late 1950s was anthropogenic, that is, caused by man. This idea, now accepted by virtually every investigator, was unpopular with the US administration and so in another pre-emptive strike they leaked the draft report to the press a year early. The first time the IPCC chairman, Rajendra Pachauri, learned of this Washington leak was when he read it on the Internet, one more unilateral trick meant to diminish the news value of the report when it was finally released. Soon paranoids will outlaw global warming as un-American.

[131] **Greenland icebergs in retreat**. It means rising sea levels, further tipping points in global warming, and a potential reversal of the Gulf Stream (making Europe much cooler). (Photo of Greenland, C. Jencks October 2006; diagram after *The Times*).

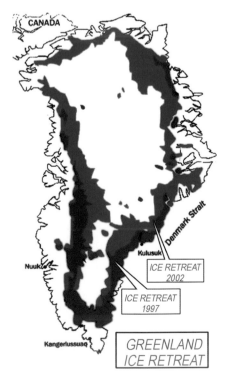

They will have trouble convincing the population, since five of the six warmest years have occurred since 2001, with 2005 and 1998 being the two hottest on record (and as I write 2006 looks set to join them). Now, with several studies of the growth of tree rings and the measurement of ice cores, it is possible to see these recent deviations in perspective. Over the last thousand years two significant variations from the norm have been discovered. There was a medieval warm period, from ad 900 to 1200, and a 'little ice age' from 1550 to 1850. During the last period, citizens could skate all over the Netherlands, joined up by frozen canals, and enjoy the community that was created across the frozen Thames. It is the rare climate blip that does nobody well. The recent global warming is, however, an unprecedented deviation from the norm. Because of positive feedback, the melting glaciers and thawing permafrost plus the increasing desertification, there have been *several* critical tipping points. These are good indicators of more to follow. The question that all earth scientists try to answer, and no one can, is how long do we have before the big one? Ten, twenty, thirty years at the most? Gaia, as the typical self-organising system, will jump up the hill of global warming in several giant steps. And one of these will tip it over the other side, into catastrophe, unless strong action is taken. [132]

Such numbing statistics reinforce the doomsday mentality, but they should not make it uncritical since choices are always to be made. Indeed, this is where Critical Theory can play a role helping people

[132] **Global warming, history and tipping points**. The graph, with exaggerations in scale, brings out the medieval warming period and the little Ice Age, and today's unprecedented rise in temperature since the mid-1970s. Further jumps, or tipping points, will reach a critical threshold and runaway warming if action is not taken. Yet the diagram also brings out the fact that global warming is created by several dynamic elements and it jumps in stages. Any jump may precipitate a crisis and then an empowered regional and global institution. Particular catastrophes, like world wars, initiate particular structures like the UN and Bretton Woods. (C Jencks)

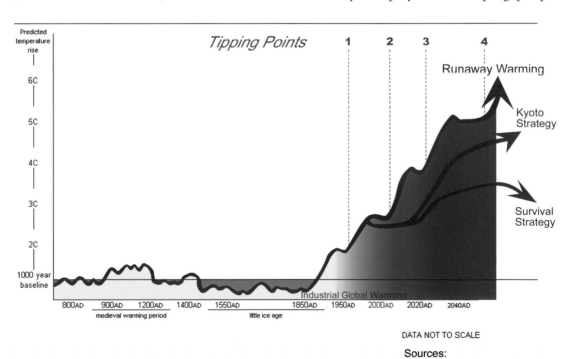

keep their heads, remembering that all crises work themselves out in stages and differentially. Where most people see a single scenario, variable paths are revealed. The Kyoto Protocol is a case in point. As a political fudge meant to harness world consent there was an argument for such a global consensus; but now that its targets are being disregarded (inadequate though they were) alternative strategies must also be tried. This was the advice of Frances Cairncross, president of the British Association for the Advancement of Science in her address to its annual festival in 2006.[98] Describing the Kyoto agreement as 'ineffectual', she called for a realistic acceptance of 'a hotter, drier world', and 'adaptation policies' – ones that have had far less attention than mitigation strategies. Five policies were suggested including wildlife corridors, flood plains, coastal defences, and accepting new drought-resistant crops and tougher building regulations. Such adaptations were suggested, obviously, for the UK and might not be relevant elsewhere, but the point is that global warming will produce varying outcomes. Indeed, climate change has hidden other divisive trends that may well divide the globe even more than it is now. For instance, the different capitalist systems that exist today can be expected to pull in various directions, and they may diverge along the post-modern/modern/pre-modern divides outlined in the fourth chapter.[99]

A range of outcomes is as likely as similar ones. When the meltdown finally comes, it is often assumed there will have to be a corresponding global response. Two standard models predict either a world dictatorship (an authoritarian model of some sort), or the slide into anarchy and neo-primitivism, a world of brutalised nomads and war-lords. But, as John Gray puts it, this idea of one outcome may be just one more 'global delusion'.[100] Moreover Gaia, as the world self-organising system of ecology, could reset itself at any number of positions varying with latitude. The runaway greenhouse effect may be catastrophic for much of the globe, as James Lovelock the originator of the Gaia Theory is predicting, but perhaps not for all of it. It is true that so-called sustainable development is a contradiction for 7 to 12 billion people. Lovelock argues that the only realistic policy is 'sustainable retreat' for the happy few, to the Arctic poles.[101] In any case, whether Lovelock is any better at predicting than others, the various forms of capitalism, competing against each other, are unlikely to save the global commons any more than they have saved previous commons. Unless, like reducing the hole in the ozone layer, the task is relatively painless.

Future land loss to water

Florida

Holland

anghai

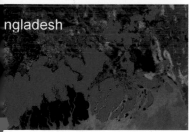

ngladesh

[133] **Lost land** (in red). Sea level rises by 20 feet are predicted, possibly as soon as 2050, with the melting of Greenland and the Arctic Circles. Much of Florida, Holland, Shanghai and Bangladesh might disappear, London and New York would be flooded, along with other major population centres. (C Jencks after Al Gore, *An Inconvenient Truth*, Rodale, USA, Bloomsbury, UK, 2006)

Dealing with doomsday fatigue and the likelihood of a variable catastrophe are part of the same situation, and they call for a critical, graded response. They suggest that, in analysing meltdown, emphasis should be placed on detailed scenarios for each country and region as well as the globe as a whole. It will bring increasing rain for some, desertification for others, new growth in the northern climes, along with generalised misery. But, if every nation perceives its particular possible fate tied in with the neighbouring ones, it would reinforce the regional powers that are starting to emerge. Again the EU is the model here for a transnational heterarchy of organisation. Even though the meltdown is a global affair, the painful restraints that are necessary are most likely to be enforceable at a level where people can see and feel their common fate.

A critical modernism has to be realistic about both catastrophe and the alternatives it would present. The Second World War resulted in all sorts of global bodies, the UN and those transnational organisations I have discussed. If there are hints of a future in this past it concerns the way particular disasters at a precise time become levers for institutional change. In 1941 the US and Britain, faced with the catastrophe of war, became great defenders of international law. Roosevelt and Churchill drafted the Atlantic Charter, limiting the use of national military force, and these agreements served as the inspiration not only for the future UN but the international criminal court and many other multilateral bodies. Each disaster leads to a different structure. Depending on which one happens and where it is most devastating, and whether the institutional ground is well prepared, one can imagine a new global body becoming empowered. Call it Rioyoto for short (Rio and Kyoto protocols combined), it might suddenly emerge fully grown from the ineffectual organisations of the past *and* the particular catastrophe. Who might lead it remains imponderable: the Chinese, if Beijing is suffocating, the EU, if they are freezing, the US, if New York and Florida are disappearing. [133] It may be too late, as Lovelock and others insist, but it is also likely that the globe will not take any collective action until just after the first, collective disaster.

Critical Modernism as a continuous dialetic

Throughout this book I have moved back and forth between the culture of modernism and the larger picture. This constant shift in focus parallels the way modernism reacts to both its own internal discourse, problems of its own making, and the greater issues in the outside world. In this concluding section I will focus down on the hidden tradition of critical modernism within architecture before widening out again to the global situation. As I have been suggesting throughout the book, a double focus makes critical modernism both critical of previous modernisms *and* world culture, and this constant dispute and simmering anger can be seen in every single 'ism that became a wasm'.

Take Futurism, a typical modern movement. It reacted against the general complacency of La Belle Epoque and demanded in 1910 that we destroy museums, libraries and the easel painting of the Impressionists – all for the sake of the Future. Filippo Marinetti, the Futurist leader, glorified war as revealing a new beauty of hygiene and dynamism. Six years later, at the height of the First World War, the Dadaists equally disgusted by the general culture but now from a new position, mounted a contrary movement for pacifism – inevitably – yet with a new agenda based on chaos, chance and nonsense. The Futurists and Dadaists shared several values and tactics – the importance of creative destruction and montage – and they related to the anarchists, as did Mussolini for a time. However, as in a dialectic typical of all modernisms, while the following movement criticised the former it also borrowed from it.

Recall Lyotard's definition of post-modernism:

> What space does Cezanne challenge? The Impressionists. What object do Picasso and Braque attack? Cezanne's . . . A work can become modern only if it is first postmodern. Postmodernism thus understood is not modernism at its end but in the nascent state, and this state is constant.[102]

The state of criticising the immediate predecessor is one part of every modern movement and bending away from it creatively is another part. This double aspect makes for constraints. It means that modernisms, like the Mafia, must honour their fathers as they kill them off, become near to them just as they create distance. And that leads to the notion, formulated especially in modern literature by Harold Bloom, of how the follower may recognisably swerve from his predecessor.[103] Influenced by a great poet, a Shakespeare or TS Eliot, the follower has the double problem to be original but show respect, overcome the extreme power of the former creator, yet carry on the tradition. Swerving from your source is the consequence. Hence the coherent way Surrealism rejects Dadaism yet continues part of its agenda; or Dadaism rejects Futurism yet prolongs many of its attitudes. Think of this coherent flow as a twisting superhighway or a bubbling underground channel. It supports the adage that the history of art always shows a reaction to previous art – an internal dialectic and conversation.

This may sound surprising especially for a modernism committed to change but reflect on the continuous history of the term, which always

[134] **Antonio Filarete's positive moderna, Ospedale Maggiore,** Milan, 1460s. Attacking the competitor, the 'barbarous modern manner' prevalent in Milan, the Gothic, his work is a revival of ancient Classicism with a difference. This modern hospital brought together several charitable institutions around a grid of open courtyards. (C Jencks)

carries an overtone of progress. For instance, the word *modernus* was given stature in the fifth century as Early Christians proclaimed their ethical progress over paganism and Roman civilisation. Then to be a Christian Modern would be to attain happiness in heaven, whereas to be famous in Rome was to achieve only provincial immortality – eternity was measurable progress over that. The modern often carries such overtones of being better, a moral improvement on the past *and* a scientific advance (in the sense that the 118 or so chemical elements today are an improvement on the Four Greek Elements of yesterday). This progressivism is revived in the Renaissance with architects such as Antonio Filarete who in the 1450s used the term *moderna* to distinguish the superiority of the classical revival. [134] Again *moderna* was tied to an ethical and spiritual superiority. When one gave 're-birth' to the ancient classical style (re-naissance), one was also becoming a born-again Christian (and Filarete's Biblical quotes about spiritual resurrection supported his idea). Progress remains a main metaphor, but the notion was becoming as complicated as it is today with the various Neo-Modernisms and Post-Modernisms. Spare a thought for Giorgio Vasari who in the 1550s had to clarify again and again the inherent contradictions in his *Lives of the Artists*. By Modern he did not mean the *contemporary* style of Gothic; that was German and bad. Rather he, like Filarete, proposed the revival of *ancient* Classicism, Classicism brought up to date. New meant old. In his words it was a 'good' or 'glorious' revival (*buona maniera moderna, il moderno si glorioso*), glorious especially when applied to his own work, and Michelangelo's – which showed progress over earlier Classicism. In the seventeenth century the term is invoked this way in the Battle of the Moderns against the Ancients. Then again in the eighteenth and nineteenth centuries it is used by architects such as John Soane, to mean the present-day, but superior, use of Classicism – the idea of improving on the Ancients. Thus, even within the history of the term, we find the paradoxical double movement. 'Modern' means at once the revival of the past, but one that is better and more progressive than it was before.

Perhaps beyond the progressive impulse there are further determinants that give coherence to history, psychological and educational channels that create the few main routes within modernisms. I believe that there are and, following structural anthropologists and others, have found some coherent strands going through twentieth-century architecture.[104] Some reasons for this are quite obvious. Architects, like artists and most people, are attracted by a loose amalgam of interrelated thoughts and practices, by other architects they admire, and they remain somewhat faithful to their adopted bloodline because of a common education and indoctrination. If one maps these loose amalgams a semantic space of oppositions can be constructed. [135] Thus (top left of the diagram) the intuitive tradition within modernism was expressionist and organic in the 1920s and attracted by fantastic and biomorphic shapes in the 1990s. Thus the logical tradition (lower right) was committed to functional and structural solutions and is now committed to parametric and light-weight architecture. These two traditions tend to be opposite and mutually critical, but are not always so, and they tend to remain coherent schools or attractor basins, but not completely. The net result is that the several modern architectures tend to fluctuate around these semantic centres, but with some variation. For instance, an architect like Le Corbusier or Frank Gehry will move between groups and schools and be hard to

[135] **Semantic space** that generates the following evolutionary tree. The structuralist method of analysis, derived from Claude Levi-Strauss and others, is based on the notion of underlying types and 'attractors basins'. Any architect may operate in several opposed traditions at once – eg Intuitive/Logical – but on the whole is attracted to consistent semantic centres. The reason is that training, friendships, the marketplace, specialisation, ideology, taste, building type and economics form 'basins of attraction,' centres of gravity.

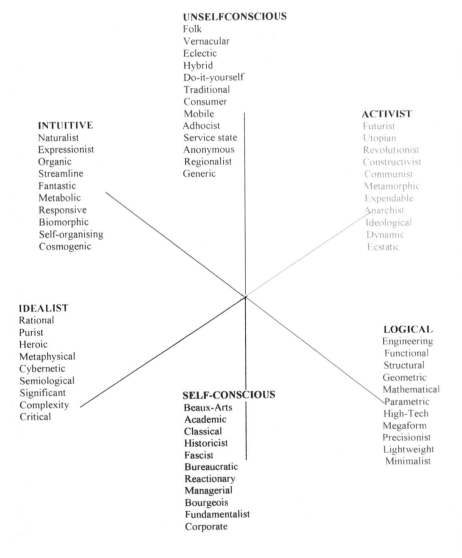

UNSELFCONSCIOUS
Folk
Vernacular
Eclectic
Hybrid
Do-it-yourself
Traditional
Consumer
Mobile
Adhocist
Service state
Anonymous
Regionalist
Generic

ACTIVIST
Futurist
Utopian
Revolutionist
Constructivist
Communist
Metamorphic
Expendable
Anarchist
Ideological
Dynamic
Ecstatic

INTUITIVE
Naturalist
Expressionist
Organic
Streamline
Fantastic
Metabolic
Responsive
Biomorphic
Self-organising
Cosmogenic

IDEALIST
Rational
Purist
Heroic
Metaphysical
Cybernetic
Semiological
Significant
Complexity
Critical

SELF-CONSCIOUS
Beaux-Arts
Academic
Classical
Historicist
Fascist
Bureaucratic
Reactionary
Managerial
Bourgeois
Fundamentalist
Corporate

LOGICAL
Engineering
Functional
Structural
Geometric
Mathematical
Parametric
High-Tech
Megaform
Precisionist
Lightweight
Minimalist

classify. This protean quality can even be an index of their worth and creativity – though, as my litany has it, not always.

If one projects this diagram sideways as an evolutionary tree and then sees how modern movements relate to each other, some coherent patterns can be found, the superhighways and underground channels of my metaphor. [136] History is neither 'just one thing after another' nor a predetermined set of roadways but, in this metaphor, a coherent set of broad boulevards that allow architects to switch lanes. Like evolutionary species they tend to clump together into groups or schools or movements but unlike biological species they can breed with anything and jump between categories. Thus the evolutionary tree shows some tendency to self-organise along the six semantic centres, but is not rigorously predetermined.

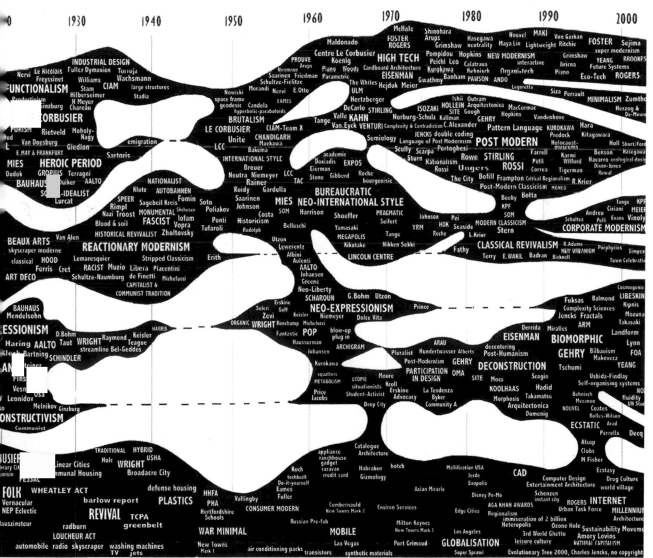

This might be contrasted with Alfred Barr's diagram of modern art, which was so influential in creating the Museum of Modern Art and a dominant ideology of Modernism (see page 44 and image [22]). By forcing a Cubist and abstract interpretation on modern art, Barr's selection preempted history. If one follows all his arrows they lead inexorably either to 'Geometrical' or 'Non-Geometrical Abstract Art', arrows that imply a zeitgeist as if history had to lead to this preferred direction. His selection rigidly excludes all sorts of movements later recognised as 'modern', not to mention representational Dadaism – an absurdity. Yet it is an absurdity that worked very well for a time, politically, especially in America, among curators and at MoMA. Barr's arrows also lead to the Big Square surrounding MODERN ARCHITECTURE, the centre of his diagram and the implied culmination of history. It is easy to laugh at such reductivism and determinism, until one remembers how successful it was in streamlining Modernism into geometrical abstraction and the International Style. This leads to another point concerning the evolutionary tree and critical modernism, the way they illuminate the great white elephant theory, MODERN ARCHITECTURE as the triumph of a single, universal style.

The white elephant theory of modernism

Many critics, and some of the public, still believe that modern architecture means white, abstract, cubic buildings and they do so because this idea was constructed effectively in the 1930s, the totalitarian period. In addition to Barr this is how a major historian of modernism, Nikolaus Pevsner, interpreted it in *The Pioneers of the Modern Movement*, in 1936. Building up to his conclusion of Walter Gropius and the Bauhaus, Pevsner dismissed other schools of Modernism, the Expressionists and the Futurists, as aberrations from the great white hope. 'There was no question that Wright, Garnier, Loos, Behrens, Gropius were the initiators of the style of the century,' Pevsner writes triumphantly and, continuing his lack of doubt, 'that Gaudi and Sant'Elia were freaks and their inventions fantastical rantings.' Betraying his white International Style agenda he justified it, in 1936, as 'totalitarian', a slip-of-the-metaphor he corrected in later editions to 'universal'. But still the hard-liner, writing the official history of the communist party, he allows how he dismissed the 'freaks' Gaudi and Sant'Elia as mere 'footnotes'.[105] Siegfried Giedion, another major historian of the movement, following the party-line five years later in *Space, Time and Architecture*, also expunged the Expressionists, calling them mere 'transitory' not 'constituent facts' of the new modernism. [106][137]

[137] **Michel de Klerk, de Dageraad Housing**, Amsterdam, 1922. De Klerk built lots of social housing that reinterprets the Amsterdam tradition; here some that turns the corner with staggered masses meant to hold a May Day Flag. Yet the Amsterdam School, Expressionism and much of Constructivism were written out of modern architecture by Pevsner, Giedion and the other main historians until the late 1960s. (C Jencks)

[138] **Gunnar Asplund, City Library**, Stockholm, 1920–28. Fundamentalist Classicism, mostly stripped of ornament and detail, responded to modernist ideas – here pure forms, the cylinder and an overlarge entrance set against a horizontal volume. Asplund's sure handling of composition and proportion made him the master of modern classicism. (C Jencks)

History, as they say, is written by the winners. But Giedion's suppression becomes especially grotesque when one reflects that the 'transitory' was often considered as half the definition of the modern. The poet Charles Baudelaire famously defined the modern as celebrating 'the eternal within the transitory', In any case, there were many counter-views that had been suppressed by the dominant white theory. At the beginning of the 1920s some English critics in *The Architectural Review* found the Amsterdam School and Expressionism epitomising Modern architecture. Well, were Gaudí and De Klerk 'freaks – or prophets?' 'Fantasists – or pioneers?' One begins to see why the blobs of the evolutionary tree are sometimes tortuous and contortedly fraught with agony. They reveal a very real power struggle that is always underway, full of ups and downs – like biological species trying to survive in the jungle of architectural discourse.

But the ironies of the great white elephant theory go deeper and are more vicious, as one can see by following the course of the middle stream of the evolutionary tree. Here one finds strange alliances within the self-conscious tradition. This stream included the monumental Classicism of those such as Daniel Burnham, Belcher & Joass and Edwin Lutyens, all good architects (routinely excluded from old Modern histories). Heavy, baroque, sometimes pompous, this was also the mainstream that Le Corbusier attacked for being immoral and Siegfried Giedion damned for being the 'ruling style'. Yet think back in history. From the old classical position of Filarete, Vasari, the Academy and John Soane this approach would have been considered progressive, especially more than the Gothic style. But from the New Modern vantage point of 1935 it was seen as reactionary. Thus Burnham and Lutyens were written out of history, out of Modernism, and became like so many political victims of the time, non-persons. If one follows the evolutionary tree through the 1940s one sees that the self-conscious tradition is still mostly versions of classicism: Edwardian Baroque leads to Beaux-Arts Classicism which gives onto monumental stripped classicism, or the fundamental classicism of Gunnar Asplund. [138] Furthermore, when the Fascists in Italy and Spain, and the leaders of Nazi Germany and Stalinist Russia self-consciously imposed their version as a state style it squeezed out contending approaches. However, with hindsight, it is clearer that this reigning state approach, like the ideologies that fed it, was really another form of modernism.

Following sociologists such as David Harvey and Jeffrey Herf, I have called these classical architects of the 1930s Reactionary Modernists.[107] Like Albert Speer they were just as committed to technology, economic progress and instrumental reason as Mies, Le

Corbusier and Gropius. The fact that Reactionary Modernists persecuted the other modernists has obscured the deeper point that they all shared some common assumptions about power, mass culture and mass production. Reactionary and functional Modernists were, in effect, disputing some common territory, a point that the evolutionary tree reveals and one that becomes especially clear when corporate modernism triumphs after the Second World War. The inheritors of the mainstream were the big corporations, and they have been so ever since.

The evolutionary tree also shows the way this dominant tends to be attracted back either to stripped classicism, or the stolid view of modernism. Although they differ Lincoln Center in New York and twenty other cultural centres in America during the 1960s, are in this mainstream; and on the edge of it is the Modern Classicism of Robert Stern and Demetri Porphyrios. Also the corporate modernism of Renzo Piano in Berlin, and even Richard Meier, is not too far away from this centre of gravity, or 'strange attractor' as I would call it. Why? The corporate forces of production and patronage favour an abstract, semi-classical sobriety; one that does not make too many demands, intellectually or culturally. Giedion's notion of the 'ruling taste' is usually pulled towards this attractor basin for reasons of taste, pragmatism and fear of the different. Above all it is attracted here for economic reasons, because big money has, in the hands of accountants, lawyers and those who decide where to put $500 million, to play it safe. There is a law of diminishing architecture, that starts at about half a million square feet

[139] **The Law of Diminishing Architecture**. The tendency for architecture to become more boring with greater size and expense occurs at over half a million square feet. For prestige building of great size – headquarters skyscrapers are typical – this means extra money is usually needed to achieve the same quality.

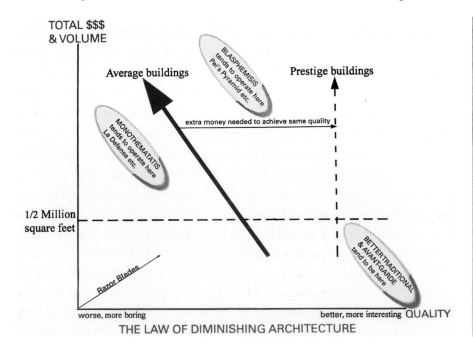

THE LAW OF DIMINISHING ARCHITECTURE

(the size of a 70- storey skyscraper) and reduces architectural creativity thereafter.[108] Like any social 'law' it is only a group tendency, and with changes in technology and structure the economic size can increase. [139] Yet like the size of animals, jumbo jets and cocktail parties there are limits beyond which quality declines, and economies of scale go into reverse. The psychological and economic forces compelling solutions towards conformity are perhaps the strongest constraints, and they channel the mainstream along predictable lines. They have created the paradox that modern buildings, born to be radical and fresh, invariably grow too big and then succumb to the great white elephant theory. Thus, because of size and power, what was meant to be creative ends up becoming reactionary. We are here back at the paradox that Gertrude Stein foresaw – 'A museum can be either a museum or it can be modern, but it can't be both' – but now from a new angle, the economic. It is perhaps the greatest internal contradiction of modernism. Savour the ironies. Siegfried Giedion certainly disliked 'the ruling taste', as much as the Futurists and Dadaists despised La Belle Epoque. Yet he wrote in order that modernism would become the dominant culture – 'the growth of a new tradition' as the subtitle of his book had it. What he could not countenance was the old saw that man kills the very thing he loves, at least when he puts it on top. To paraphrase Gertrude Stein: modernism can be the ruling taste or the new tradition if it wants, but then it can't be modern.

Critical modernism, the underground channel, once again reacted against this state of affairs, the power of conformity, and in the guise of no other than the leading modern architect, Le Corbusier. In the 1950s, just as corporate modernism was becoming the reigning approach in America and Europe, he delivered a series of withering attacks on his generation of pioneers, now suddenly those who had become the 'betrayers' of the movement. To quote him in characteristic fighting mode, quoting himself in the third person: 'In 1956 L-C was asked to accept membership of the Institute de France (Académie des Beaux Arts) in Paris: 'Thank you, never! … My name would serve as a banner to conceal the present evolution of the École des Beaux Arts towards a superficial modernism.'[109]

The 'superficial modernism' Le Corbusier was fighting, even to the end of his life nine years later, were such things as Bernard Zehrfuss' big dome, advertised, as later domes would be, as the 'greatest in the world', one promoted as large enough to 'cover the Place de la Concorde in a single span'. [140] Why was this modernism superficial? Because of the typical disjunction between bigness and smallness, image and use. The artefacts displayed inside the biggest dome, he points out, are the smallest things: 'lipsticks, benches 43 centimetres high and tables 70

[140] Bernard Zehrfuss, **CNIT Dome at La Défense**, Paris, 1955. Le Corbusier criticised the crude overdevelopment of Paris here as 'superficial modernism'. (C Jencks)

centimetres high'. Le Corbusier damned the whole grandiose misconceived project of modernism that was destroying Paris, all the way from La Défense to the Hôtel de Ville, and his damnations still have a point. His architectural indignation stems from that underground tradition of modernism, the moral strand, the very one Giedion invokes in a chapter of *Space, Time and Architecture*, called 'The Demand for Morality in Architecture'. This recounts the recurrent attacks on 'sham architecture' by Berlage, van de Velde and William Morris, ones that have echoed throughout the modernisms. Yet, while the moral commitment remains relatively constant over the years, the meaning of what is 'sham' continues to change with regularity, as style and philosophy shift. Sometimes it refers to structural dishonesty; at others to misplaced bigness as with Le Corbusier; then to social, urban or authoritarian turpitude. In short, critical modernism maintains a moral stance, a constant negative critique of its own, or others' shortcomings and this drives it forward. But its particular morality continuously moves around as the situation changes.

The ten-year rule and continuous refolution

In any case, ethics is only half the engine of change, the lesser half. The greater part, and why people sit up and take note, is the 'modernist urge', the creative mania. Creativity without criticism is blind, but criticism without creativity goes nowhere. That is why the twin engine – critical modernism – is so powerful. But, alas for our exemplars, it is also why critical modernists usually lose power in a few years.

As the evolutionary tree shows, the twentieth century does not belong to any single style, building type, such as the skyscraper, or sector. Sometimes a movement or an individual may be momentarily in the public eye, and enjoy media power, but such fame and influence rarely last for more than five years and usually for not more than two. It is true that certain architects were creative forces that lasted for longer. Mies was a power to be reckoned with in the 1920s and again in the 1960s. Le Corbusier, Frank Lloyd Wright and Alvar Aalto, who with Mies made up the big four 'masters', were seminal at more times and Kahn, Stirling, Eisenman, Foster, Gehry and Koolhaas, the little six, each had two periods of influence. [141] But even these protean characters, in order to stay relevant and on top, had to reinvent themselves about every ten years.

The notion that there is a 'ten-year rule' of reinvention for the creative genius in the twentieth century has been put by the

[141] **1970 # 1990 – The influence of potent creativity lasts about five years**. Thus, to be a force in world architecture, protean creators have to reinvent themselves about every ten years. Two periods of influence, the 1970s and 1990s, and two approaches can be seen in the work of Frank Gehry, Peter Eisenman and Rem Koolhaas – among other influential architects. Note the shift in approach from Gehry's Santa Monica House (1978) to the Disney Hall (2003); from Eisenman's House III (1971) to the Aronoff Center (1996); from Koolhaas' City of the Captive Globe (drawing Madelon Vriesendorp) (1975) to the Seattle Public Library (1999). Some of these shifts are stylistic, some philosophical, some productive. (All photos C Jencks except middle left courtesy Eisenman Architects)

1970s

1990s

Harvard cognitive scientist Howard Gardner in his book *Creating Minds* (1993). Subtitled *An anatomy of creativity seen through the lives of Freud, Einstein, Picasso, Stravinsky, Eliot, Graham and Gandhi*, it is a detailed study of these, the big seven modernists, and it shows how they often made breakthroughs or underwent creative shifts about every ten years. In *Le Corbusier and the Continual Revolution in Architecture*, I have found the same pattern in this the Proteus of design.[110] As the Hayward Gallery put it, polemically, in the title of a 1987 retrospective, Le Corbusier was *The Architect of the Century* – a pre-emptive designation before the century was over and someone like Frank Gehry given a shot at the title. Was the judgement valid? If one judges worth by the ability to reinvent oneself and influence others, the answer must be positive. I have marked in the evolutionary tree the five times Le Corbusier enjoyed this recurrent influence, greater authority than any of the other creative figures: as the leader of the Heroic Period of the 1920s; as a leading thinker of a new (and rather unfortunate) urbanism; as the leader of CIAM and mass housing after the war; as a harbinger of Post-Modernism with Ronchamp and the symbolic architecture of Chandigarh; and, just at the end of his life, with his Brussels and Zurich pavilions, the forerunner of the High-Tech movement. No other architect was as creative in different traditions; not for nothing was he seen as 'the Picasso of architecture'.

My point, however, is slightly different than Howard Gardner's. While agreeing with his analysis, I think one of the important reasons for the demonic creativity of his seven 'geniuses' is that the twentieth century was uncommonly turbulent. The diagram, and its tortuous blobs, captures these continual revolutions. Or, I should say more exactly, continuous *refolutions* because, as noted at the outset of this book, these shifts are partially also slides where much remains the same. At any one time the twentieth-century architect has had to face three or four competing movements of architecture, the sixty or so 'isms' noted in the diagram, and then also respond to changes in technology, social forces, style and ideology – not to mention two world wars and such large impersonal forces as the Internet. All of this turbulence generates the hundred or so trends and events that are indicated, mostly at the bottom of the diagram. It was an exhausting century. As the Chinese say: 'may you be condemned to live in interesting times'. To keep at the top of the profession, and moving with all this interesting change, an architect had to refolutionise his message about every ten years.

Hidden tradition or process?

The evolutionary tree shows the turbulent pattern of critical modernisms in architecture, underground streams always bubbling away and occasionally surfacing. It raises the larger question of whether today there are real alternatives to modernism, cultures that can live outside the pervasive system of modernisation. There are certainly anti-modern traditions, remnants of traditional society in the countryside untouched by modernity, and small fragments of Neolithic life. But are these real alternatives, and do they amount to separate systems of culture and production?

My view is similar to that of the sociologists I have quoted above, Herf and Harvey, that traditional attitudes and fundamentalism are now inevitable parts of the modern formation, not exceptions. One finds all the commitments to high-tech and the wired world among those forming an alternative culture and sometimes this is best summarised as Reactionary Modernism – not a real difference from the underlying condition. There are indeed important variations within modernisms, but there is no going back to pre-modern conditions. What looks like traditional alternatives – for instance the Christian, Buddhist or Muslim ways of life – have been partially absorbed into one or another of the competing streams and thus one might speak of the hyphenated condition Christian-Modernism, and so on. Modernism is here the main classifier, Christian is the weak modifier. The religious modifier does make a small difference, but does not change fundamental assumptions about progress, the importance of change, technology, globalisation – even if today the Bishop of London pronounces it a sin of global warming to take an aeroplane. The key point is that modernism as a whole has evolved from Christianity and is a kind of Post-Christian faith, as I argued at the outset. This is a one-way evolution, one cannot go back from modernity no matter how many people may wish they could. You cannot uninvent the modern economy any more than Relativity Theory. Yet, to reiterate, there are several quarrelling modernisms just as there are several competing versions of capitalism and there is unlikely to be a single grand synthesis in the future. To think so is to believe in the great white elephant theory of modernism, similar to what John Gray calls the 'global delusion' that American or Chinese or EU capitalism is the model for the rest of the globe.

It comes down to a battle of what could be called 'Prefix-Modernisms'. And, if one sort of hyphenated-modernism or another is inevitable, then critical modernism assumes more importance as a single stream among others. Could it become a conscious movement, a capital-lettered trend? It looks entirely possible given today's prevailing scepticism, one which Lyotard called the hallmark of post-modernism, and given the way analysis pervades all thought. The critical temper colours every specialised area, even if only as a trace. For instance, within architecture, and following the Frankfurt School, there have been movements variously labelled criticality, Critical Reconstruction (Berlin urbanism in the 1990s) and Critical Regionalism. During the late 1980s academic probity could be assured by placing 'critical' before almost any subsequent word. But the last mentioned phrase, theorised by Kenneth Frampton (following Tzonis and Lefevre) is put forward *not* as a movement but as a 'fragmentary and marginal practice.'[111] As Frampton defines the features of Critical Regionalism it is both a typical post-modern trend with contextual and local aspects that resist the universal tendencies of modernisation, and also one that resists what he calls the 'scenographic' aspects of post-modernism itself. Thus for him it is doubly critical, and its resistance takes the form of using tactile elements against the visual, and tectonic elements against the scenographic. There is something to be said for this strain of revisionist modernism. Indeed, the regional has been promoted as an alternative to the international since the 1940s – even by Walter Gropius himself. But as a conscious, collective and political movement, regionalism does not exist as a coherent architectural force. Furthermore, although individual architects whom Frampton cites, such as Jørn Utzon, Alvaro Siza and Tadeo Ando, may have fragmentary allusions to regional elements, such architects are perceived more correctly as Late Modern rather than Critical Regionalists. Most importantly, they do not form part of a collective, local movement.

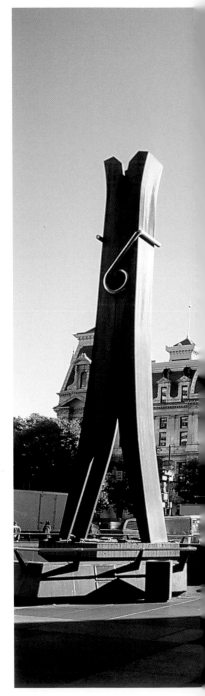

A similar point could be made about architects, such as Peter Eisenman, who tie their 'criticality' to operations on the language of architecture. They resist stereotyping and forge critical moves in architectural discourse, but they do not constitute a collective movement of 'critical' mass (to play on the other sense of the word). As George Baird summarises the debate between the 'critical and the post critical' architects, it remains mostly within academic walls, and has yet to engage with a wider public.[112] The problem for the intellectual critique is that it is dismissed, however wrongly, as mere negative resistance and not understood as the counterpart of creative extension. As Baird recounts this struggle it has been too easy for the 'post-critical' pragmatists to dismiss the 'negativity' of their adversaries and, following Rem Koolhaas, promote instead 'the projective' scheme, in effect the positive imagination of architectural projects. This touches a generic problem for artists and architects today, especially in the advanced economies, since they are so isolated as individuals or constrained within small groups. Their influence

usually extends just to other professionals and almost never to the wider community or into politics. Hence their criticism is usually limited to marginal differentiation, to the critique of other academic positions and not something more radical and outside their specialisation.

Such limited criticism is nevertheless important and, in any case, it corresponds to the negative dialectic that partially drives critical modernism forward: Futurism slating Fauvism, Dadism refuting Futurism, Surrealism attacking Dada etc. It also supports the idea that critical modernism is not a conscious movement – one 'ism' among others – but a radically dispersed practice. It is distributed in many places and exists in many individuals, if only for a short time. At a minimum it is the process of learning through absorbing and criticising other modernists, a system of immanent feedback, each move reflecting on the previous one. Positively, this dispersed practice opens up a space of imaginative freedom where creative individuals have a degree of autonomy and integrity. Furthermore, it is a primary role of the critic and historian to discover this critical creativity where it can be found, to judge and then to celebrate it.

Sooner or later, however, these creations are bound to be absorbed within the global system of Late Capitalism and cultural consumption to end up as items in the museum-go-round. If one doubts that sobering thought, reflect on what happened to DADA, the *soi-disant* ugly, anti-bourgeois, anti-art. Its works have, since the mid-1970s, been gulped down and digested as beautiful by all the world's MOMAS – and without a burp. That is the power of consumption today, swallowing what is meant to be poison but loving it as champagne. As amazed French critics remarked, when Oldenburg's *Clothespin* was put up as a monument in the centre of the most symbolic and politically charged site in Philadelphia (with the statue of William Penn surveying the scene), it showed that any act of art can be absorbed. [142] A banal, meaningless and expensive pin, 45 feet high in Corten steel, was erected – why? One imagines it was a good sign that the city had understood, and accepted, avant-garde Pop. Another reason was that the shape looked powerful against the dumb, white offices (today one should never underrate the primacy of the aesthetic gesture). Negatively, one might surmise, it was erected because there was nothing officials found pressing in Philadelphia life to celebrate: the clothespin became the default option. This object, like the iconic buildings that dominate global architecture, once again proves the point of the art critic, Arthur Danto: 'today anything can be a work of art'. If Oldenburg's *Clothespin* is anything to go by then culture, critical or not, has only a marginal ability to change (or even startle) the greater society.

Critical Modernism –
a conscious movement?

One cannot be sure if critical modernism will remain a swirl of underground streams bubbling along, an immanent dialectic, or become a more conscious movement – Critical Modernism. If it were the latter then it would take on many of the post-modern themes I have touched on. Let us imagine a hypothetical movement of a modernism come of age, one aware of its own problems and continuously critical of reigning assumptions in the wider land of the dominant Bush. This might seem an idle speculation. But here, where I write these concluding lines, in Berlin, and the land that Donald Rumsfeld characterised as Old Europe, it does not seem so fanciful. Berlin suffered several modernist traumas in the twentieth century and almost alone among such unfortunate cities has begun to acknowledge both its positive and negative history. Monuments, museums and exhibitions constantly remind the German nation in its capital city what it has done on both sides of the balance sheet. I have already discussed Daniel Libeskind's Jewish Museum as a key point in this process of growing consciousness and it is worth quoting from an official document describing another such building, Peter Eisenman's *Memorial to the Murdered Jews of Europe*. It asks 'why is the memorial dedicated only to the murdered Jews?' and answers:

> After a long debate, the German Bundestag decided in 1999 to dedicate the memorial to the murdered Jews of Europe. This underlines that acknowledging the uniqueness of this crime and historic responsibility is central to the Federal Republic of Germany's self-understanding.[113]

Such a debate, and 'self-understanding' of the 'historic responsibility', is rarely found in other countries. Compared to Germany, Japan and Italy have hardly acknowledged their war crimes, and the US and UK, for instance, have only begun to come to terms with their slavery, imperialism and destruction of the native Americans. These countries may feel they have no great transgression to answer for; nor do they cultivate a historical consciousness about such possible misdeeds. By contrast, the long German debate especially since the mid-1980s has been painful and open-ended. It raises the question of whether a whole country or people can be collectively guilty, or a 'culprit nation', as it was called. Or, equally hard to judge, whether other victims of the Nazis – the Sinti, prisoners of war, gypsies and homosexuals – should be honoured equally next to the murdered Jews,

[143] Laurie Chetwood, **London Oasis**, 2006. An energy beacon and an installation symbolising and performing the clever use of natural resources. Solar power is taken in through the wing-cells, which also double as rainwater collectors. The energy, also coming through the wind turbine at the top, is dramatised by the glowing fibres on its way to the storage batteries at the base; a hydrogen fuel cell provides more energy by stripping electrons from the hydrogen present in methanol. The mast acts as a thermal chimney and water is stored in irrigation tanks. (© Edmund Sumner/ Chetwoods)

with a European scaled memorial. Something along these lines is now contemplated. Will this result in tokenism, or a culture of pseudo-shame, or false apology; or perhaps a national victim-cult?

All of this has been argued. But whatever one's conclusions, and some have said the greatest monument is the debate itself, it is important in the context of a Critical Modernism that more than ten such buildings, or areas in Berlin, retell versions of this past. Most impressively they do so without much rhetoric.[113] Neither piety, nor maudlin pity is on display, there is not the usual undercurrent of voyeurism. It is true that Holocaust museums and war memorials were built in some numbers around the world during the 1980s, but they have not been absorbed into the wider national consciousness and governmental debate as they have in this German capital. Self-awareness of one's place in cultural space and time is the precondition of a possible Critical Modernism, and Berlin has done more to raise this critical consciousness than any other place. Such consciousness has implications for Critical Modernism.

If it becomes a conscious movement then it will be set around abstract principles, not a single style. I will mention five generalisations, and clarify them with particular works completed by 2005 or later.

1. *External issues.* As the inheritor of the post-modern critique a conscious movement would take on many specific aspects of the pluralist agenda; for instance, fighting for the locale against the dominant centre, campaigns against the destruction of city fabric and the ecological community, launching attacks on the reigning ideologies. That is to say Critical Modernism would continue to focus its efforts on areas *outside* specific cultural disciplines as a critical practice. It is obvious from the 1960s that general issues radicalise specific subcultures, just as it is apparent that the 2003 Iraqi invasion raised critical consciousness. Yet, at the same time, a cultural movement would have to be realistic, need to acknowledge that its interventions were marginal if symbolically crucial. The irony of this limited position, especially with respect to such chronic problems as global warming, has to be accepted. [143]

Irony is a grudging way to deal with an unfortunate truth. The fact is that where Earth Summits and Kyoto Protocols, oil companies and Al Gore, Green gurus and politicians have failed to slow the greenhouse effect, pressure groups, not to mention architects and artists, will not succeed. PM irony is more acceptable than posturing, or pretending that sustainable development, in a world of 6 billion consumers growing in size, is sustainable. It allows one to take a strong symbolic position without deluding either oneself, or others, that it will actually change the situation. It allows one to take on the struggle of our time, without succumbing to the lie that it can be easily won. There are many other areas outside culture where Critical Modernism can take such a stand – on social and political issues, where lying is also institutionalised.

For instance, as I have argued, it can criticise the notion that the war on terror actually decreases terrorism, rather than amplifies it. Critical Modernism could continue to broadcast the fact that the number of people worldwide who die as a result of international terrorism is only a few hundred per year – a tiny figure when compared with those who die in civil wars or from automobile accidents. Indeed, actuaries who assess risk can show that in 'almost all [recent] years, the total number of people worldwide who die at the hands of international terrorists anywhere in the world is not much more than the number who drown in bathtubs in the United States'.[115] Irony, given the water shortages, indeed. But more ironic is the fact that the CIA, FBI and fourteen more intelligence organisations in the US produced a report saying the invasion of Iraq and the war on terror had increased terrorism, and published it at the very moment that President Bush and Prime Minister Blair were asserting that this war increased safety.[116] The hard truth of our time is that once committed to a failed policy politicians get locked into the law of increasing guilt and cannot get out because to do so would be to admit their previous and then continuing culpability. The inability to acknowledge one was wrong, respond to criticism and change direction increases the guilt with the passage of time and, it has been argued, was a prime mover of the Holocaust.[117] Everyone has to suffer as a result of this tragic flaw in our character and democratic systems, one that cannot be too strongly criticised.

2. *Relevant iconography*. The obvious reason that Critical Modernism, like all movements worthy of the name, might go outside its field of specialisation is that its first motive is towards the human condition. It can only carve out a critical space from this larger perspective, it can only take a critical position on subject matter, a second motive, if individuals think across fields, use each one to question another. How does one know that the scientific metaphors I have criticised at the outset of this chapter – the big bang and selfish gene – are degraded comparisons, and questionable in themselves? From questioning *within* science and philosophy, and from seeing where these metaphors lead from *without*, that is in the rest of life. To return to architecture – how does one become conscious that a right-

[144 a, b, c, d] Cai Guo-Qiang, **Head On**, a three-part installation at the German Guggenheim, Berlin, 2006. A wolf pack leaps to the attack, only coming to its downfall when it hits the glass wall. The drawing (above) **Vortex**, was created by detonating varieties of

gunpowder (seen in the explosion) below stencils of wolves, thus giving the ghost image of a prehistoric cave painting. The 99 life-size wolves were constructed from painted sheepskins stuffed with hay and given marble eyes.
(Photos C Jencks, © Cai Guo-Qiang)

angled world has its limits? By challenging it with triangles or curves or fractal subsets; by thinking outside the box (as did Frank Lloyd Wright). How did Impressionists challenge the representational system of perspective? Or Cubists challenge the Impressionists? And so it goes.

Forging a relevant iconography means addressing the local context with methods that challenge its cultural space and time. A case in point is the Berlin installation by the Chinese artist Cai Guo-Qiang, keyed into the themes of twentieth-century Germany history, particularly the aggression of herd behaviour. [144] The artist studied several areas in Berlin including Checkpoint Charlie, the Soviet Memorial and the site of the former Gestapo Headquarters. This last place, an excavation that has now become a permanent exhibit called Typography of Terrors, was instrumental in starting the larger German debate in the 1980s: how, when memorialising the usual national attainments can one also have a policy of marking the tragedies and crimes?

Cai's response to conflict and killing elicited one of his well-known gunpowder drawings, controlled explosions that leave imprints on canvas, in this case silhouettes of wolves chasing and being destroyed by the chase. The idea of a pack of wolves swarming towards its prey in a large arc is turned into something of a time-lapse installation frozen in mid-leap. The iconography may be somewhat obvious, the allegory of a Germany run amok only to 'hit the wall', as his title has it – *Head On*. But there are some surprising subtleties, such as the way the gunpowder drawing recalls the cave paintings of prehistory and the installation as a whole literally pulls the visitor in. One follows the pack in and under the springing animals to explore them close up and from all sides, thus becoming part of the chase – and its victim. In several ways this is an iconography with a direct connection to its subject matter, and a theatrical confrontation with the nationalist wolf always on the run.

3. *Multivalence*. As I have emphasised, so much of thinking consists in opposing one code to another and so much of consciousness is an awareness of difference and contradiction. The negative dialectic and the positive creation both set up an opposition of codes that heighten consciousness, for criticism *is* the juxtaposition of meanings, and having a conscience *is* listening to that interior dialogue of codes as they battle in the mind while, all the time, trying to be an impartial judge. If the critical work sets up an analogous or parallel dialectic, it follows that the third motive of a Critical Modernism would be *internal* to a discipline, focusing on the way a specific work of art contrasts its texts. Close reading, textual analysis as an interrogation of the work

while creating it, leads to its complexity. The critical in this sense is allied to the creative, to the discovery of new links in a work that is unfolding in the creator's mind and on the canvas. Concentrating on internal meanings may highlight the double coding of post-modernism or the cross-coding of many texts. In both cases it reveals 'organised complexity,' that is, the inherent quality of objects (illustrated in the diagram on cosmic axiology, above, [102]. Cross-coding links more and more meaning, either finding the similarities or foregrounding the differences. Criticality thus concerns reaching an apogee of complexity between order and chaos – multivalence – neither sliding into over-

simple cliché nor gratuitous complication – univalence. As I have stressed, this is not a precise point and, in any case, it is one judged by a variable audience of naïve and educated readers. Yet, imprecise as this judgement is, it becomes a duty of the critic to elucidate the critical depth that is the mark of quality.

Take the Frank Gehry design for the Stata Centre at MIT, a very complex *but* complicated building. [145] Given the convolutions, the positive points might be overlooked, but as a typical post-modern solution to high density, the scheme breaks down a huge volume into a village scale and provides an internal street life for the students and academics. Gehry has been effective in achieving the informality and interaction called for in his brief. Where scientists and students were separated by specialisation, they now have many common spaces both small and large. Here they interact or meet spontaneously. Gehry's informal village articulation supports this social complexity functionally at the many contact points; and represents it architecturally with his signature elements: the punched out windows, the splayed entrances and fractured improvisation. The ten visible pavilions are also pulled together at the base to create these common public spaces. As a whole the building carries through the theme of a densely related city fabric, in its symbolism and layout becoming very much the hybrid assemblage which was sought. At some points the building becomes more complicated than complex, especially when competing elements shout for attention, or when some rooms have too many oblique corners. But, over the years, this labyrinthine urbanism is likely to absorb its diverse population very effectively, that is as long as it is managed so that individuals and groups can look after the fabric and make it their own.

4. *Overturning usage.* These buildings at MIT also underscore the fourth and most visible motive of a potential Critical Modernism: its creative potency, its 'modernism that is new'. I put the phrase in scare quotes because, after two hundred years following Wordsworth's injunction 'to make it new', a sceptical audience is aware that this is often more of a claim than a result. Most modernism, especially that safe, white, cubism marketed in the 1930s (and again in the 1960s and 1990s) is rather predictable. Originality has correspondingly been put in question by a few post-modernists such as Cindy Sherman and the critic Rosalind Krauss. Yet however marginal novelty and creativity are, however much a matter of degree, they are clearly valuable motives in culture, just as they are interesting in nature. Moreover they can be disguised within very familiar forms.

[146 a, b, c] Peter Eisenman, **Memorial to the Murdered Jews of Europe**, Berlin, 1998–2005. A field of grey that dissolves into the city at the four edges – here the Tiergarten – becomes a work of Land Art that gently embraces visitors and draws them into contemplation. The multiple entries and many uses of these blocks – appropriated for sitting, jumping and eating on – displaces the one-liner of cube, death and shame, allowing a more nuanced relationship with the subject. Information centre and street of stelae carry through the metaphor, field of traces. (C Jencks)

On one reading, Eisenman's Holocaust monument in Berlin could not be more obvious, indeed Modernist. [146] It consists of concrete slabs – the ubiquitous white cube it appears, multiplied 2,711 times and turned different shades of grey. They vary only in vertical dimension, from 1 to 15 feet, and are in the proportions of a coffin. My first impression, when I saw the plans and read about the scheme, was that this field of slabs might be a bit remorseless, a constant hammer-blow on the German conscience of one grey grave after another. Or, perhaps as the press photos portrayed it, like a First World War graveyard, an Op-Art 'aesthetics of death'.

Yet it is more appropriate and creative than these aerial shots reveal Subtle surprise is its hallmark. As one walks into this field of stelae the ground undulates somewhat downwards, the coffin shapes tilt a bit here and there and get taller towards the centre of the site, as if there were something down there worth discovering. It feels vaguely as if one were descending into frozen slabs of water, slowly submerging under the horizon-line of the earth. But no, Eisenman's intention was to create a monument that gives no greater meaning to the Holocaust. 'The space isn't a graveyard. I didn't want any names: it should be absent of meaning,' Eisenman said, only allowing the metaphor of getting lost and disoriented, as he once was in an Iowa cornfield. 'That moment was very scary. There are moments in time when you feel lost in space. I was trying to create the possibility of that experience, that frisson, something that you don't forget.'[118] Curiously, although one does experience this *Memorial to the Murdered Jews of Europe* as bleak and perhaps frightening, one is never lost because of the visible grid of streets and avenues, and this clear orientation plays a critical role in furthering contemplation. My biggest surprise, on descending into the site several times, was discovering how intimate all these stelae could be as an entire field; and the polished cubes, how much more engaging they were than in the aerial view, the remorseless one-liner. Because the space between the slabs is so narrow, everyone has to walk the site alone, enforcing an existential individuality on contemplation, making one a singular witness. Moreover, the result is that other people suddenly appear and disappear between slabs as freeze-frame shots, as if their life and death were fleeting, cut-off at both ends.

The overall effect of these stelae is quite different from their mental appearance, not the clichés of a photo-op but small parts of a larger experience, one that constantly elicits various thoughts as one sees the background, one contemplates what has happened framed in different settings – set against the trees of the Tiergarten, the cars and buses rushing around the block, the children jumping from one to the next, or the self-important buildings and moving cranes. Thoughts can be held in continuity amid this pressing reality, making of the Holocaust something part of urban life as it really was. This striking field of grey carries forward such realistic attitudes worked out during the 1980s, that a sober and factual approach to war crimes was preferable to editorialising.[118] In the underground information centre, aspects of the Holocaust are presented in the same way; for instance, last letters or diary entries of victims can be read under glass panels set in the floor reflecting the proportions of the stelae overhead. Sensitised to the shape, one begins to notice that most of the office windows surrounding the site also have proportions of the grave.

In effect, Eisenman has used the most familiar form of Modernism in an extreme way, as ground rather than figure, and thereby overturned its associations, 'making new' the already said. As I have stressed in the first chapter, much portentous nonsense was placed on the minimalist cube in the twentieth century, the way it symbolised 'the presence of the absence' and a plethora of other absent meaning; for once, with this Land Art, such signification has found its proper social role, a task appropriate for the Wittgensteinian silence – and again, Amen to that.

5. *Honouring by critique*. It goes without saying that a younger generation will be critical of this architecture and vary their models away from it. Indeed, one finds the followers of Eisenman and Gehry swerving down the road as they construct their own diverging route ahead. Ben van Berkel and Caroline Bos, of UN Studio in Holland, do some quick turns in their 2006 polemic *Design Models* veering sharply away from 'safety' on the left rail and 'criticality' on the right.

> What we don't like is risk-free architecture. In the long run, it makes no difference if that 'safe' architecture is of the commercial variety or disguised as 'critical' architecture, its criticality amounting to a recitation of the received opinions that have been echoing for thirty years.

After this palpable hit at Eisenmanian criticality, they go on to nudge the fashionable expressionism of Gehry, pushing it onto the verge.

> The meaninglessness of architecture that avoids risk is most eloquently expressed by the fact that it has recently [and] noiselessly converted from a once staunchly defended modernist formal appearance, to a once vehemently opposed expressionist, or organic, formal appearance.

[147 a, b, c, d] UN Studio, **Mercedes-Benz Museum**, Stuttgart, 2001–6. Next to the highway, this sleek waving volume has the gentle nips and tucks of a high-speed racer. Like a giant car-ramp its organisation is based on continuous flow. Here visitors start at the top, in the manner of the Guggenheim Museum, and then can travel down on several routes around a trefoil plan. At some points there are concrete twists and double helical ramps, and the continuously varying structure and window-wall are further tropes of today's complexity architecture. In short, the building is not an experimental leap into the unknown, more a convincing extension of current design ideas of fluidity used with great skill on a building where they are appropriate. (Courtesy UN Studio, photos © Christian Richters)

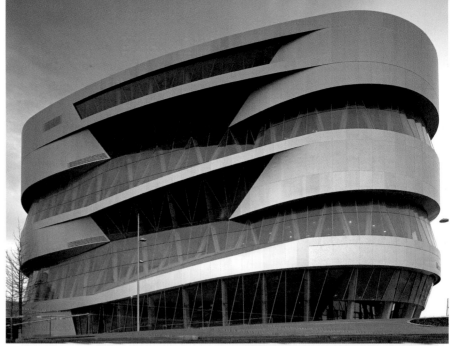

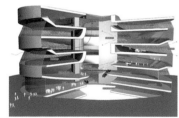

How true (in part). Then comes their final generational swerve, an answer to their critics, and an acceleration onto the new open road – into the unknown!

> Although we, and some of our contemporaries, have occasionally been labelled pragmatists, insinuating that what we are is a bunch of morally lax, uncritical opportunists, it seems to us that only those who continually practice an experimental approach – concentrating all our efforts in a completely unknown outcome – are the ones who can truly be said to be the idealists … [120]

Experimental approach, how romantic, how positively Unknown! What I like about this polemic, not surprisingly, is the way it neatly illustrates my thesis of critical modernism as both the immanent negative dialectic plus the swerve. These two points are borne out just as much by the architecture illustrating their polemic of *Design Models*. For what do we find in their recently completed museum for Mercedes-Benz in Stuttgart, and its romp through the history of 160 vintage models and 40 racing vehicles, its 'legends and *Mythen*' of the German motor car? Nothing else than a 'kind of' Eisenmanian set of diagrams and process-oriented moves carried through in a 'sort of' expressionist swirl like Gehry. [147] I use these weasel words of Fuzzy Logic advisedly, for the younger designers work is dependent on, but different from, their predecessors. This combinatorial logic, this double move that carries on some ideas just as it rejects others, is the fifth and most obvious part of a conscious tradition. And my irony at these designers' expense is intended to be more affectionate than vicious, since, like all creators out to cut a new space, they had to convince themselves of their radical otherness before they could convince others.

This example also reaffirms how critical modernism relates to its capitalised-lettered counterpart, how modernisms of all persuasions are under the burden of having to invent a marginal differentiation and call it new, of being beholden to their predecessors while they kill them off. This quarrelling and competing, however, can obscure the tacit understanding below the surface, the apparent disagreements are like ritualised shadow-boxing. It's a fight, to paraphrase Umberto Eco, where each pugilist knows that his opponent knows that landing blows is only the bizarre modern way of showing a deeper appreciation (as Barbara Cartland would not say, of showing love).

Let me put the same problematic with other metaphors. Because critical modernism is a trans-historical category there is no single person, group or set of attitudes that can encompass its goals, can synthesise its dialectic process across time. It is driven by opposite forces, a critical temperament, analysis, and disgust with present conditions; but also by the modern part of the equation, its creativity, the forward thrust of the combination. Thus the effective cocktail where the critical Vermouth tempers the modern Gin and the hybrid is still a powerful drink. Or, put another way, because modernisms follow each other so quickly and relentlessly today they could lead to a critical tipping point, a hyper-consciousness about the process itself. Then the underground stream would suddenly rise up through the surface as a visible wave. When that point of consciousness is reached, a Modernism^2 or Modernism^3, it becomes aware simultaneously of its own shortcomings and virtues and its prolonged adolescence of two hundred years turns into a new coming of age. While the political counterpart to such a cultural movement is a long way off, in some parts of the world that maturity may well be upon us.

NOTES

Chapter 1

1   The Arctic Circle ice retreat has increased since measurements started in 1979, and radically since 2005, opening up a 'new black gold rush' as well as land grab by the eight adjoining nations. The cowboy opportunities are enumerated by Ben Macintyre in, 'As the Arctic ice retreats, the old Great Game begins to boil over', *The Times*, 11 February 2006, pp 46–7.

2   Jean-François Lyotard, *The Postmodern Explained to Children, Correspondence 1982–1985*, Turnaround (London), 1992, pp 30–1.

3   For complexity science as a centre of post-modernism see below Chapter 5, 'Cultural and natural complexity'. My interviews with these scientists, and Lyotard, were broadcast in 'Mr Jencks' Jumping Universe', BBC Radio 3, 11 May 1997, producer William Catlin, Loftus Productions, London.

4   To give an idea of the ubiquity of the term in the early 1990s, I might mention three of the seventeen anthologies that appeared recently. Because of date I start with my own *The Post-Modern Reader*, Academy/St Martin's Press (London/New York), 1992, which has thirty articles ranging from post-modern film to science and religion; Thomas Docherty's *PoStmOdErNnism, A Reader*, Harvester Wheatsheaf (Hemel Hempstead), 1993, has thirty-four articles ranging from post-modern politics to avant-gardism; Joseph Natoli and Linda Hutcheon, *A Postmodern Reader*, SUNY Press (Albany, NY), 1993, has twenty-five articles ranging from 'postmodern blackness' to 'The Postmodern *Weltanschauung*'. Three 'readers' with some overlap of authors appeared within twelve months of each other. That rate of scholarly production never happened with modernism, even in its heyday. Yet the popular and professional press tend to magnify the less savoury aspects of post-modernism, either the deconstructive nihilism of some philosophers or that of consumer society. See, for instance, the issues of the TLS, 16 October and 18 December 1992 and that of *The Independent on Sunday*, 16 November 1992, p 21.

5   Linda Hutcheon, *A Poetics of Postmodernism, History, Theory, Fiction*, Routledge (New York and London), 1988, p xi.

6   Such post-modern liberalism has been explored by the Canadian philosopher Charles Taylor and is the keynote of my *Heteropolis: Los Angeles, the Riots and the Strange Beauty of Hetero-architecture*, Academy Editions (London and New York), 1993.

7   Gerard-Georges Lemaire, 'Le Spectre du post-modernisme', 'Decadence', *Le Monde Dimanche*, 18 October 1981, p xiv.

8   Clement Greenberg, 'Modern and Post-Modern' presented as the fourth Sir William Dobell Memorial Lecture in Sydney, Australia, on 31 October 1979 and published the following year in *Arts Magazine*.

9   Walter Darby Bannard, 'On Postmodernism', an essay originally presented at a panel on post-modernism at the Modern Languages Associatio's annual meeting in New York, 28 December 1983, published later in *Arts Magazine*.

10 Aldo van Eyck, 'RPP – Rats, Posts and Other Pests', 1981 RIBA Annual Discourse published in *RIBA Journal*, *Lotus* and most fully in *AD News*, 7/81 (London 1981), pp 14–16.

11 Berthold Lubetkin, 'Royal Gold Medal Address', *RIBA, Transactions II*, Vol 1, No 2 (London), 1982, p 48.

12 Berthold Lubetkin, 'RIBA President's Invitation Lecture', 11 June 1985, unpublished manuscript, p 13. Published in part in *Building Design*, London. The comparison is with Stalin's giving Corinthian columns to the people. The Prince of Wales provokes the following memory: 'I can't help recalling the diktat of Stalin fifty years ago when he said "The assumption that the specialists know better drags theory and practice into the bog of reactionary cosmopolitan opinion." The proletariat acquired the right to have their Corinthian colonnades …'

13 'Is Post-Modern Architecture Serious? Paolo Portoghesi and Bruno Zevi in Conversation', *Architectural Design*, 1/2 1982, pp 20–1, originally published in Italian in *L'Espresso*.

14 Roman-esque meant 'corrupted Roman' in its first usages, circa 1819; Gothic like Gothick was another term of abuse having several origins, first applied in the Renaissance, based on an assumption about the Goths and the way they corrupted Roman architecture and the arts. Baroque and Rococo were seen as degenerate classicism – the disordered curves and shell like *rocaille*. Impressionism was merely based on impressions of light, not a representation of reality; Fauves were 'wild men;' Cubism was like simplistic sugar cubes, and so on. Some of this is discussed by E.H.Gombrich in 'Norm and Form' The Stylistic Categories of Art History and

their Origins in Renaissance Ideals, *Norm and Form*, Studies in the art of the Renaissance, Phaidon, London, 1966, pp. 81-98.

15 Henri de Saint-Simon, *Opinions littéraires, philosophiques et industrielles*, Paris, 1825, quoted in Donald Drew Egbert, *Social Radicalism in the Arts: Western Europe*, Alfred A Knopf (New York), 1970, p 121.

16 Ibid, pp 121–2.

17 Quoted from Adolf Loos, 'Ornament and Crime' in Ulrich Conrads, *Programmes and Manifestoes on 20th Century Architecture*, Lund Humphries (London), 1970, pp 19, 20.

18 Piet Mondrian, quoted in Reyner Banham, *Theory and Design in the First Machine Age*, Architectural Press (London), 1960, p 150.

19 Theo van Doesburg, ibid, p 152.

20 De Stijl, ibid, p 151.

21 Le Corbusier, *Towards a New Architecture*, translated from the French by Frederick Etchells, Architectural Press (London), 1959, first translation 1927, p 12.

22 Ludwig Mies van der Rohe, 'Industrialized Building', 1924, reprinted in *Programmes and Manifestos on 20th Century Architecture*, Lund Humphries (London), 1970, p 81.

23 Colin Rowe, *The Architecture of Good Intentions*, was published nine years after these words were first written; Wiley Academy (London), 1994.

24 'Dialogues with Philip Johnson', in Charles Jencks, *The New Moderns*, Academy Editions/Rizzoli (London and New York), 1990, pp 153–4.

25 Jean-François Lyotard, *The Postmodern Condition: A Report on Knowledge*, Manchester University Press (Manchester), 1984, p 79. The book was first published in French in 1979.

26 Ibid, p 81.

Chapter 2

27 My own writing and lecturing on Post-Modernism in architecture started in 1975 with 'The Rise of Post-Modern Architecture'. This was published in a Dutch book *Architecture – Inner Town Government*, Eindhoven, July 1975, and a British magazine, *Architectural Association Quarterly*, No 4, 1975. Subsequently Eisenman and Stern started using the term and by 1977 it had caught on. For a brief history see the 'Footnote on the Term' in *The Language of Post-Modern Architecture*, fourth edition, Academy Editions (London) and Rizzoli (New York), 1984, p 8.

28 Umberto Eco, *Postscript To The Name of the Rose*, Harcourt Brace Jovanovich (New York), 1984, pp 67–8.

29 Linda Hutcheon, *A Poetics of Postmodernism, History, Theory, Fiction*, Routledge (New York and London), 1988, pp 3–22.

30 See John Barth, 'The Literature of Replenishment, Postmodernist Fiction', *The Atlantic*, January 1980, pp 65–71, and Umberto Eco, 'Postmodernism. Irony. The Enjoyable', *Postscript to The Name of the Rose*, Harcourt Brace Jovanovich (New York and London), 1984, first published in Italian, 1983. Umberto Eco's *The Name of the Rose* became a best seller of the kind of pm fiction that Barth and Eco describe in their criticism.

31 See 'Folding in Architecture', *Architectural Design*, 3/4, 1993, *Profile 102*, especially the writing of Jeffrey Kipnis and Greg Lynn.

32 For my critiques of post-modern kitsch see 'Post-Modernism on Trial', *Architectural Design*, 1991 and *The Language of Post-Modern Architecture*, 6th edn, 1991, last chapter.

33 For architectural examples see my *The Architecture of the Jumping Universe*, Wiley Academy (London), 1995. Also Steven Johnson, *Emergence, The Connected Lives of Ants, Brains, Cities and Software*, Penguin Press (London), 2000, which discusses Jane Jacobs and is typical of the many books on complexity theory.

34 These figures were supplied at *The Frank Gehry Exhibition* at New York's Guggenheim Museum, 2001.

35 In the first edition of *The Language of Post-Modern Architecture*, 1977, I foresaw this as a primary cause of the shift in architecture, but it had to wait twenty years before a complex, non-standard building such as Gehry's could be produced almost as economically as a repeated, rectilinear one. Carlos Hurriaga, a project architect who worked on this in Bilbao, told me its complexities added only about 10-15 per cent to the cost.

36 Because of this change in emphasis I used the phrase 'the new paradigm in architecture' to signal the turn. Several key buildings showed its promise – those by architects I have already mentioned, Frank Gehry, Peter Eisenman and Daniel Libeskind – and those on the outskirts of the new paradigm, the Dutch architects, not only Rem Koolhaas, but Ben van Berkel and MVRDV. There were those who had moved on from Deconstruction – Zaha Hadid, Eric Owen Moss, and Morphosis – and those, such as Norman Foster, who had turned high-tech into 'eco-tech'. Will Alsop, Coop Himmelblau and the Japanese architects such as Kisho Kurokawa,

Shoei Yoh, Masaharu Takasaki and Arata Isozaki were intermittently engaged with the approach as were Australian architects ARM (Ashton Raggatt MacDougall) and LAB, who completed a seminal work of the new movement, Melbourne's Federation Square. Why could they be seen as continuing the agenda of Post-Modernism? Because they developed the complexity paradigm (see above); because they produced sculptural iconic buildings that had some significance (the enigmatic signifier); and because they used the computer to personalise their mass production. Of course, they might avoid the pm moniker, but that did not mean they escaped the practice. I have discussed this stage of Post-Modernism at length in several articles and the seventh edition of *The Language of Post-Modern Architecture* (2002), and the reader can see the complexity of overlapping movements in the evolutionary tree in the final chapter.

37 Linda Hutcheon, *A Poetics of Postmodernism, History, Theory, Fiction*, Routledge (New York and London), 1988.

38 Julian Stallabrass, *High Art Lite, British Art in the 1990s*, Verso (London and New York), 1999, p 205.

39 Nick Glass and Cole Moreton, 'An Artist? I'm a brand name, says Hirst', *The Independent on Sunday*, 1 October 2000, p 11.

40 Stallabrass, *High Art Lite*, Verso (London and New York), 1999. pp 108–115, for a discussion of multiculturalism, Ofili, and the following quote.

Chapter 3

41 Kwame Anthony Appiah, 'The Case for Contamination', *RSA Journal*, London, April 2006, pp 38–44; idem, *Cosmopolitanism: Ethics in a World of Strangers*, Norton (New York), 2006.

42 For a good discussion of post-modernities, albeit from a modern perspective, see David Harvey, *The Condition of Postmodernity, An Enquiry into the Origins of Cultural Change*, Basil Blackwell (Oxford), 1989, pp 201–308.

43 Daniel Bell, 'Notes on the Post Industrial Society' I&II, *The Public Interest*, Spring, 1967; *The Coming of the Post-Industrial Society*, Basic Books (New York), 1973; Alvin Toffler, *The Third Wave*, William Collins (London), 1980.

44 Will Hutton, *The State We're In*, Jonathan Cape (London), 1995.

45 For a discussion of the conceptual muddle and further US statistics see Andrew Hacker, 'The Rich and Everyone Else', *New York Review of Books*, 25 May 2006, pp 16–19.

46 Sheelah Kolhatkar, 'Thanks a billion', *Times 2*, London, 17 August 2006, pp 4–6; also in *Atlantic Monthly*, 2006.

47 Alexandra Frean, 'We're all middle-class now as social barriers fall away', *The Times*, 5 May 2006, pp 12–13. See William Nelson, *Middle Britain*, report of the Future Foundation, Spring 2006.

48 An early use of Post-Fordism is by Michael Davis in 'Urban renewal and the spirit of postmodernism', *New Left Review*, no 151, 1985, pp 106–13. In German see J Hirsch, 'Fordismus und Postfordismus', *Politische Vierteljahresschrift* 26, 1985, pp 160–82.

49 For these figures see Joel Kotkin and Yoriko Kishimoto, *The Third Century*, Crown (New York), 1988, p 65.

50 Gianni Vattimo, *The End of Modernity: Nihilism and Hermeneutics in Postmodern Culture*.

Chapter 4

51 Most historians see the nation-state as the invention of the modern world and chart its present-day decline for being, at once, too big and too small to deal with issues such as global warming and local legitimacy. See Paul Kennedy, *The Rise and Fall of the Great Powers, Economic Change and Military Conflict from 1500 to 2000*, 1988.

52 Zygmunt Bauman, *Modernity and the Holocaust*, Polity Press (Cambridge), 1989.

53 Jean-François Lyotard, *The Postmodern Explained to Children, Correspondence 1982–1985*, Turnaround (London), 1992, pp 30–31, 40, 91.

54 Professor EO Wilson has analysed the various studies on extinction and come up with these figures; see his *The Diversity of Life*, Allen Lane (London), 1993, p 280.

55 Freedom House Surveys are conducted annually. For the 100-year comparisons see Gregory Fossedal, *The Democratic Imperative – Exporting the American Revolution*, Basic Books (New York), 1989, p 16.

56 Anatole Kaletsky, 'Ice-cool under terror attack', *The Times*, 13 July 2006, p 20.

57 Tom Baldwin, 'US admits Iraq is a terror "cause"', *The Times*, 29 April 2006, p 46. This article starts, 'Three years after its invasion of Iraq the US Administration acknowledged that the war has become "a cause" for Islamic extremists worldwide and there is a risk of the country becoming a safe haven for terrorists hoping to launch fresh attacks on America … '

58 Letter published in *The Independent*, 20 January 2003, p 13. Along with the president of RIBA, Paul Hyett, I organised this pressure group and wrote the letter. The

59 others who signed were Lord Rogers, Sir Terry Farrell, Professor William Alsop, Rick Mather, Paul Finch, Eva Jiricna, Mohsen Mostafavi, Zaha Hadid, Rem Koolhaas, Sir Richard MacCormac, Ken Powell, Richard Murphy, Frank Gehry, George Ferguson, Edward Cullinan. For the full text see 'Opinion' on my web site, www.charlesjencks.com

59 Robert Cooper, *The Breaking of Nations*, Atlantic Books (London), 2003, pp 26–37; quotations are from pp 27 and 54.

60 Robert Cooper, 'The next empire', *Prospect*, London, October 2001, pp 22–6.

61 Mark Leonard, *Why Europe Will Run the 21st Century*, Fourth Estate, UK, 2005; PublicAffairs, USA, 2005.

62 'By the end of the British presidency of the EU, just 34 per cent of Britons supported their country's European membership. Only one nation emerged as more Eurosceptical – Austria, which has now taken over the presidency', *Manneken Pis*, *Prospect*, February 2006, p 52.

63 For typical reports on EU corruption and fraud, see Simon Bain, 'EC accounting worse, says whistleblower', *Glasgow Herald*, 19 April 2006; Anthony Browne, 'Gone east: how E7bn EU cash melted away with the Cold War', *The Times*, 21 April 2006; Raphael Minder, 'MEPS vote to keep generous allowances', *Financial Times*, 13 April 2005; Nicola Smith, 'Inside the EU's travelling circus, MEPs squander £120 million a year flitting between Brussels and Strasbourg', *Sunday Times*, 22 May 2005, p 3; Anthony Browne, 'EU accounts still riddled with fraud and errors, say auditors', *The Times*, 16 November, 2005, p 42; Anthony Browne, 'EU travelling circus comes to town and loses £105m for taxpayer', *The Times*, 26 April 2006, p 13.

64 See the 2005 *Transparency International Corruption Perception Index* on the Web for the recent listing. Corruption is defined as 'the abuse of public office for private gain' and is made in an annual survey undertaken by the Berlin group. The perception by businessmen has Iceland as the top, the most squeaky-clean nation. The following list gives an idea of recent rankings: New Zealand, 3rd; Switzerland, 7th; UK, 12th; Germany, 16th; USA, 17th; Japan, 22nd; Israel, 28th, Italy 41st. Italy, stands at the watershed, and the rest of the 110 nations are considered to suffer from serious, debilitating public and private corruption. Bulgaria, 55th; Egypt, 72nd; China, 78th; India, 92nd; Azerbaijan, 137th; Bangladesh, 158th; Chad, 159th. As the authors note, corruption is a major cause of poverty as well as a barrier to overcoming it.

65 Anthony Browne, 'Through a glass darkly in the "Berlaymonster"', *The Times*, 4 August 2004, p 12. The most powerful European Commission meets on the 13th floor rooftop conference room, so this is probably where the Euro stops.

66 Robert Cooper, 'All Together Now: Europe', *Sunday Times*, 25 February 2005.

Chapter 5

67 For his list of the new public intellectuals see John Brockman, *The Third Culture: Beyond the Scientific Revolution*, Simon & Schuster (New York), 1996.

68 The Harvard astrophysicist David Layzer uses the term in his title, *Cosmogenesis, The Growth of Order in the Universe*, Oxford University Press (Oxford), 1990; Teilhard de Chardin adapted it from HP Blavasky and her *The Secret Doctrine, The Synthesis of Science, Religion and Philosophy* (1888), really a book on the occult. See also Brian Swimme and Thomas Berry, *The Universe Story, From the Primordial Flaring Forth to the Ecozoic Era*, Harper (San Francisco), 1992 and Thomas Berry, *The Dream of the Earth*, Sierra Club Books (San Francisco), 1988.

69 In measuring quality and organised complexity one already assumes an audience: a reader of a book or viewer of a work of art or a building. Obviously, as reception theory shows, the naïve and educated viewer bring very different assumptions and mental encyclopaedia to the work being measured. For my purpose I assume in this discussion a well-educated reader who knows what a work by Jackson Pollock is like as much as a black hole. The naïve reader does not perceive the same complexity as does an educated one. A discussion of reception theory and audiences would take us far beyond the confines of this book, but one should say that the elitism implied by the educated reader is non-snobbish and open in the sense discussed below and by Umberto Eco. For Gell-Mann's book see footnote 81 below.

70 'Algorithmic complexity theory', a new branch of mathematics, quantifies the complexity of a sequence of numbers by the length of the shortest computer algorithm that can generate the sequence. The mathematician Charles Bennett of IBM claims it can measure evolutionary complexity and, therefore, progress, in terms of DNA information. See Paul Davies, 'Life's Little Complexities', *The Independent*, 13 February 1989, p 15. For a discussion applied to literature see Tito Arecchi, 'Chaos and Complexity' in *The Post-Modern Reader*, ed. Charles Jencks, Academy Editions/St Martin's London and New York), 1992, pp 350–3. For the related idea of 'Effective Complexity' and 'Algorithmic Information Content' see Murray Gell-Mann, *The Quark and the Jaguar, Adventures in the simple and the complex*, Little, Brown Company (Boston and London), pp 34–7, 58–9.

71 For these new ideas on evolution see Israel Rosenfield and Edward Ziff, 'Evolution Evolving', *New York Review of Books*, 11 May 2006, pp 12–17.

72 Zeeya Merali, 'Abstract art appreciation is all about the hidden fractals', *New Scientist*, 29 October 2005, p 12. The LA team investigating Pollock forgeries quantified the complexity of his colour patterns by fractal dimension and found he had one of the highest or most complicated dimensions.

73 Toyo Ito, 'Beyond Modernism', *El Croquis 123*, Madrid, 2005, p 174.

74 Ilya Prigogine and Isabelle Stengers, *Order Out of Chaos, Man's New Dialogue with Nature*, Bantam Books (New York), 1984.

75 Eric Chaisson, *Cosmic Evolution: The Rise of Complexity in Nature*, Harvard University Press (Cambridge, Mass), 2001. Chaisson postulates that the expanding cosmos creates the energy flow that powers evolution and that it can be used as a unifying principle, and measure, of growing complexity. In other words, he argues for a universal measure for the positive arrow of time, what he calls 'the energy rate density'. It is not simply the gross amount of energy a system has – 'But if we look at energy flow in relation to mass, we find a real and impressive trend of increasing energy per time per mass for all ordered systems over more than 10 billion years of the universe's existence. This "energy rate density" is a useful way to characterise or quantify the complexity of any system be it physical, biological or cultural: it is a potential common currency between them. Energy, the ability to do work, is the big commonalty in the natural sciences. And in an expanding, non-equilibrium universe, it is "free"energy that drives order to emerge from chaos'. [Eric J. Chaisson, 'The Great Unifier', *New Scientist*, 7 January 2006, pp 36–8.

76 A good description of the BZ Reaction and self-organisation as a universal concept is Philip Ball, *The Self-Made Tapestry, Pattern Formation in Nature*, Oxford University Press (Oxford), 1999, especially pp 50–73.

77 Bertrand Russell, 'Why I am not a Christian', lecture delivered in South London, 1927, republished in book form by Allen & Unwin (New York), 1957; quotation is from p 107.

78 Stuart Kauffman, *At Home in the Universe: The Search for the Laws of Self-Organisation and Complexity*, Oxford University Press (New York), 1995.

79 Freeman Dyson, *Infinite in All Directions*, Harper & Row (New York), 1988; Paul Davies, *The Cosmic Blueprint*, Simon & Schuster (New York), 1988, pp 197–203, and *The Mind of God: The Scientific Basis for a Rational World*, Simon & Schuster (New York), 1992 (the last chapter includes references to Fred Hoyle's views). For further references see my *The Architecture of the Jumping Universe*, Wiley Academy (London and New York), 1995. The late Allan Wilson from Berkeley California published some of this work in the 1980s in *Scientific American*, especially October 1985; see diagram.

90 Mark Henderson, 'Pyow pyow pyow … hack hack hack', *The Times*, 18 May 2006, p 3.

81 For the general ideas of complex adaptive systems, CAS, see Murray Gell-Mann, *The Quark and the Jaguar, Adventures in the Simple and Complex*, Little Brown (London), 1994.

82 Hans Christian von Baeyer, *Taming the Atom*, Random House (New York), p 162.

83 Paul Davies, *The Mind of God: The Scientific Basis for a Rational World*, Simon & Schuster (New York), 1992.

84 For an accessible and striking discussion of these points see Paul Davies, *The Cosmic Blueprint*, Simon & Schuster (New York), 1988, pp 81–92, 189–96.

Chapter 6

85 See Colin Brown, 'Estate Agents more trusted than politicians', *The Independent*, 16 September 2006. 'The government has not recovered from a loss of trust during the Iraq war which may be doing lasting damage to the reputation of ministers, according to Sir Alistair Graham, chairman of the committee on standards in public life, which commissioned the survey.' See also *Daily Mail*, 15 September 2006. A 2004 poll in Western Europe found the 'trust in politicians' averaging an even lower 15 per cent; a Blog of May 2005 also found politicians trusted less than estate agents. Similar conclusions were contained in a BBC News poll of 18 March 2005: 'Voters don't trust politicians'. In this case the poll indicated the distrust was felt by 80 per cent of the population.

86 For the quotation and debate see below and George Baird, 'Criticality and its Discontents', *Harvard Design Magazine* 21 (Fall 2004/Winter 2005), pp 16–21.

87 If one supposes sound is the most important metaphor to convey the origin, it still was not a 'bang' but a 'hum', and at much too low a frequency to be audible. The physicist John Cramer, at the University of Washington, has made a recording of the sound for an eleven-year-old boy fascinated by hearing bangs, as boys are. The result, based on WMAP's microwave data, sounds like 'a large jet plane flying at 100 feet', and then falls off like the sound of a passing ambulance. Big Bang? Big raspberry. See Marcus Chown, 'Forget the big bang, tune into the big hum', *New Scientist*, 1

November 2003, p 16.

88 See for instance the admirably eclectic compilation by James Steele, *Ecological Architecture, A Critical History*, Thames & Hudson (London), 2005. This includes recent architects and groups, starting with Charles Rennie Mackintosh, who had the trace of an ecological concern, a huge gang but one without a common outlook.

89 Digitised architecture is now ubiquitous as are the various non-standard morphologies developed from it. Issues of *Architectural Design*, London, are regularly devoted to the subject (see *Emergence*, May/June 2004; *Morphogenetic Design*, Vol 76, No 2, 2006). I have discussed these trends in the last two chapters of *The New Paradigm in Architecture*, Yale University Press (London and New Haven), 2002, and there is a growing and substantial literature devoted to the subject.

90 See, for instance, Peter Eisenman, 'Autonomy and the Will to the Critical', *Dialogue*, Taiwan, May 2000, pp 58 ff. Eisenman recommends another text on the critical: 'Terragni and the idea of a critical text', in Peter Eisenman, *Giuseppe Terragni, Transformations Decompositions Critiques*, Monacelli Press (New York), 2003, pp 295–301. The 'critical' here is the interiority of architecture, opening up the question of the language of the formal, the textual net of traces and deformations of them that the architect operates on, independent of semantic meaning. Obviously this leaves out iconography and social meaning, and therefore the other half of the critical in my discussion.

91 Consellaría de Cultura e Deporte, *Galicia's City of Culture, The culture from the country of land's end* (fundación cidade da cultura de Galicia), brochure explaining the project, Santiago de Compostela, 2006. This document brims with regionalist pride – '60% of the population speaks Galician regularly and 95% can understand it … The First Galician nationalist proposals arose around the middle of the XIX century, the *Rexurdimento* … When democracy was restored in 1975, Galicia was recognized as a historical nationality …' etc. Functional questions about this ambitious scheme are pressing, the programme is not yet up to the large scale of the project. Ridiculously arcane functions are proposed, like an archive of old Galician newspapers, hardly the kind of thing to attract pilgrims up a suburban hillside. The existing Museum of Galician History now in downtown Santiago hardly attracts enough people, and even fewer are likely to come when it is relocated. Also, the so-called New Technology Building and Music Theatre, 'presently under re-definition' as the brochure admits, probably will have trouble at the turnstiles. Indeed, if such functional questions are not soon convincingly answered the whole project may succumb to the Millennium Curse that has plagued Britain and other iconic sites.

92 See Eisenman Architects, *Codex, The City of Culture Galicia*, Monacelli Press (New York), 2005, especially pp 27–35. Druids were a first-century English tribe to whom Caesar referred, leading eighteenth-century amateurs to think they inhabited prehistoric sites in France, among other places.

93 Umberto Eco, 'Intertextual Irony and Levels of Reading', *Umberto Eco on Literature*, Secker & Warburg (London), pp 212–235, 234. The article was first presented as a lecture in 1999 and discusses, among other things, my ideas of post-modernism and sets double coding in a context of metanarrative, dialogism and intertextual irony.

94 This idea is supported in different degrees by the philosophers and writers David Chalmers, David Ray Griffin, Michael Lockwood, Thomas Nagel, William Seager, Galen Strawson and Peter Unger.

95 Colin Renfrew, *Figuring It Out*, Thames & Hudson (London), 2003; see also Mel Gooding and William Furlong, *Song of the Earth, European Artists and the Landscape*, Thames & Hudson (London), 2002.

96 Beyond the well-known proponents of Critical Theory, there is the Critical Rationalism proposed by the philosopher Karl Popper in the 1960s. This was a quasi-scientific method with two parts. First scientists were to explain rationally a theory, then criticise it fearlessly, a method they supposedly followed. Also called Fallibilism and Falsificationism (because it seeks to falsify its hypotheses), it was in turn criticised for not being the way scientists actually work, or come to believe and follow theories. Nevertheless, Critical Rationalism, like Critical Theory in general, contains the truth that scientists do, from time to time, criticise their hypotheses and certainly have a critical temperament (if selectively so). See Karl Popper, *Conjectures and Refutations*, Routledge & Kegan Paul (London), 1963, pp 26, 49, 103, 194, 215, 355, 375. Obviously, political and social theories are held dogmatically like religious faiths and only open to marginal criticism, but it is interesting that even here there is some competition between theories and those of different countries.

97 Lewis Smith and Ben Hoyle, 'World has only 20 years to stop climate disaster', *The Times*, 31 January 2006, p 7. Michael Meacher, 'Ten years to prevent catastrophe', *The Times*, 10 February 2006, p 21. See also the report by the US National Center for Atmospheric Research in Boulder, Colorado which predicts that the Netherlands, London, New York, Florida etc will be under water by 2100 as seas rise 6 metres. *The Times*, 24 March 2006, p 12. Again it is caused by glacier melting in

Greenland, the Arctic Circle and Antarctica. The ten-year count till doomsday was also reiterated by further experts in September 2006: 'Ten-year deadline on global warming', *The Times*, 5 September 2006, p 31. By about the year 2026 climate scientists have predicted that the carbon dioxide emissions will reach 440 parts per million volume and make global warming self-sustaining.

98   Mark Henderson, '3C. Earth's danger point. Now scientists say it is going to happen', *The Times*, 4 May 2006, p 3. The figure of 400 million starving people is estimated by Sir David King, Britain chief scientific advisor.

99   Frances Cairncross as quoted in 'Adapt or fry', *New Scientist*, 9 September 2006, p 6; 'Global Warming "cannot be stopped"'; also *The Times*, 4 September 2006, p 25. It is obvious that her five adaptation policies are as inadequate to the situation as the Kyoto Protocol, but that is no reason not to put them on a critical agenda with others.

100   *Post-modern states*, Europe and Japan, would likely keep their bureaucratic combinations of social democracy and a regulated neo-liberal economics. Global warming might lead them to ever-tighter regulations and huge public projects at the scale of the TVA hydroelectric projects in America. A few large schemes may work. *Modern states*, like China, are likely to take draconian measures of an authoritarian kind, as is already under way in preparations for the 2008 Olympics. The US, Israel, India and Australia are likely to cherry-pick their compliance with international norms, as they do now, looking for a technological fix. Russia, with its authoritarian monopoly capitalism, will act more like China, as a controlled super state. Finally, *pre-modern and failed states* are not particularly capitalist, of course, and will not act as integrated countries, as they face the worst crises of all.

101   John Gray, 'The Global Delusion', *New York Review of Books*, 27 April 2006, pp 20–3. Gray, taking arguments from the recent books of Daniel Cohen and Suzanne Berger on globalisation, also criticises the reigning assumption that globalisation means a single process and one world outcome.

102   James Lovelock, *The Revenge of Gaia*, Allen Lane (London), 2006.

103   Jean-François Lyotard, *The Postmodern Condition: A Report on Knowledge*, Manchester University Press (Manchester), 1984, p 79. The book was first published in French in 1979.

104   Harold Bloom, *The Anxiety of Influence: A Theory of Poetry*, Oxford University Press (Oxford), 1973.

105   My idea that there are coherent routes within modernisms rests on four sources. Claude Lévi Strauss' writings on structural anthropology reveal hidden continuities and structures. George Kubler's 'shape of time' is based on the 'fibrous bundles' of historical continuity (corresponding to my evolutionary blobs). Charles Osgood, in 'the measurement of meaning', reveals common semantic spaces that unite thoughts and meaning across time. And the notion of strange attractors, attractor basins of coherence, is another support for the self-organising schools within historical change.

106   Nikolaus Pevsner, *Pioneers of Modern Design*, Penguin Books (London), 1960. This confession is on page 17 and the book was first published in 1936 as *Pioneers of the Modern Movement*.

107   Seigfried Giedion, *Space, Time and Architecture*, Harvard University Press (Cambridge, Mass), 1967, pp 5–18. Like Pevsner, Giedion has a derisory mention of the Expressionists, on pages 485–7. I have analysed these uncritical suppressions and others of Modern historians in 'History as Myth', *Meaning in Architecture* (London and New York), 1969, pp 244–65. Written under my mentor at London University, Reyner Banham, who wrote his thesis under Pevsner, the former enjoyed my critique of his mentor and himself – is this critical modernism at work in historiography?

108   See for instance Jeffrey Herf, *Reactionary Modernism, Technology, Culture, and Politics in Weimar and the Third Reich*, Cambridge University Press (Cambridge), 1984. David Harvey uses the concept in several books.

109   I have put the case for this 'law', really a tendency, in 'The Power Law of Bad Architecture', *The Architectural Review* (Spring 2001 and earlier in *The Language of Post-Modern Architecture* (1977) and following editions. After a certain size, about a half a million square feet, the bigger the building the less the architecture, unless the client is willing to spend a proportionally larger percentage of money to make up for the multiplying costs. There are economies of scale to this point, then the savings turn into increased costs. With new efficiencies in production and structure this point obviously rises.

110   Le Corbusier, *My Work* (also titled *Creation is a Patient Search*), Architectural Press (London), 1960, p 219.

111   Charles Jencks, *Le Corbusier and the Continual Revolution in Architecture*, Monacelli Press (New York), 2002.

112   See especially Kenneth Frampton, 'Critical Regionalism: modern architecture and cultural identity' in *Modern Architecture: A Critical History*, Thames & Hudson (London), 1985, pp 313–27. The architects he features as critical include Jørn

Utzon, the Barcelona School, Alvaro Siza, Luis Barragán, Harwell Hamilton Harris, Batey and Mack, Harry Wolf, Gino Valle, Carlo Scarpa, Mario Botta and the Ticinese Regionalists, Tadao Ando and the Greek Regionalists such as Pikionis. See also an earlier version in Frampton's 'Towards a Critical Regionalism: Six Points for an Architecture of Resistance' in Hal Foster (ed), *The Anti-Aesthetic*, Bay Press (Seattle), 1983. Also the critique by Fredric Jameson, 'The Constraints of Postmodernism', in *The Seeds of Time*, Columbia University Press (New York), pp 189–205.

113   George Baird, '"Criticality" and its Discontents', *Harvard Design Magazine* 21, (Fall 2004/Winter 2005), pp 16–21. The debate goes back to an earlier Michael Hays wrote at the same time Kenneth Frampton was writing on Critical Regionalism, 'Critical Architecture: Between Culture and Form', *Yale Architecture Journal, Perspecta 21*, 1984. Those whom Baird characterises on the 'critical' side of the debate beside Peter Eisenman include Manfredo Tafuri, Michael Hays, Diller and Scofidio and Michael Sorkin, while those on the 'post-critical' side include theorists Michael Speaks, Robert Somol, Sarah Whiting and many of the pragmatic Dutch followers of Rem Koolhaas (discussed under 'Superdutch' in much literature). Oddly, Mies van der Rohe became an exemplar for the 'critical' even though his Seagram Building was elsewhere interpreted, by Lewis Mumford and others, as the apotheosis of the bureaucratic spirit. How the term 'critical' could be used in architecture in a reactionary way is also evident in its common designation for buildings that observe strict urban guidelines. This was especially true of the movement of *Critical Reconstruction* dominant in Berlin in the 1990s, the planning rules that often mandated repetitive urban blocks, standard facades, common cornices, windows and materials. Under this rubric, Post Modern urbanism of the 1980s was interpreted as rigid formulae although there are several notable exceptions. Worth mentioning are the three city blocks, also connected underground, of Pei Cobb Freed, Jean Nouvel and Oswald Mathias Ungers and the infill blocks of Michael Wilford, Frank Gehry and Christian de Portzamparc.

114   Official Pamphlet, *Information: The Memorial to the Murdered Jews of Europe*, Berlin 2005; www.stiftung-denkmal.de

115   In addition to the Jewish Museum and Memorial to the Murdered Jews, there are the Typography of Terrors, fragments of the Berlin Wall, the Stasi Museum, the German Historical Museum section on the twentieth century, the Checkpoint Charlie Museum, the Russian graffiti preserved inside the Reichstag, the Missing House (a public artwork by Christian Boltanski), the Neue Wache Memorial, the Soviet War Memorial, a memorial to those murdered by euthanasia in the Philharmonie and countless works of art in museums, such as that by Anselm Kiefer, and public places. Also of note is the way streets are named after those who resisted the Nazis: Hannah Arendt, Karl Liebknecht, and a man who was a second father to me, Varian Fry.

116   John Mueller, 'A False Sense of Insecurity', *Regulation*, Fall, 2004, pp 42–6. bbbb@osu.edu

117   The National Intelligence Estimate, from the office of John Negroponte, asserts that 'the Iraq war has provided Islamic militants with a "cause célèbre" and created a new generation of Islamic terrorists.' See Paul Harris, 'Iraq war created a terrorist flood, American spymasters warn Bush', *The Observer*, 24 September 2006, p 35; and for the quotes, Tim Reid, 'Read it yourself, says Bush as threat report made public', *The Times*, London, 27 September 2006, p 2.

1189 Zygmunt Bauman has argued that the law of increasing guilt locks people into early decisions that cannot be easily reversed, and then further shuts them in because any admission of guilt would mean their series of previous actions were also wrong. This 'law' is of course only a social tendency but one can see it operating especially in the political sphere and with the Mafia where change is highly penalised. See Zygmunt Bauman, *Modernity and the Holocaust*, Polity Press (Oxford), 1989.

119   Quoted by Deyan Sudjic, 'Feuds? I've had a Few', *The Observer*, 19 December 2004, p 8. In published texts Eisenman speaks about the instabilities created between two grids, making 'for a place of loss and contemplation' ... no goal, no end, no working one's way in or out ... no further understanding, since understanding the Holocaust is impossible'. See, for instance, Cynthia Davidson, *Tracing Eisenman*, Thames & Hudson (London), 2006, p 290. This conclusion about the unspeakable nature of the Holocaust is similar to what Libeskind has said about it; indeed, the two Berlin memorials are similar in their highlighting the cubic abstraction of a grave, yet different in other representational ways.

120   The public as well as architects and the elite preferred the factual approach; see Nikolaus Bernau, *Holocaust Memorial Berlin*, Die Neuen Architekturführer Nr 70, Stadtwandel Verlag (Berlin), 2005, p 4.

121   Ben van Berkel, Caroline Bos, *UN Studio, Design Models: Architecture Urbanism Infrastructure*, Thames & Hudson (London), 2006, p 12.

INDEX